From Television City in Hollywood...

ALL IN THE FAMILY

ALL IN THE FAMILY

The Show that Changed Television

By **NORMAN LEAR,**
the Cast, and the Crew as told to **JIM COLUCCI**

Foreword by **JIMMY KIMMEL**

UNIVERSE

CONTENTS

Foreword by Jimmy Kimmel 6

Norman Lear in Conversation
with Jim Colucci 8

The Pilots & Season 1
BECOMING THE BUNKERS
7 Episodes that Made a Hit 14

Seasons 2–3
"YOU'RE REALLY GOING TO DO THAT?"
14 Episodes that Pushed Buttons 48

The Script 90

Seasons 4–6
"YOU CAN'T PUT THAT IN THE SCRIPT!"
12 Episodes about Human Nature 94

The Costumes 136

Seasons 7 & 8
THE HUMAN EXPERIENCE
10 Episodes that Shook Things Up 148

The Set 190

Season 9
AND THAT'S A WRAP
4 Episodes that Closed the Arc 194

All in the Family's Legacy
THE LAUGHTER CONTINUES
5 Encores 204

Acknowledgments 220

Credits 222

About the Authors 223

FOREWORD

When *All in the Family* aired on CBS, I was too young to understand that it was a brilliant and groundbreaking show that embraced controversial subjects and forced America to confront the uncomfortable. I just knew that it was funny. I grew up in a house in Brooklyn not far from the Bunker house in Queens, and while I was unaware of his ignorance when it came to race, religion, gender, and just about everything else, Archie's malaprops made me laugh. "Patience is a virgin" and "Go take a flying leap off the Golden Goose Bridge!" are lines that took permanent residence in my brain.

As I got older, I gained appreciation for how much more substantial this show was than the television fare that came before (and after) it. The characters were rich, the language authentic, and the actors exceptional. The first time I heard Carroll O'Connor speak, I was shocked to learn that Archie's New York accent wasn't "real." It may have been the moment that I realized *television* wasn't real. The popularity of *All in the Family* was enduring and, thanks to reruns in syndication, Archie, Edith, Meathead, Gloria, and the many great charac-

ters who stopped by the house ("Oh jeez...Maude") became part of my nightly syndicated TV diet.

Thirty-plus years later, my friend the writer and actor Justin Theroux and I were talking about the show. We agreed that we'd heard too many people say, "You could never do that now." That assessment always bothered me. Why couldn't you do it now? For many of us, this show is what connected the dots between racism and ignorance. Archie Bunker was the character your dad was and you didn't want to be. In the hands of a genius like Norman Lear, the uncomfortable enlightens us.

I called Mr. Lear (nervously) and his partner Brent Miller and asked if they would be interested in restaging an original *AITF* script, live on ABC with an all-star cast. Norman responded as though he'd been expecting the call, gracious but mildly doubtful that anyone could follow Carroll O'Connor in the role of Archie. As luck would have it, Norman had recently seen *LBJ* (directed by Rob Reiner) and thought Woody Harrelson might be the one guy who could pull it off. I said, "I know Woody!" and texted him immediately. Woody is not a person who quickly returns texts. Or at least my texts. He returned this one instantly and enthusiastically, and off to the races we went.

ABC needed no convincing; they jumped onboard. Every role seemed impossible to fill. The shoes were huge but the opportunity to work with Norman Lear and Woody Harrelson made it an easy sell. When Marisa Tomei agreed to play Edith Bunker, we couldn't believe our fortune and decided to stage an episode of *The Jeffersons* too. Our first choices to play George and Louise said yes right away. Jamie Foxx and Wanda Sykes moved into the deluxe apartment in the sky. We asked the great Jim Burrows to direct and he said yes. It was an embarrassment of riches. Will Ferrell and Kerry Washington as Tom and Helen Willis, Ike Barinholtz and Ellie Kemper as Michael and Gloria Stivic. Anthony Anderson, Sean Hayes, Jovan Adepo, Fran Bennett, Jackée, Amber Stevens West, Stephen Tobolowsky, Kevin Bacon, Jesse Eisenberg, and the ageless Marla Gibbs in a surprise reprise of her classic turn as Florence.

On the day of the show, most everyone was terrified. When it was over, we were ecstatic. Norman and I hosted the evening, and I am exaggerating in no way when I say it was the most pleasurable experience I've ever had on television. When Woody and Marisa sat down at the piano and we heard the words "Boy, the way Glenn Miller played…" I looked over at the incredible man in the white hat, and the tears in his eyes brought tears to mine. And then, a little more than six months later, we did it all over again. This time Woody, Marisa, Ellie, and Ike were joined by Justina Machado, Kevin Bacon, and Jesse Eisenberg—and directed by the brilliant Pamela Fryman.

The pages that follow are filled with this same kind of energy, told by the many people who made the series so brilliant, from Norman himself to *All in the Family*'s producers, directors, writers, costars, guest stars, and crew. Joining them in the book are the voices of today's leading showrunners and members of our own *Live in Front of a Studio Audience* team—further testament to this show's timeless inspiration.

I am forever grateful to Norman Lear for allowing me to be a small part of a show that means so much to me, my family, and our country. Norman is one of the finest men I've ever had the good fortune to know, *All in the Family* is one of television's greatest shows, and anyone who says otherwise can go take a flying leap off the Golden Goose Bridge.

—JIMMY KIMMEL

NORMAN LEAR
IN CONVERSATION WITH
JIM COLUCCI

ABOVE: Cast of *All in the Family* with Bud Yorkin (left), Norman Lear (center), and John Rich (second from right)

JIM COLUCCI: *All in the Family* is based on a British sitcom called *Till Death Us Do Part*. What about that show attracted you so strongly?

NORMAN LEAR: My partner, Bud Yorkin, was in Britain while we were working on a film deal, and he told me he had seen this wild show. His description of it made me think of my own youth, with my father who had a touch of what I'd go on to create in Archie Bunker, in that his language was full of Archie Bunker–isms. It was so close to home, I thought, "Oh, my God, I've got to do something like that!"

The character Alf Garnett wasn't really Archie Bunker; I'd had some thought of what Archie Bunker (or Wally Justice, as he was named at the time) could be. But when Carroll O'Connor came in to meet with me, sat down and read half a page, then I knew what the character looked like. Carroll brought his talent to it.

He was a New York– and Dublin-trained actor, but when he opened his mouth to read, he was no longer the cultured man who had walked in. His voice, his eyes, and his whole body language changed, and out poured Archie. I don't think he was off the first page before I said, "If we can make the deal, you've got the role." There was absolutely no doubt in my mind that he was Archie Bunker.

JC: At this same point in your career, you had been offered a three-picture deal to make movies for United Artists, but you turned it down to take a gamble on *All in the Family*. Why were you always so determined to make this show?

NL: I loved the situation, I loved the characters, and I loved the script I'd written, which ended up being far more about the Lears who lived at 68 Woodstock Street in Hartford, Connecticut, than it was about Alf Garnett and company. And then, having made the first three pilots, I absolutely fell in love with the two actors, Jean Stapleton and Carroll. I was committed. I just had to work with those actors.

JC: What was the process like, casting Jean Stapleton as Edith?

NL: This wonderful casting agent Marion Dougherty brought in a number of actors I read in New York for the part of Edith—who in the very beginning was named Agnes. I had seen Jean in *Damn Yankees* on Broadway, so I was excited to meet her. She liked the script and the role, and our meeting was magical.

JC: In your memoir, you mentioned that of everyone associated with the show, Jean was always the one who had faith that it would get picked up.

NL: Yes, absolutely. That's so Jean, so much in her nature, to be an optimist. But to a person, we all cared about what we were doing and knew we were doing something big. Something that was very different from "The roast is ruined, and the boss is coming to dinner!" which had been a kind of staple for situation comedies.

JC: You wrote in your memoir about Carroll having a unique and sometimes difficult acting process; he would dislike the script in the beginning of the week, until somehow making peace with it and becoming Archie. And you also wrote about yourself being what you call a "clutch writer," where you stew, or call your therapist, and go crazy until a writing deadline, and then it can just pour out of you. Would you call Carroll a "clutch actor," meaning that part of his process was to fight against the script and have problems and stomp his feet, and then he could pull it out at the end? It seems like maybe the two of you were cut from the same cloth. Maybe that's what caused some of the friction?

NL: I hadn't thought about that. Yes, absolutely a similar approach. When Carroll passed, I went to visit his wife, Nancy, at home. There was a whole group of people, but I stayed later. Once we were alone, and she could spend a couple of minutes with me, Nancy said, "I'm going to show you something." She took me into

ABOVE: **Norman Lear** (left) and **Bud Yorkin** (right).

his study, behind a locked door. And there was a letter from me on Carroll's desk. It was a love letter. I had told Carroll that, despite all our disagreements, I adored the Archie Bunker he was giving us and thought the world of his talent. Nancy wanted me to see that Carroll saw that letter every day of his life.

The difficulty was part of Carroll's process, that's all. How could I look at what he brought to the show week after week after week and not be overwhelmed by gratitude that we had found each other?

JC: Over the years, Archie seems to get a little bit more—*liberal* is the wrong word, but he gets a little more accepting. There's a moment in the fourth-season episode "Lionel's Engagement" when George Jefferson uses the N-word, and Archie turns to Edith and says, "Listen to that. I ain't used that word in three years." And by the end of the series, Archie is raising a Jewish daughter. Was that a plan, to evolve Archie and make him not always the bigot he started out to be?

NL: That evolution was very, very much not an accident. I was always careful to be sure that Archie was not a bad dude. He might have been another Archie Bunker had he been raised in Ohio. But he was raised in this area, at this time, shaped by reading the *New York Daily News* and the *New York Daily Mirror*, and the *Journal-American*. God, I'm remembering how many newspapers existed in New York!

JC: I've heard you say that of all the characters on your shows, you see yourself most in your lead character in *Maude*, Maude Findlay. In *All in the Family*, one might think you were most like Mike, because he's the liberal, fighting with the conservative. But Gloria is Archie's actual biological child. Are you Mike, or are you Gloria?

NL: I've never been asked that question. Both Maude and Mike were "horseshit liberals." By that I mean reflexively liberal, without knowing enough to back it up. That's true of me, too—it's true of all of us who pretend we know everything when we're arguing a point of view, and we don't. I've never known as much as I seem to know when I'm talking about it. So I would guess as a male I think of myself, reflexively, as more Mike. But there's Gloria in me, too.

JC: One of the keys, I think, to making Archie likeable, in addition to Carroll's performance, is the fact that Gloria loves him. She knows he's undereducated and ignorant, yet he's still her daddy. She loves him and she comes home every night to his house. So her acceptance of him seems very important to the show.

NL: It is. I didn't like my father telling me he was going to take my mother out for "chinks" on a Sunday evening, meaning he was taking her to a Chinese restaurant. I couldn't bear that he had to say that word. This was true of his language generally. And yet I never stopped loving him.

JC: Where did the character of Edith come from?

NL: Edith is an amalgam of my mother, my grandmother, and my aunts. I adored my grandmother, and she and Edith shared a lot in common, with the purity of their love. There was no doubt 24/7 that she loved you. It was just who she was, and she had no trouble saying it, with every ounce of her.

JC: That makes sense, because some of the things you quote your mother saying are bitingly funny, but not necessarily open and naive like Edith.

NL: Yes, when I found out that the TV Academy was going to start a Hall of Fame and that I was going to be among the first inductees along with such greats as Lucille Ball and Milton Berle, I called my mother and told her the whole story, excited. And she said, "Listen, if that's what they want to do, who am I to say?"

JC: What did Jean Stapleton bring to Edith?

NL: She added the enormous talent of Jean Stapleton. Edith was a character I had written, but she was also a character Jean Stapleton happened on and made her own. Each of those four characters was a combination of what I had drawn and what the actors brought to it. And I think that that marriage is what's responsible for a great performance.

JC: It's ironic that some people might rightly describe Edith as a simple woman—and yet she's so complex in the way she handles both Archie and life's big issues with great understanding.

NL: Somebody once said, "Each man is my superior in that I may learn from him." I was very young when I heard or read that for the first time, and it's been with me ever since. Because it seems so true to me, that somebody with far less education, far less sophistication, could still be counted on. You could still expect to be startled and to learn something. Just paying attention, listening.

JC: Sitcoms of the '60s had all been so white, and then *All in the Family* featured people of color, including Lionel Jefferson in the pilot. Were you consciously breaking ground about bringing people of color to the screen?

NL: I really don't know whether I was conscious of it. It was just natural and normal. When I thought about what made Archie a bigot, it was that he was afraid of life, afraid of tomorrow, afraid of what's new. He was comfortable with what existed. And Black people moving next door—that was too new for him. He couldn't deal with progress and change. When today became yesterday, you had to accept what the future brought you. And that was not easy for him. He was yesterday's child.

JC: One of the things I think is so important about the way Lionel is written is how he deals with Archie.

Lionel could just be offended by him, but then we wouldn't like Archie. Instead, Lionel knows how to laugh at Archie and make fun of him to his face, even if it goes over Archie's head.

NL: Lionel's deep friendship with Mike and Gloria perhaps gave him a lot of understanding to be able to live with Archie in the way he did. And I love that you're calling attention to the fact that he knew how to laugh at him. That was, I think, a secret of his character and personality, and his adulthood. He had the attitude of somebody who really understood.

JC: One of the things I've always noticed about the show is that so many times, when someone tells off Archie and it goes over his head, as that person exits, Mike and Gloria laugh. It seems to me to be such a smart choice in the acting or directing.

NL: Well, they all had to find a way to live with him. I lived with that, too. I had a very difficult father. He went to prison when I was nine years old. When I was twelve, and he got out, my mother, my sister and I met him at the railroad station in New Haven. We were going to New York to live with another couple and their two children

until my father found a job. Nonetheless, on the train, he sat with my mother for a while, then sat with each of us, my sister and me. When he was sitting with me, he said, "Well, Norman, you're going to be bar mitzvahed next year. I'm going to take you and your mother and your sister for a trip around the world. We'll be gone a year."

Well, that line, "We'll be gone a year": It's like I heard it yesterday. That moment has so carved a hole in my head. I remember it so clearly because even then, at the tender age of twelve, I knew something was off. And we never went on any trip.

JC: So is that how you dealt with it, by laughing at it, like Mike and Gloria do? Would you find it funny in order to cope with it?

NL: You know, it's likely that I did. Because what followed through all the years was my dealing with that kind of— what I call the foolishness of the human condition. I've always recognized it well enough to write about it.

JC: Sixties sitcoms tended to be about a lot of witches and warlocks and spies, but not real life and not racial tensions. Did you think you'd have trouble getting *All in the Family* on the air?

NL: I didn't have to *think* about having trouble getting it on the air—I had trouble getting it on the air! It came with the territory. But that's what happens. That part of Archie Bunker existed in the capitalist culture as well—the fear of taking a chance on something new. That never came easy in either business or family matters. People have resisted progress always.

JC: So how did you get first ABC, and then CBS, to take a chance on the show?

NL: That's where good fortune came in. A new man, Robert Wood, had just come into power running CBS. He wanted to do something that said, "Robert Wood is here." There was this *All in the Family* pilot, which we had made twice for ABC. Putting it on the air on CBS was Wood putting his stamp on the network. And that was important to him.

JC: How did you cast Rob Reiner and Sally Struthers?

NL: My family has long been friends with the Reiner family, and I have known Rob since he was eight years old. When we made the first pilot, Rob would have been too young. But now, in late 1970, he was absolutely right for it. And the same thing happened: one reading, and that was it. I knew I had found Mike. And with Sally, I had seen her on *The Tim Conway Comedy Hour*. Sally was the one actor who, before even meeting her, I was certain was going to be Gloria.

JC: Speaking of things that differ from earlier shows, CBS had just finished canceling all its "rural shows," which were all shot like films, with one camera. And here comes *All in the Family*, which returned to the multicamera tradition pioneered by *I Love Lucy*. It really does feel like watching a stage play, often just on that living-room set with just those four characters.

NL: We were extremely conscious of that. We were doing one-act plays for a live audience. Everything to the extent possible took place in one scene.

JC: Is that the reason for the extreme close-ups you used on the show? As opposed to, say, *The Mary Tyler Moore Show*, which was a different kind of ensemble comedy and which often used wider shots of its characters?

NL: Yes, that came from me. There's nothing I've done that didn't have that same look. In the moments in life that test your character, and test your relationships, you're looking in the other person's eyes. Life becomes a close-up in those situations. So that's what I thought we needed to do to express it correctly. We had great performers, so we tried to get a camera in close, so you could see what was going on in their eyes.

JC: Shows often find their stories when individual writers come to work and talk about their real-life experiences. Many shows, too, particularly dramas, try to rip stories from the headlines. How did *All in the Family* come up with its storylines?

NL: I instructed the writers to pay close attention to everything that was going on in the house, what was going on with the kids or their mates if they were married, and to read at least one newspaper every day. It wasn't enough for a story to be topical if there was no effect on the family. We looked for stories that touched the lives of the mothers and fathers and kids living together. We came in talking about what was going on in our world, and then adapted that to what could be going on with the Bunkers.

JC: When the show first aired, in January 1971, there was that warning up front, something about how it was "suggested for mature audiences." How did you feel about having that label on the show?

NL: That's the way it had to be, and that was a network decision that had nothing to do with us. They felt they had to do it. But in the end I thought that made the show more interesting. "Well, if they have to warn us about this, I gotta see why!"

JC: What was the initial reaction to the show?

NL: Well, audiences loved it. At our tapings, I used to love to stand in the back of our live audience and wait for the guffaw, the belly laugh, because I would see a couple hundred people coming out of their chairs, going forward, and then coming back, which is inevitable in a huge laugh with a big crowd. And I remember thinking that was as spiritual a sight as anything I'd ever seen. All those people, strangers to each other, laughing at the same moment, their bodies moving as one.

JC: I know there were some critics who at first didn't get the show, who thought you were glorifying a bigot.

NL: Yes, that occurred a great deal. They said we made a hero of a bigot, and then they came to realize that that's not at all what the show was doing.

JC: In the pilot, Archie gives Edith a card with a poem, "Together," which in real life is a poem you once wrote for your father to give to your mother. Did your mother notice the poem in the episode? Did she call after the premiere?

NL: She didn't call me. I called them. And I had to say, "Did you see the show?" "Well, of course, darling. Of course we saw the show." And I don't recall whether I said, "Then why didn't you say something about it?" But that's the way she was. She withheld. When other people were around she made a big fuss about my sister and me. But I don't remember a single "I love you" when we were alone.

JC: Sitcoms often start to show strain as they age, yet *All in the Family* aired some of its most beloved episodes in season eight. Why did you decide to leave the show after that season?

NL: Bud and I had several other shows on the air, and one or two just beginning that needed so much of my attention. *All in the Family* had many great writers and producers who had been there for years, and I knew they could handle it.

JC: Would it be possible to do a show like *All in the Family* today?

NL: I don't know why not.

JC: Even though we've become so much more politically correct about language and about discussing hot topics?

NL: I understand why you're asking the question. I'm so fascinated with the fact that the question could still exist. Because we did it before, I have to believe it could happen again. But the conversation about whether it can happen again suggests that we both know it would be difficult.

JC: Do you still sit down and watch *All in the Family*? How do you feel when you watch it?

NL: I don't sit and watch it. But I did, preparing for this conversation. I saw a couple of episodes and I was overwhelmed by them as if I'd never seen them—certainly not because I had anything to do with them. But just because to watch Carroll O'Connor and Jean Stapleton—I mean, they were so good!

JC: Are you watching it almost like an audience member now, or do the memories flood back?

NL: Almost like an audience member. That's the way I've always been. I sit down and say, "Take me." I'm much more lost in the performance, when it's performances of this consequence.

JC: What did it mean to you to have Archie and Edith's chairs in the Smithsonian?

NL: As you asked that, I got such a tinge of joy, just to think that they're there. Right now, at this minute, there are people looking at those chairs. At the Smithsonian! It's an enormous honor in my life. That's the best of awards.

JC: Is that something your mother would have been impressed by? Or would she have said, "Listen, if that's what they want to do . . . "

NL: That's what she would have said . . . for the laugh.

The Pilots & Season 1

BECOMING THE BUNKERS

7 Episodes that Made a Hit

After we shot the first pilot, *Justice For All*, ABC asked me to make script changes to soften Archie, who at the time was named Wally, but I politely refused. We recast Gloria and Richard (later renamed Mike) and we shot another pilot, *Those Were the Days*. This time executives were simply frightened of the possibility of a bad reaction to a bigot on the tube. Now, when I think about how it turned out, everything happened for the best. Between shooting the first two pilots in 1968 and '69 and when *All in the Family* finally aired in 1971, the country was that much further into political and social change, and had a new president, Richard Nixon, for Archie and Mike to argue about. Although the show was not the immediate hit it would become, I knew we were doing something right. If the average sitcom was about "Mom had a little accident with the fender on the car, and how can we keep Dad from finding out about it until it's fixed," we were instead, as I instructed our writers' room, looking for the kinds of personal, real stories about what happened to us, our family members, and our neighbors.

—NORMAN LEAR

The Unaired Pilots
"Justice for All"
"Those Were the Days"

———

Season 1, Episode 1
"Meet the Bunkers"

———

Season 1, Episode 5
"Judging Books by Covers"

Season 1, Episode 6
"Gloria Has a Belly Full"

———

Season 1, Episode 8
"Lionel Moves Into the Neighborhood"

———

Season 1, Episode 13
"The First and Last Supper"

ARCHIE AND EDITH INTERRUPT RICHARD AND GLORIA'S PRIVACY BY
COMING HOME FROM CHURCH EARLIER THAN EXPECTED.

"JUSTICE FOR ALL"

WRITTEN BY: **Norman Lear** • DIRECTED BY: **Norman Lear** and **Gordon Rigsby**

STARRING: **Carroll O'Connor** as **Archie Justice** • **Jean Stapleton** as **Edith Justice** • **Kelly Jean Peters** as **Gloria**
Tim McIntire as **Richard** • **D'Urville Martin** as **Lionel**

TAPE DATE: **September 29, 1968**

"THOSE WERE THE DAYS"

WRITTEN BY: **Norman Lear** • DIRECTED BY: **Bud Yorkin**

STARRING: **Carroll O'Connor** as **Archie Justice** • **Jean Stapleton** as **Edith Justice**
Candice Azzara as **Gloria** • **Chip Oliver** as **Richard** • **D'Urville Martin** as **Lionel**

TAPE DATE: **February 16, 1969**

NORMAN LEAR: Sometime in the late '60s, I heard about *Till Death Us Do Part*, a British show that centered on a bigoted father and his liberal son who fought about everything. Immediately I thought, "That's my dad and me." My dad, H.K., used to call me "the laziest white kid he ever met." I'd accuse him of putting down a whole race of people just to call his son lazy, and he'd just yell back, "That's not what I'm doing, and you're also the dumbest white kid I ever met!" I knew I had to do an American version of this show. I wrote about seventy pages of notes—and incorporated those real life words of my dad's, which ended up in the pilot script—and asked a well-known agent, Sam Cohn, to represent the project.

In 1968, between early August and the end of September, we secured the rights, ABC commissioned a pilot, and I wrote and cast the episode. With Carroll O'Connor and Jean Stapleton as the leads, it was taped

before a live audience. There were two more pilots, two more years, and another network, CBS, before it got on the air.

The original title of the show was *Justice for All*. We were going to start the show by zooming in on a doormat on the porch that said "Justice," the family name. But when we shot the second pilot, we changed the show's name to *Those Were the Days*, to match the theme song. And then, when the show went to CBS, someone—I don't remember who—suggested naming the show *All in the Family*. At that time we also changed the family's name to Bunker, referring to Archie's opinions being based on "bunk."

In his oral history for The Interviews, **CARROLL O'CONNOR** *remembered:* I went to see Norman at his office on Sunset Boulevard. He had talked with me about the character, and he said some people thought he should

JUSTICE FOR ALL

First Draft

OPEN ON:
~~FADE IN:~~ HELICOPTER SHOT

CAMERA MOVES over the familiar skyline of New York City; moves out to Queens; and ZOOMS into a specific unit among blocks of identical attached two-family houses. DISSOLVE through to interior: the residence of the Justice family, a stamped-out, two-bedroom-one bath lower middle class unit, approximately 20 years old. ~~It is~~ furnished largely in Grand Rapids mahogany, *not* ~~most of it twenty years older~~ than the building. The only modern piece in the room is a 27-inch color TV set with remote control. It's on a swivel so as to face the dining room area as well as the sofa and easy chair.

As we open, RICHARD CULLY, the son-in-law, is hovering over the dining table adjusting the four place settings. A few strands of party streamers criss-cross above the table as a token sort of party gesture. It is mid-day -- and, as we will soon learn, Sunday. From the kitchen we hear the whirring sound of a blender.

>   RICHARD
>   (Calling toward kitchen)
>   Hey! What're you doing in there; you're
>   gonna beat those eggs to death. ~~if you're~~
>   ~~not careful!~~

The whirring stops.

>   GLORIA'S VOICE (O.S.)
>   I want everything ready when they get here.
>   All I have to do now is dump the eggs into
>   a pan.
>   (She ENTERS with a basket
>   of bread and rolls)
>   We can toast the bread right at the table.
>   Let's see now -- juice, eggs, bacon,
>   sausage, ~~link not patty, dad hates sausage~~
>   ~~patty -- yup, we're all set.~~

Link, not patty. ~~RICHARD~~ *He hates sausage patty, remember?*
~~He also hates paper napkins, remember.~~

>   GLORIA   *U-huh -- although it isn't easy*
>   ~~Oops, forgot. Thank you. It's hard to~~
>   *remembering* ~~remember~~ everything it takes to please Dad.
>   ~~(as she picks up the napkin~~
>   ~~she spots something else -- a~~
>   ~~small thin package)~~
>   ~~Oh -- Mom's present from Dad -- where'll I~~
>   ~~put it?~~

GLORIA
He gave it to Lionel.
He's going to deliver
it later, with some
fresh cut flowers,
just to make it more
romantic.

>   RICHARD
>   *What about the present you bought for him*
>   ~~this~~ *to give your mother?*
>   ~~[struck through text]~~

ARCHIE: An argument is nothing but shouting and hollering.

EDITH: Like what you're doing now.

ARCHIE: I am *not* shouting and hollering, goddammit!

EDITH: Now you're swearing too.

ARCHIE: You are a pip, you know that? A real pip!

be from Texas, since he was a bigot. And I said no, make him a New York Cockney, just like the guy in the English show was a London Cockney.

Working with Jean was one of the great pleasures of my life. I think Jean made *All in the Family*. Because she was exactly the right counterpoint for Archie Bunker. And her character was all-important. She was the proper, sensible, moral reaction to this nonsensical, immoral man. And with just as important a role as the immoral man's.

In her oral history for The Interviews, **JEAN STAPLETON** *remembered:* Before *All in the Family*, I was still in that category of character actress. It was easy for me to play, for instance, a bag lady, or to make myself look older. I liked my category, because it was interesting. And

very gratifying, too, because there was more richness in those characters than just a bland leading lady.

I remember reading the script, and was amazed by its quality. A comedy based in character and situation. And I thought to myself, "Wow, this, on TV? How wonderful!" Even then I thought that.

CARROLL O'CONNOR: We shot the first pilot in a theater on 58th Street in New York. ABC had turned it into a television studio, with room for an audience. We had an audience, and they howled that night.

I was in Europe when Norman said that ABC had said to him, "We want to do it again, with two other kids." So when I came back from Europe, in February, we went to the ABC Studios in Los Angeles and taped another pilot with another boy and girl. ABC rejected that, too.

CANDICE AZZARA: Carroll O'Connor and Jean Stapleton were wonderful—both incredible theater actors who were nothing like the characters of Archie and Edith. I couldn't get over how different Carroll was offstage, because he was very sophisticated. Jean, too, was such a brilliant actor, and she taught me something while we were doing this pilot. Sometimes I want something to be so real that I take too much time on a moment. And in one such moment in rehearsal, when I'm supposed to say something admiringly to Richard, Jean said to me, very quietly while she was folding her napkin, "Just say it." I had been overthinking the moment, and she was encouraging me to say the line on the impulse. She said it very quietly, because she didn't want anyone to hear. And I love when actors help each other like that. Otherwise, actors could go off and not do the truth about the scene, and why not get it correct? I was a young kid, just figuring out my craft, and I was so appreciative of that.

From what I heard about the three pilots, this second one was unusual in that they calmed it down a little. Gloria's husband, Richard, was a big, handsome guy, played by a former football player. The tone was a little more serious, and I didn't think it was as funny. The taping went well, but I just kept on thinking, "When am I going to go back to New York?" I had my heart set on being in the theater, and had never really thought about doing a series.

When the show got picked up by CBS with Rob and Sally in the roles, I was so happy to see it go that way. Everything just came together, and it made sense to me. I think Sally Struthers is much better than I was

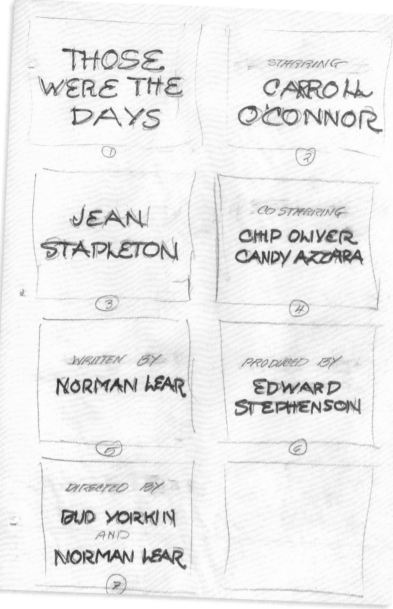

in the role, for one thing because her look was better, looking so much like Carroll. When I've met Sally, I've told her how I feel she was more adorable and much more right for the part.

In his oral history for The Interviews, former CBS Vice President of Programs **FRED SILVERMAN** *remembered:* Norman Lear and his agent came over to see CBS President Bob Wood, and I was in the meeting. We saw *All in the Family,* and I couldn't believe what I was seeing. Compared to the crap we were canceling, this was really setting new boundaries. To Bob Wood's credit, he said, "I love the show. We've got to put this on the air. This is good for television, and it's good for the nation." He had a major fight with CBS Chairman William S. Paley, who hated the show. But Bob prevailed, and they kind of snuck it on the air, in January.

NORMAN LEAR **helped change the face of television. At last, you could write something "real" after** *All in the Family***! Changing television is huge, and we owe that to Norman.**

—*SOAP* AND *THE GOLDEN GIRLS*
CREATOR SUSAN HARRIS

"THE OPENING SONG"

MUSIC BY: **Charles Strouse** • LYRICS BY: **Lee Adams**

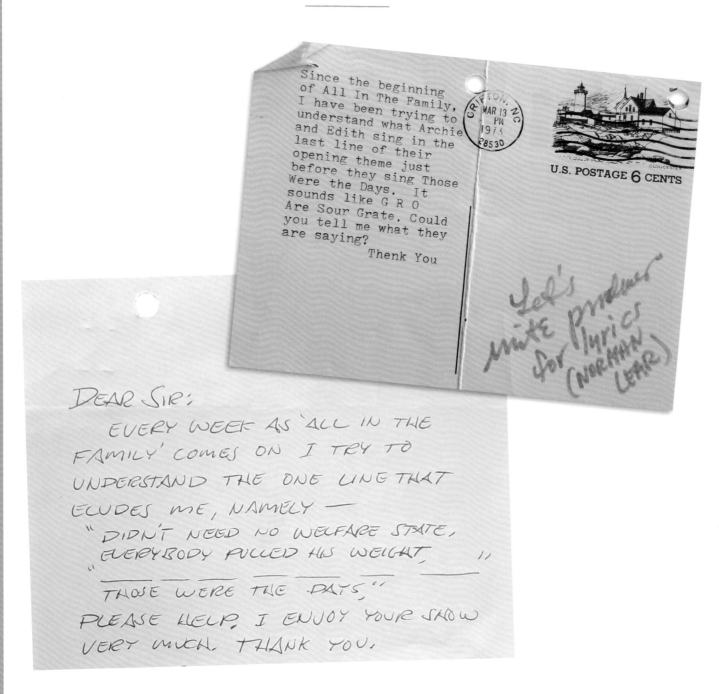

Since the beginning of All In The Family, I have been trying to understand what Archie and Edith sing in the last line of their opening theme just before they sing Those Were the Days. It sounds like G R O Are Sour Grate. Could you tell me what they are saying?

Thank You

Let's write producer for lyrics (NORMAN LEAR)

DEAR SIR:
EVERY WEEK AS 'ALL IN THE FAMILY' COMES ON I TRY TO UNDERSTAND THE ONE LINE THAT ELUDES ME, NAMELY —
"DIDN'T NEED NO WELFARE STATE, EVERYBODY PULLED HIS WEIGHT, _____"
THOSE WERE THE DAYS,"
PLEASE HELP. I ENJOY YOUR SHOW VERY MUCH. THANK YOU.

NORMAN LEAR: I was friendly with Charlie Strouse, who had written the music for Broadway's *Bye Bye Birdie* with his lyricist partner, Lee Adams, and who would go on to do the same for *Annie*. I asked him to write a theme song for *All in the Family*, and he asked me what the character of Archie was like. I said he's afraid of change, and of progress. So Charlie and Lee wrote this song, which conveys a deep nostalgia for another time: "Those Were the Days."

FADE UP:

(ARCHIE & EDITH AT PIANO)

MUSIC: "THOSE WERE THE DAYS"

ARCHIE

All right, I hear you!

BOY, THE WAY GLENN MILLER PLAYED

SONGS THAT MADE THE HIT PARADE!

GUYS LIKE US, WE HAD IT MADE --

THOSE WERE THE DAYS!

(DISSOLVE TO: FILM: AND SUPER TITLE
                CARDS:)

MUSIC: CONTINUES: 1. ALL IN THE FAMILY

EDITH   2. STARRING
AND YOU KNEW WHERE YOU WERE THEN   CARROLL O'CONNOR

ARCHIE   3. JEAN STAPLETON
GIRLS WERE GIRLS AND MEN WERE MEN,
                                      4. CO-STARRING
BOTH   BOB REINER
MISTER WE COULD USE A MAN   SALLY STRUTHERS

LIKE HERBERT HOOVER AGAIN!   5. DEVELOPED FOR
                                          AMERICAN TV
ARCHIE   AND
DIDN'T NEED NO WELFARE STATE,   PRODUCED BY
                                             NORMAN LEAR
EDITH

EVERYBODY PULLED HIS WEIGHT

BOTH

GEE OUR OLD LA SALLE RAN GREAT!

THOSE WERE THE DAYS!

Season 1, Episode 1

"MEET THE BUNKERS"

ARCHIE AND EDITH INTERRUPT MIKE AND GLORIA'S PRIVACY BY
COMING HOME FROM CHURCH EARLIER THAN EXPECTED.

WRITTEN BY: **Norman Lear** ● DIRECTED BY: **John Rich**

STARRING: **Carroll O'Connor** as **Archie Bunker** ● **Jean Stapleton** as **Edith Bunker**
Sally Struthers as **Gloria Bunker Stivic** ● **Rob Reiner** as **Michael Stivic** ● **Mike Evans** as **Lionel Jefferson**

ORIGINAL AIR DATE: **January 12, 1971**

WARNING: The program you are about to see is *All in the Family*. It seeks to throw
a humorous spotlight on our frailties, prejudices, and concerns. By making them a source
of laughter, we hope to show—in a mature fashion—just how absurd they are.

NORMAN LEAR: Right before things started heating up again for *All in the Family*, I had been offered a three-picture deal by the movie studio United Artists—and in fact, friends and family members were encouraging me to take that, rather than choose the riskier option of this TV show. But knowing that I had that in my back pocket helped me stand up to CBS on several occasions. The first had been when CBS, having seen the second episode we shot, wanted to air it as the show's premiere instead, because it was gentler. But I argued to CBS that we were going to

have to jump into the deep water and get wet together. And by airing the true pilot first, not only would we be showing the full 360-degree view of Archie Bunker which I intended, but after all, I told them, "You can't get wetter than wet."

In this pilot episode—actually, in all three versions of the pilot we shot, which used almost exactly the same script, with some edits for the purposes of time—Gloria and her husband are home alone on a Sunday morning, which is also her parents' twenty-second anniversary. The one real difference here is that the husband is a Polish-American man named Mike instead of the earlier version of the son-in-law character, an Irish-American named Richard.

Mike and Gloria have planned a surprise for Archie and Edith, a celebratory brunch. Gloria has finished preparations earlier than she thought, and she and Mike kiss, which leads to them going upstairs. But moments later, they hear the door open; Archie and Edith are home early, because he didn't like the service.

When Archie sees them come running downstairs, with Mike buttoning his shirt, he remarks, "11:10 on a Sunday morning!" Well, the network wanted that line out, and I couldn't believe it. They said the line would cause the audience to think about exactly what Archie

ALL IN THE FAMILY

ACT ONE

FADE UP:

(GLORIA IN DINING ROOM SETTING TABLE.

MIKE ENTERS FRONT DOOR.)

MIKE

Gloria -- I hurried back.

GLORIA

Good, you can take out the garbage.

MIKE

Garbage ~~isn't~~ IS NOT exactly what I had

in mind. Come here.

GLORIA   MIKE: why not?

Not now, Michael. I want everything

FOR
ready when the folks get back from

church.

(COMES D.S. TO TABLE)

It's different, isn't it, an

anniversary brunch.

MIKE
Yeah, well I think
Your mother will love it, But

Doesn't
your father -- ~~a lot~~ he cares about

anniversaries. You hadda buy ~~him~~

For him
the present to give your mother.

her
And I had to ~~pick out~~ the card.

And he doesn't even know about any

of this. What do you think he's

                    GLORIA

He'll have a fit. But ~~he~~ *then* wouldn't

get her anything and it'll make

Mom's day.

                    MIKE

~~Why~~ *What* are you running from me? Come

here.

(HE KISSES HER)

                    GLORIA

We've been living with your folks

since ~~we've been~~ *we're* married. ~~How~~ *we*

~~often do we get the house alone?~~ *Don't get the house alone that much!*

                    GLORIA

We're not alone. Lionel's upstairs.

                    MIKE

Lionel? Why?

                    GLORIA

He's fixing the portable TV for

Dad.

                    MIKE

(Reacts)
~~Great.~~

                    GLORIA

And later ~~Lionel's going~~ *he's gonna* to take

the present, ~~pick up~~ *get* some fresh-cut

flowers and deliver them together,

just to make it more romantic.

thought had been happening at 11:10 on that Sunday morning. That became the first huge fight the network and I had. Program Practices had other concerns about the episode, which we'd settled, such as, "Archie's comment on the shortness of Gloria's skirt should not be as anatomically personal as, 'Every time you sit down the mystery's over.'" But even though our premiere date was set—Tuesday, January 12, at 9:30 p.m., right after *The Beverly Hillbillies*, *Green Acres*, and *Hee Haw*—by that Monday, CBS was still insisting that they would have to remove the "11:10 on a Sunday morning" line.

I was on my way home to see the first episode live on television, airing three hours after it had aired in New York, and I didn't learn until I got home that when it had aired in the East, the network had left the line in after all. This was before car phones, and when I had left the studio and the last telephone call with the network, we had still been arguing about it. I said that if they took out the line in New York, I would not be in the next morning.

The line had been left in, and no state seceded from the union. I never understood the kind of fear they had showed that day. What did they think would happen? What would the American people do? Would they burn a building? Would they throw rocks at anything resembling CBS?

A sweeter note in the episode came from the poem that Edith reads from the anniversary card, which came right from my real life; it was an actual poem called "Together," which I had written as a kid for my father to give my mother for their anniversary. Here I am now at ninety-eight, and I can remember the whole thing. "The thirteen years I've been with you we've shed many a tear, it's true / But life for us has just begun. We've yet to have all our fun / As long as we're together. / And when, my dear, we're old and gray, and life for us is sunny weather / We'll look back on our lives and say / it's been a gay, gay lark together." I never forgot that.

"ALL IN THE FAMILY"

CHARACTER BACKGROUND

Archie Bunker is 48 years old. Edith is 45. They have been married for 24 years, married after World War II, when Archie had returned from service overseas. They attended the same high school and Edith remembers Archie from that period, although Archie claims no memory of it.

Edith has long ago made her peace with Archie's force and bluster. Inside she understands, and a later show will illustrate this, that his bluster is merely a defense. Outside, it's impossible to live with but Edith manages the impossible. She manages it, by only being about 50% there all the time. The rest of her is off somewhere. Edith probably had a father like Archie so her training in living with the condition is extensive.

Archie was with the 15th Air Force overseas and, from time to time, he may speak of the missions his outfit flew over Berlin, Frankfurt, the Brenner Pass, etc., only to have someone remind him that he was in the supply department and never actually got off the ground himself.

When Archie was mustered out of the service, his uncle got him a job as an elevator operator in one of the best local Manhattan commercial buildings--a distinguished address. Archie is still there.

ROB REINER: I knew Norman from the time I was eight years old, because he and his wife were friends with my parents, and I used to play with his daughter Ellen. When *All in the Family* was made twice as a pilot for ABC, I auditioned for one of those, and didn't get it. Then some time went by, and they were doing it again at CBS. At the time I was working as a writer on a show called *Headmaster*, starring Andy Griffith, and had appeared in one episode as a young teacher. I showed Norman that, and he said I'd improved. So I went back and auditioned, and got the part in the CBS pilot. And actually, Penny Marshall, who I was dating at the time and would later marry, auditioned to play Gloria, and didn't get the part.

I was twenty-three when the show went on the air, and it meant a lot to me to get that part. We all saw from the start that we were doing something special. There's an expression people use, "playing for the band," which means you're too hip for the room, but at least the band is going to laugh. We felt that way, excited to be part of something really good, but also something that would last a few weeks and then go away, because it was just too far out.

Forget about pushing the edge of the envelope—we ripped up the whole envelope! And CBS tried to sneak the show on the air. They aired a huge disclaimer at the beginning. Basically it was, "Pay no attention to the show. None of the views expressed in the show are part of what CBS thinks. If you want to watch it, fine—but we wouldn't recommend it." We thought it would all be over after thirteen weeks, and then goodbye and good luck. And in fact, it wasn't until we won the Outstanding Comedy Series Emmy in May, and they replayed those thirteen episodes over the summer, when people eventually caught on to it.

SALLY STRUTHERS: I had been a regular on *The Tim Conway Comedy Hour* on CBS in 1970. I did sketches on the show, and I was also part of the show's opening, which was designed to look like it was being done for pennies. Tim had had shows on the air before, and all of them were over in thirteen weeks; he even drove a car with "13WEEKS" as his license plate. So that was the joke, that his show was such an underdog, it had no budget. The announcer would announce "Ladies and gentlemen…the Tim Conway Dancer!" and then it would be just me, in a ridiculous-looking tap-dancing costume. But the suits in New York didn't get the joke. They called the producers and said, "That girl makes the show look cheap! You've got to get rid of her!" And so I was let go.

But as the adage goes, when a door closes, God opens a window. I got a call from my agent that there was a man named Norman Lear casting for a TV series

called *All in the Family*. The day I first went in to read for Norman, I had laryngitis. In his outer office, I got handed the audition pages—a yelling scene. And I guess when I read it for Norman, trying to yell but with no voice, that in itself was funny. It certainly was not planned, but it must have made him remember me.

I didn't hear anything for a while, and I don't know how many young ladies he saw for the role of Gloria, but I think it was many. Finally, I got a phone call that I was in the final four. I would be reading again at CBS in front of Norman, his partner, Bud Yorkin, and a whole bunch of CBS suits. Rob Reiner was already cast as Mike, and when I walked in, they were going to throw a subject at the two of us and we would just make up dialogue. The problem was, I knew one of the other four women was Penny Marshall, Rob's girlfriend. I knew them personally, and that they already knew each other's rhythms. So of course Penny would land the role!

Psychologically, the moment I saw Penny that day, I gave up. I knew I didn't stand a chance—and I guess that made me relax, and improved my performance. Later, after I was cast, I asked Norman, "How the hell did I land this role? Was I the funniest one in the auditions?" And he explained that the writers had considered what would make better storylines—if Gloria were closer to her mother, or if she were Daddy's Little Girl? "We decided Daddy's Little Girl had more story opportunities," Norman explained. "And you look an awful lot like Carroll. You've got the same round face with blue eyes."

But the best casting story for *All in the Family* has to be about Mike Evans. He was just a kid who was hitchhiking to Santa Monica one day, wanting to go to the beach. He was hitchhiking on Santa Monica Boulevard, and some other kid driving by stopped and picked him up. The guy told Mike he could take him only as far as Century City, because he was going to read for a new television show. Mike found that very interesting, so the guy said, "Well, why don't you come with me?" So Mike walked into Norman Lear's outer

> **ARCHIE:** I made up a name like Roundtree Cummerbatch?
>
> **MIKE:** That's right, you made it up to put down a Black man.

26

The Hanupper Manufacturers' Bank and Trust Building is one of the few buildings in Manhattan that still has the grace to retain elevator operators--and more than that, an Elevator Starter. Archie, for the past 13 years, has occupied this top post. His take-home pay is about $7,300.00 a year, a high for the profession, but it isn't enough to sustain the Bunkers.

For the past five and a half years, or so, Archie has been moonlighting as a cab driver on most Saturdays and an occasional Sunday and on some holidays. This pulls Archie up to almost $11,000.00 a year on a good year. A figure of which he's quite proud.

On Gloria's next birthday, she'll be 21 years old. She and Mike have been married less than a year. Gloria was a delicate child through most of her early years and her mother hasn't quite gotten over it. She babies her some, which isn't that upsetting to Gloria. Upon graduating high school, Gloria saw no reason to go to college. Instead, she took a one year stenographic course and she now works a day or two here and there, averaging about three days a week, for a Kelly Girl type service. Gloria's ambition is to be a good wife to Mike. Their relationship is very physical and the fact that they both have a need to touch a lot drives Archie up the wall.

Mike, by the way, is Michael Stivic, a Slavic type whom Archie insists upon calling a Pollack. Mike's family actually came from Estonia and though certainly Slavic, he is not sure if he's Polish. He is 23 years old and, having grown up largely on the streets in a rough neighborhood, he barely made it through high school and felt no urge to continue on to college when he graduated. Instead, he went to work with two uncles as an apprentice in the Hod Carriers' Union. When the military called, Mike was lucky--flat feet. Otherwise, he might be in Canada.

From 18 to 21, Mike tried many things. Nothing took but he began to find a kind of direction out of a growing desire to help humanity. As noted, Gloria and Michael are married under a year. Now 23, Michael is enrolled in N.Y.U. where his major is somewhere between the humanities and sociology. With Gloria passionately in agreement with his aims, Mike hopes someday to do something worthwhile for humanity--to become one of Ralph Nader's Raiders, for example; or to join the Peace Corps in some meaningful capacity; etc.

Mike is not a student of long habit and so he finds college difficult. He attends school six hours and studies six hours and he also moonlights when he can, pumping gas at a friend's station. With the little he makes and the few half days that Gloria works each week, they have enough to keep them in "pin money." So, while they pay no rent, they at least have the small amounts needed to take care of their own entertainment, most of their own clothing, etc. and now and again, Mike may even be able to make a gesture; such as, taking the folks out to dinner.

Lionel is about ~~Richard~~ MIKE'S age, perhaps a year younger. His father has been manager of the Hemstead Apartments--about six blocks away, for some years and Lionel has been doing odd jobs in the neighborhood since he was 12. When Mike moved into the Bunker household and met Lionel, they became fast friends. This friendship was further cemented when they learned that each went to N.Y.U. Lionel's visits to the house, then, occur as a result of some work Lionel is doing there or simply as a result of his friendship with Mike and Gloria. The frequency of Lionel's visits irks Archie, but never so much as when Mike and Gloria double date with Lionel and a girl.

Within the first 13 episodes, Lionel's family will buy the house next door to the house next door to Archie. But even before, that big moment will be preceded by another episode in which Lionel's father advances from his position as a janitor in an apartment building to the owner of a small neighborhood cleaning store.

In the first 13 episodes, we will also expect to do a show in

ARCHIE: That's a nice suit you got on, by the way. Where'd you get it?

LIONEL: Harlem. I got two more just like it. One in yellow, one in purple. You know, for when I'm with my people.

which Archie's job is threatened. In the second year, he will lose it, at which point he will have to be trained (with men far younger than he) for some other kind of employment.

Much of the above information will take many episodes to unravel for the audience. Little of it is necessary for their understanding except as it fits the show's purposes to reveal background.

office, and they handed him a script. Mike wrote his name down, because he watched the other guy do so. And when they called his name, Mike went in and read it—and landed the role. He had been hitchhiking to the beach, and fate intervened. And that guy who gave him the ride probably kicked himself for the rest of his life.

In his oral history for The Interviews, **JOHN RICH** *remembered:* We called Mike in and told him he got the part. I took him aside and said, "Listen, everybody else in this rehearsal is accomplished. They've been onstage before. They know how to wait for laughs." I said, "When that audience laugh comes at you, it's like a thunderclap. You've got to know when to wait. If we don't hear the straight line, we haven't got the joke." So I said, "Just don't talk too soon. Come in when it's time."

We did the night, and every one of my professionals talked into laughs. He did not. He was great that night.

ORMAN'S SHOWS MADE ME SEE just how relatable and deep a sitcom could be, and I continue to aspire to that in my own writing. On *One Day at a Time* we certainly continue the *All in the Family* tradition of people with opposing and disparate political views hashing out their differences in the living room or at the dinner table. And when things get real, we try to keep them as real as possible. Like Norman, we want our viewers to deeply feel with the characters and relate to them.

Nowadays there are so many political-commentary and social-awareness discussions on social media and talk shows, but dramatizing that in a way that feels real—and tells a higher truth than just scoring points back and forth—remains a very difficult thing to pull off successfully. In my opinion, the reason for *All in the Family*'s success was not because of its "edginess" but because of its relatability. Everybody knew, and knows, a guy like Archie, as well as the other characters. If it were to work again today, it would have to achieve that same thing, which of course is a high bar.

But as Norman will tell you, his favorite word is "next." As in, don't dwell on the past, but go on to the next things. Norman lives to keep learning, and that is reflected in his shows that continue to hold up a mirror to the world and reflect new things.

—*ONE DAY AT A TIME* (2017–20) CO-CREATOR MIKE ROYCE

In her oral history for The Interviews, **JEAN STAPLETON** *remembered:* At first we actors had nothing to go on, but Edith had a zinger, about one line a page, that just broke Archie's hot air. Every time, it was a laugh. And so I think I said the lines in quite a wry and wise manner, knowingly giving a zinger. It burst his bubble, and that's the way I played the pilots and the first shows, because I had nothing else to base Edith on. You don't know much about these parts. I tried to find it in what she was doing, but the character evolved in the first thirteen weeks, as they did for all of us. I didn't even use the nasal quality in my voice. We saw one episode of the English series called *Till Death Us Do Part*, and that wonderful actress who played the wife was as abrasive as her husband. And so that was a hint about how to go about this. But when we got into rehearsal, and the fact that we were in New York, where I knew everybody hurried, the abusive demands on Edith pushed her into a run. She was hurrying to get things on the table. That's how the little run arose, and became part of the character. And I added the nasality because I had used it in *Damn Yankees* for comic purposes, and I thought well, I'll give her that nasality. I'll steal it from myself.

LIONEL: Now there you are, Mr. Bunker, you should be proud of the fact that you're Jewish.

ARCHIE: But I ain't Jewish!

EDITH: I didn't know you was Jewish.

"JUDGING BOOKS BY COVERS"

AFTER JUDGING MIKE AND GLORIA'S EFFEMINATE FRIEND TO BE GAY,
ARCHIE DISCOVERS THAT HIS OLD BAR BUDDY, HIS FOOTBALL IDOL, IS HOMOSEXUAL.

WRITTEN BY: **Burt Styler** and **Norman Lear** • DIRECTED BY: **John Rich**

GUEST STARS: **Anthony Geary** as **Roger** • **Philip Carey** as **Steve** • **Bob Hastings** as **Tommy Kelcy**
Billy Halop as **Barney** • **Billy Sands** as **Nick** • **Linn Patrick** as **Jerry**

ORIGINAL AIR DATE: **February 9, 1971**

NORMAN LEAR: Gay people were then and are now a part of everyday life, which is why we did this episode. It's not that we were looking for subjects that would startle or stun an audience. We just wanted to look at real life and deal with subjects that mattered. So while in 1971 this story may have been something new to television, it wasn't new in the neighborhood. You didn't get to be as old as I was and not know someone who was gay.

Now, what could be better dramatically and comedically than Archie, after going on and on about Mike's friend at the bar, then not only learning that a guy he admired for years as a great football player and a strong male is gay, but to learn it as they were arm wrestling, right there in their moment of "double maleness"?

Steve is a big guy who could easily slam Archie's arm down, and *boom*! He did. I like that Steve was very matter-of-fact about his sexuality, and didn't hate Archie for his attitude. He had long since learned to live his life.

In arguing about Roger, Archie says, "I never said a guy who wears glasses is a queer. A guy who wears glasses is a four-eyes. A guy who's a fag is a queer." I'll never forget that line. I don't remember having trouble with too much of the language in this episode from the network—but I do remember being surprised that not everybody knew the expression *four-eyes*.

MIKE: You know something, Archie, just because a guy is sensitive, and he's an intellectual and he wears glasses, you make him out a queer.

STORY LINE NUMBER 2   4.
                                                    (8/6/70)

This is the story of Mike's friend, Roger. Roger is a kid who

wears glasses, has a fair complexion and is fairly intellectual.

Wally is convinced he's a queer and doesn't want him around. Early

in the show, perhaps at the bar where wally stops for a beer we

meet a buddy of his, a truck driver named Clancy. Clancy is big

and tough and we learn of course at the end of the show that he

has been a homosexual for some time. Wally learns it for the first

time too. It could take place when Mike brings his friend, Roger,

into the bar and Wally makes a couple of remarks to Clancy. Clancy

takes exception and in their ensuing dialogue Wally learns the

truth. This story should explore the current American attitude

toward maleness and what constitutes a man, all the phoney values

that exist. Viet Nam and draft dodging, and protesting and so forth

can be a part of the dialogue here because Wally drags it in. Being

a soldier, being able to kill, standing up for one's country, etc.

All of this is equated to manliness in Wally's mind.

Somehow indian wrestling should top off this episode. I don't know

whether it's Wally who Indian Wrestles with Roger or Roger who

Indian Wrestles with Clancy as Wally cheers Clancy on -- but I

see an Indian Wrestling match taking place at the end of this show.

The problem with this one is to discover that Clancy is a homesexual

in such a way that it is not either a set-up or is simply announced

that it has to develop dramatically. It may be that Mike has always known this about Clancy and that he sets up a situation wherein Wally finds out. As a matter of fact it would be wrong if Mike knew it. It wouldn't ring true really. The one that could know that Clancy was a homosexual is Roger. And if Mike brings Roger into the bar and Roger sees Clancy, he could mention it to Mike. Then when Mike hears it and we, the audience, here hear it at the same time, Mike would register surprise and pleasure and we know that he intends to do something about it by way of surprising Wally with the truth... This leads to a kind of run down now.

In an early scene in the house, Mike announces Roger is coming over. Wally calls him a queer, they argue about queers and war and Viet Nam, and etc. Wally blows the argument by going down to the bar for a beer. We CUT TO the bar where a few of his cronies hang out, including the bartender. Wally comes in. Big greeting, a few remarks, we see how close Clancy and Wally are (when Wally leaves, Edith asks him to bring back a few beers for her. He pays no attention and we know he isn't gonna do it) After Wally is at the bar for a while, Mike and Roger come in. Mike has come to get the beers for Edith. While they're waiting at the bar, Roger notices Clancy and makes some mention of him. Mike is surprised that he knows him. Roger answers that there's something about the world of minorities being a small one. Roger reacts surprised and pleased. END OF ACT ONE.

EDITH: That
big football player
is a flower?

ANTHONY GEARY: I had just left college in Utah and come to L.A. in a play. Then I got this script, and was really shocked and excited about it. In those days, to be gay, you would hear everything in terms of negative reactions. It might make you not want to get out of bed in the morning, because it was so oppressive and so minimizing as a human being. I know because I *am* gay, and I had to face some fear about this role—but then I realized I had to do it, because it was just too good and too special. This show was new and was already jumping into deep water.

I had to figure out exactly how gay Roger would be, although I loathe saying that, because any of us who is gay or knows gay people knows that there's no one way to be gay. But in that script, Roger had to elicit strong feelings from Archie. So I tried to make him just the friendliest kind of guy imaginable, flamboyant, with lots of gestures, excited about life, a younger-than-spring-time kind of guy. I asked the wardrobe department to give me a longer scarf than they had initially provided, so that when I came through the door and started talking with my hands, I could really get that thing flying. I figured Roger was going so fast and having such a good time with his little life that he didn't even hear the negative kinds of things Archie would say. It was silly, and cartoony in a way, but it seemed to work.

After a while in rehearsal, Norman called me aside and said, "I love what you're doing. It's absolutely perfect. Don't change a thing. There are a lot of feelings around this episode from the network all the way down. We're taking a big risk here, but you're being very courageous." That relieved me of all my fear, and then I was able to go forward. It ended up being an extremely positive experience for me. This episode has turned out to be an iconic piece, and I'm proud of it. I quite like "Roger the Fairy." He is precious to me.

Burt Styler is working on that story and in discussing it
with him there were a few additional ideas that grew out
of it, which I'd like to note here.

I see a scene toward the end of the piece taking place in
a bar in which Wally's friend recognizes Roger. This is
a switch on the earlier idea that it was Roger who recognized
him. Wally's friend recognizes Roger and Wally is surprised.
He wants to know how his friend knows Roger. The friend says
that he used to go to the same bar that he went to. Wally
expresses surprise and the friend expresses surprise that
Wally is surprised. The friend intimates that he's queer.
Wally scoffs. The friend scoffs back, unable to believe that
Wally who has known him for 20 years didn't know this. The
friend even goes so far as to say that in all of those years,
in all of the times I've been to your house, etc. have you
ever seen me with a date. Wally's answer is that he knows a
lot of bachelors and he just shrugs the bad joke off. The
friend is willing to forget the whole thing. Now it's Wally
who presses. "Come on. What are you kidding about a thing
like that for?" I see this scene written with very little
dialogue. A lot of reactions back and forth. A lot of "come
ons" from Wally. I even see Wally getting up and walking
around his friend, sizing him up. Maybe even jabbing him on
the shoulder as it gives him an excuse to feel his muscle.
But in any event refusing even to the end to believe that
the guy is anything but a hundred percent male.

ARCHIE

How long you known this friend of
Mike's, this Roger?

STEVE

Oh, a coupla years. Ever since he
started coming into the shop.

ARCHIE

A couple of years. All right now,
you're a man of the world -- you
know the kid's a la-de-da. Don't you?

STEVE

Is that what <u>Mike</u> thinks of Roger?

ARCHIE

Mike? Don't be silly. I hate to
tell you what Mike thinks. Come on
let's go at it again. Give me a chance
to get even.

(HE LAUGHS AND PUTS HIS ARM UP AGAIN. STEVE LOCKS
HANDS WITH HIM AGAIN.)

STEVE

(BEMUSED)

What <u>does</u> Mike think, Archie?

ARCHIE

Well, first of all he thinks his
friend Roger is straight. And
then --

(STRAINING AGAINST STEVE)

    You'll bust him wide open for this

    when you hear it --

(LAUGHS THROUGH THE STRAIN)

    I don't know where he comes up with

    these brainstorms!

              STEVE

    What is it, Arch?

              ARCHIE

    He has the infrontery to infer that

    you -- that you're a --

(HIS ARM GOING OVER - PUSHING IT UP)

              ARCHIE

    -- I can't even say it.

              STEVE

(SIMPLY)

    He's right, Archie.

              ARCHIE

(REFUSING TO HEAR)

    Huh!?

              STEVE

    He's right, Archie.

(ARCHIE'S HAND GOES OVER WITH A ZONK)

              ARCHIE

    You mean about Roger.

              STEVE

    About everything.

5/5/72
dear Norman + John —
Score another one
for our side!

J Hirsch

MARCH 21, 1972

DEAR SIRS:

PLEASE CONVEY MY PRAISE AND WARMEST REGARDS TO THE PRODUCERS AND CAST OF YOUR TELEVISION PROGRAM "ALL IN THE FAMILY" FOR LAST SATURDAY'S SUPERB PRESENTATION WHICH CASTED A FAVORABLE AND HONEST LIGHT ON HOMOSEXUALITY TODAY.

CERTAINLY, AS ANY "GAY BAR" OWNER WILL TELL YOU, THERE ARE MILLIONS OF BEAUTIFUL HOMOSEXUALS IN THIS WIDE WORLD AND THE RANKS OF HOMOSEXUALS ARE GROWING GREATER EVERY DAY!

INDEED, WHAT A MAN DECIDES TO DO WITH HIS OWN BODY IS HIS OWN JUDGEMENT AND BUSINESS AND BEYOND THE PROVINCE OF ANY AGENCY!

CERTAINLY, THERE IS ROOM FOR EVERYONE IN THIS WORLD! YOUNG AND OLD, HETEROSEXUAL AND HOMOSEXUAL!

WHAT IS MORE, THE HOMOSEXUAL IS NATURE'S ANSWER TO CONTROL OF THE OVER-POPULATION OF THIS CROWDED WORLD! HUMAN LOVE WITHOUT REPRODUCTION!

CONGRATULATIONS! CBS HAS COME A LONG WAY IN THE HUMAN FAMILY TOWARD JUSTICE AND PEACE FOR EVERYONE!

VERY TRULY YOURS,

(AN ORGANIZATION OF PROFESSIONALS WHO ARE ALSO HOMOSEXUALS)
(DOCTORS, LAWYERS, PILOTS, ETC.)

(8,000 COPIES)

"GLORIA HAS A BELLY FULL"

WHEN GLORIA ANNOUNCES HER PREGNANCY, SHE AND MIKE INFURIATE ARCHIE BY STARTING TO LOOK FOR THEIR OWN APARTMENT. BUT WHEN SHE THEN SUFFERS A MISCARRIAGE, IT'S UP TO HER LOVING FATHER TO COMFORT HER.

WRITTEN BY: **Jerry Mayer** • DIRECTED BY: **John Rich**

GUEST STARS: **Mike Evans** as **Lionel Jefferson** • **Holly Near** as **Mona**

ORIGINAL AIR DATE: **February 16, 1971**

NORMAN LEAR: The idea for this episode arose from our wish to show a loving side of Archie. I thought getting Archie to a moment with Gloria where he could express his feelings, and allow that much emotion to emerge, was just wonderful for both the character and the actor. And as I say those words, I am right back there, utterly in that scene. I can see Carroll so clearly in that moment with Sally. This was also the first time the show gave Sally an opportunity to stretch and show how strong she was. I like using the word "swell" to describe Sally, because swell means great; swell means wonderful; swell means perfect. And Sally was all of the above.

One other trivial bit about this episode: The argument between Archie and Edith about whether Archie prefers patty sausage or link had originally been in the show's first two pilots, between Archie and "Richard," but had been cut. So we reused it here. It goes back to my youth with my father, because he had a distinct preference for link.

JERRY MAYER: I pitched this story to *All in the Family* because I thought it could be a good combination of comedy and then seriousness. Norman liked it, we discussed it, and I went back and wrote the first draft. but Norman rewrote it into a second draft, realizing that they could really turn the end into a tearjerker with Archie, which was a good idea. And that second draft is what they shot.

HOLLY NEAR: In casting the part of Mona, I think the producers wanted to go hippie. I think they were trying to bring in what would symbolically appear to be progressive, to go in opposition to the head of the household. My character was talking about natural childbirth and how beautiful and wonderful it all was, in contrast to Edith's then-more-traditional point of view, where she was happy to have been sedated during Gloria's birth.

I was on *All in the Family* near the very beginning, and I ended up being so impressed with the show. I know that progressives could watch and enjoy it, and so even could conservatives who might see themselves in Archie. But what was interesting for me were those people who didn't fall in either category, who found themselves being exposed to race and gender and sexuality. *All in the Family* contributed to conversations that hadn't been had before. Let's say someone is watching at home an episode with a gay character. The conservative in the household is glad that Archie disapproves; the progressives are saying, "This is incredible that this is happening!" And somewhere in there is a person, maybe a mom who sides with her husband on conservative issues, but she'll be the one that her kid comes home to and comes out to. Now somebody has said the word "gay," and it's in her consciousness because she saw it on *All in the Family*. I think the show was very helpful to a lot of people.

ARCHIE: I always order patty!

EDITH: And I was so sure it was link.

ARCHIE: Edith, I'm going to say "patty" once more—once more, you understand—and if you say "link"…if you so much as think "link"…

EDITH

Archie, we have to tell you something.

ARCHIE

Edith you've been yakking at me for weeks

to get this thing settled between me and

this big galook. Now what have you got to

tell me that's more important than getting

it done before the baby?

EDITH

Well --

(LOOKS TO MIKE TO TELL HIM)

MIKE

It That's just it, Archie. (BEAT)
We're not having a baby now, Archie.
There won't be a baby.

ARCHIE

Whattaya mean no baby?
What you mean won't be a baby? You
do
didn't go through something unlegal,

you big dumb Pollack!

MIKE

No, no. Nothing like that, Archie
You mean abortion?

ARCHIE (RIDING)

Can't you have a conversation without

using words like that? Now what's

going on around here? I'm asking you

if you did something to otherwise

ARCHIE
(HE SENSES, BUT CAN'T FACE IT)
Then what are you talking about?
Edith, what are you looking like
that for?

EDITH
Gloria lost the baby, Archie.

(BLUSTERING ON) ARCHIE
But she ain't even had the
baby yet - how can she lose it??
(KNOWS THERE'S NO ANSWER - TAKES ANOTHER TACK)
Who'd you have over here, anyway?
What doctor?
That Viennese phony with
the hair and the wire glasses?
I wouldn't believe a man like
that if my life --

(THE DOCTOR HAS BEEN COMING DOWNSTAIRS
IN THE B.G. ARCHIE SEES HIM NOW AND
BECOMES INSTANT-HUMBLE)
Oh. You - must be Doctor...

DOCTOR
Herman.

ARCHIE
(SMILING)
Yes. Well. How's my little girl?

CUT TO:

(GLORIA IN HER BED. CLOSE SHOT.)

SOUND: DOOR OPENS

(GLORIA SMILES. PAN FROM HER TO
ARCHIE IN THE DOORWAY)

GLORIA

Hi, Daddy.

ARCHIE

Hi, sweetheart - you O.K.?

GLORIA

I didn't do a very good job,
did I?

ARCHIE

Who said so? Say, did that little
Vienna sausage say anything to ---

(A BEAT)

GLORIA

No, no. Now ~~stop it.~~ And you
can stop fidgeting, too. What is
it you want to say?

(BEAT)

ARCHIE

Nothing.) Well, I ---

GLORIA

You love me.

(ARCHIE SIMPLY STANDS THERE AND GRINS)

I love you, too, Daddy.

FADE OUT:

Season 1, Episode 8

"LIONEL MOVES INTO THE NEIGHBORHOOD"

ARCHIE IS NOT HAPPY TO LEARN BLACK PEOPLE ARE MOVING NEXT DOOR—EVEN IF THEY ARE THE BUNKERS' LONGTIME FRIEND LIONEL JEFFERSON'S FAMILY.

WRITTEN BY: **Don Nicholl** and **Bryan Joseph** • DIRECTED BY: **John Rich**

GUEST STARS: **Mike Evans** as **Lionel Jefferson** • **Isabel Sanford** as **Louise Jefferson**
Vincent Gardenia as **Jim Bowman**

ORIGINAL AIR DATE: **March 2, 1971**

ARCHIE: They ain't gonna be happy here. What are they gonna do?
What are they gonna do for recreation? There ain't a crap game
or a pool hall in the whole neighborhood. There ain't a chicken shack
or a rib joint within miles.

LIONEL: No ribs? Lawd Almighty, what is we gonna do?

NORMAN LEAR: Archie's racist actions here, helping to circulate a petition to keep a Black family from moving into the neighborhood, was something that had long been going on in America, and was still going on then. The '70s were still rather early when it came to integration of neighborhoods in many places. And there was conversation everywhere about neighborhoods changing.

In the episode, Mike even cites studies showing that when the first Black families move into a neighborhood, property values actually increase, because those families tend to be prosperous. But my father had built houses for some years, so I knew that misconceptions were definitely out there, something I understood to be a supposed "truth" in our culture.

And the reason Archie's reaction to the Jeffersons moving in next door was so effective for comedy was that it was so well-understood. It was not discussed, it was pushed aside, and people pretended those conversations didn't exist—but they were totally recognizable to many viewers.

ROB REINER: The way this episode depicts Archie's racism is very un-PC. Some of the things Archie says, screaming about how "watermelon rinds are going to be flying out the window"—it's the most racist, horrible stuff you can possibly imagine. I don't think you could get away with having even an obviously racist character say things like that now—and yet, there certainly are people who are like that now.

ALL IN THE FAMILY IS TELEVISION THAT MATTERS. The show enlarges your heart and makes you more sensitive to other people's perspectives and humanity. The humanism of it has been inspiring to me, and the skill with which it can make you laugh and feel strongly in back-to-back moments.

When I was co-creating *King of the Hill*, I was aware of using a family dynamic to bring a lot of perspectives to controversial current topics. We also had a conservative father grumpily dealing with a changing world, and when I broke stories, I would explicitly think about how *All in the Family* would manipulate the story to put pressure on Archie's worldview. With *The Office*, where I was bringing a British show to the U.S. the way Norman Lear did, I was thinking from the start about issues of translation from British sensibilities to American, which I'm sure he thought about. And then I had as a central character a culturally insensitive middle-aged man who was often being used by the show to make more sensitive and socially progressive points. And *Parks and Recreation* started with NBC president Ben Silverman's insistence that *All in the Family* birthed a lot of other shows and that we needed to do the same for NBC, and it contains a lot of political optimism.

—*KING OF THE HILL*, *THE OFFICE* (U.S. VERSION) AND *PARKS & RECREATION* CO-CREATOR GREG DANIELS

Season 1, Episode 13

"THE FIRST AND LAST SUPPER"

WHEN LOUISE'S HUSBAND, GEORGE, REFUSES TO ATTEND A DINNER WITH
THE BUNKERS, SHE BRINGS HIS BROTHER, HENRY, TO POSE AS HER SPOUSE, PROVING
THAT ARCHIE IS NOT THE ONLY STUBBORN PATRIARCH ON THE BLOCK.

WRITTEN BY: **Jerry Mayer** ● DIRECTED BY: **John Rich**

GUEST STARS: **Mike Evans** as **Lionel Jefferson** ● **Isabel Sanford** as **Louise Jefferson**
Mel Stewart as **Henry Jefferson** ● **Bill Benedict** as **Jimmy McNabb**

ORIGINAL AIR DATE: **April 6, 1971**

ARCHIE: Every picture I've seen of God, he's white.

HENRY: Well, maybe you were looking at the negative!

HENRY: What makes you think God isn't black?

ARCHIE: Well, because I was made in God's image, and you'll notice I ain't black.

HENRY: Well, don't complain to me about it.

NORMAN LEAR: From very early on, we had had Isabel Sanford in mind to play Louise, but then we had trouble getting the right actor to play her husband. And at first we tried to avoid naming a Louise until we had a George.

Isabel was superb as Louise. From the first time she appeared on the show, in "Lionel Moves Into the Neighborhood," it was apparent. In that episode, she had a scene where she came to the Bunkers' house to get the house keys and to borrow a pail for cleaning. And from the first time I saw Isabel in that scene with Jean and Carroll, offstage in rehearsal, it was magic. I knew there had to be an important relationship there.

What I remember most of all from these early days of the show was watching the actors, especially the first time coming into the rehearsal hall. It would be the first time we saw the actors up and moving, mouthing the words that we loved in the script. It was fabulous, like being a visitor to show business. And this script had such a great back-and-forth in the dialogue, such as when Archie and Henry argue over whether God

and Jesus could be Black. It was fun to watch—and of course we don't know for sure to this moment whether God is white, or Black, or green.

In her oral history for The Interviews, **ISABEL SANFORD** *remembered her casting differently:* The first time I was on *All in the Family*, I was playing Louise Jefferson's sister.

Then they called me to come back again. I said, "Do you know who you're calling? This is Isabel Sanford." And the girl said, "Yes, I know, I know. They told me to call you to come out for an audition."

I said, "All right, but you know I was out there already."

"We know, we know," she said.

"You see, I want things to be straightened out before I go," I said. "I don't want to be embarrassed."

She said, "I know, but they said they want to see you again."

So I went back in. This time, I saw John Rich, the director. I said, "But John, I was just here the other week. And I was the aunt, the sister to Louise Jefferson!"

And he said, "Well, who's going to remember that?"

After that, I didn't audition for the role of Louise. John just called me in to see me and speak to me. He didn't audition me, because I auditioned already. He knew what I could do.

I spoke with John about the role of Louise. I said to him, "You know, I wouldn't come running in, asking George how was his day. Black women don't do that. And I wouldn't go running into the kitchen to get him his beer or whatever he wanted. We don't do that." He said he understood, and took that all in. That's the discussion we had about Louise. I patterned Louise after me, the way I was with my husband.

4 October 1971

ALL IN THE FAMILY
CBS-TV
New York, N.Y.

Gentlemen:

I have just recently been introduced to ALL IN THE FAMILY and I love it.

Beneath its innocent guise of "situation comedy" it is a tremendous commentary on our contemporary social scene. It is entertaining, and at the same time, constructive.

CBS and the program's sponsors are to be commended for the courage to support such a program.

I suspect that you get more than a fair share of negative letters each week re: this program; hence, this note of support. Don't give it up. We all need ALL IN THE FAMILY.

ALL OF *ALL IN THE FAMILY*
The Unaired Pilots and Season 1

The Unaired Pilots
1968 & 1969

"Justice for All"
WRITER: **Norman Lear**
DIRECTORS: **Norman Lear, Gordon Rigsby**
TAPE DATE: **September 29, 1968**

★

"Those Were the Days"
WRITER: **Norman Lear**
DIRECTOR: **Bud Yorkin**
TAPE DATE: **February 16, 1969**

Season 1
1971

Episode 1
"Meet the Bunkers"
WRITER: **Norman Lear**
DIRECTOR: **John Rich**
AIR DATE: **January 12, 1971**

★

Episode 2
"Writing the President"
WRITERS: **Lee Erwin, Fred Freiberger, Paul Harrison, Lennie Weinrib, Norman Lear**
DIRECTOR: **John Rich**
AIR DATE: **January 19, 1971**

★

Episode 3
"Archie's Aching Back"
WRITER: **Stanley Ralph Ross**
DIRECTOR: **John Rich**
AIR DATE: **January 26, 1971**

★

Episode 4
"Archie Gives Blood"
WRITER: **Norman Lear**
DIRECTOR: **John Rich**
AIR DATE: **February 2, 1971**

★

Episode 5
"Judging Books by Covers"
WRITERS: **Burt Styler, Norman Lear**
DIRECTOR: **John Rich**
AIR DATE: **February 9, 1971**

★

Episode 6
"Gloria Has a Belly Full"
WRITER: **Jerry Mayer**
DIRECTOR: **John Rich**
AIR DATE: **February 16, 1971**

★

Episode 7
"Mike's Hippie Friends Come to Visit"
WRITERS: **Don Nicholl, Bryan Joseph, Phil Mishkin, Rob Reiner**
DIRECTOR: **John Rich**
AIR DATE: **February 23, 1971**

★

Episode 8
"Lionel Moves Into the Neighborhood"
WRITERS: **Don Nicholl, Bryan Joseph**
DIRECTOR: **John Rich**
AIR DATE: **March 2, 1971**

★

Episode 9
"Edith Has Jury Duty"
WRITERS: **Don Nicholl, Bryan Joseph, Susan Harris**
DIRECTOR: **John Rich**
AIR DATE: **March 9, 1971**

★

Episode 10
"Archie Is Worried About His Job"
WRITERS: **William Bickley Jr., Norman Lear, Don Nicholl, Bryan Joseph**
DIRECTOR: **John Rich**
AIR DATE: **March 16, 1971**

★

Episode 11
"Gloria Discovers Women's Lib"
WRITERS: **Norman Lear, Sandy Stern**
DIRECTOR: **John Rich**
AIR DATE: **March 23, 1971**

★

Episode 12
"Success Story"
WRITER: **Burt Styler**
DIRECTOR: **John Rich**
AIR DATE: **March 30, 1971**

★

Episode 13
"The First and Last Supper"
WRITER: **Jerry Mayer**
DIRECTOR: **John Rich**
AIR DATE: **April 6, 1971**

The Emmys
1971

Outstanding New Series
NORMAN LEAR, PRODUCER

★

Outstanding Series - Comedy
NORMAN LEAR, PRODUCER

★

Outstanding Continued Performance by an Actress in a Leading Role
JEAN STAPLETON

---

from Box # 302 (Sony)
(1971)

EMMY OPENING   1971

FADE UP:

(EDITH IS RUSHING TO TV, PICKING UP
TV GUIDE AND CALLING OUT EXCITEDLY.
ARCHIE IS READING NEWSPAPER)

EDITH

Hurry up everybody! It's going
to start in a minute -- the 1970-71
Emmys -- direct from the Palladium
(SINGS FLATLY)

"Hooray for Hollywood."
(ARCHIE ENTERING)"

ARCHIE

Alright, Edith, settle down. The
Emmys. It's just another one of them
dumb shows -- a bunch of millionaire
actors runnin up and huggin and kissin
and thankin each other and cryin! I
want to tell you something, if one of
them guys start to cry tonight with
them making Ten Thousand Bucks a week,
I'm gonna turn off that set.

Seasons 2–3

"YOU'RE REALLY GOING TO DO THAT?"

14 Episodes that Pushed Buttons

We knew we were a ratings hit when we started the second season. Total strangers would, again and again, stop me to talk about the show, recognizing me even then by the white hat I so often wear. People stopped me everywhere. But the enthusiastic reaction to the show didn't really change anything. We all had our work to do, and it was the same work, the same struggle to come up with a good idea—and it sounds crazy to say "struggle" when you're sitting in a room, trying to make each other laugh. That's what it was all about: a laugh with a good idea.

—NORMAN LEAR

Season 2, Episode 5
"Flashback: Mike Meets Archie"

Season 2, Episode 7
"Edith's Accident"

Season 2, Episode 9
"Mike's Problem"

Season 2, Episode 12
"Cousin Maude's Visit"

Season 2, Episode 14
"The Elevator Story"

Season 2, Episode 15
"Edith's Problem"

Season 2, Episode 21
"Sammy's Visit"

Season 3, Episode 4
"Gloria and the Riddle"

Season 3, Episode 7
"The Bunkers and the Swingers"

Season 3, Episodes 9 & 10
"Flashback: Mike and Gloria's Wedding"

Season 3, Episode 15
"Archie in the Hospital"

Season 3, Episode 20
"Archie Is Branded"

Season 3, Episode 23
"Gloria the Victim"

"GOD BLESS AMERICA"
(Playback)

(UP ON)

                    MIKE

Oh YEAH, Now
~~Uh huh!~~ I see what your idea of a

free country is. You're free to say

anything you want, but if anyone

disagrees with you -- they're either

thrown into jail, or called a meathead, RIGHT?

                    ARCHIE

That's right. Because this is

America! Land that I love...

                              MIKE

                    I love it, too, Mr. Bunker...

                    and it's because I do I

                    protest when I think things

                    are wrong, the right to dissent

... stand beside   is the principle on which this

her, and guide her country was based. Listen to

... through the   me! It's in the Bill of Rights.

night with the   Why do you think we broke away

light from above. from England to begin with?

From the mountains, Because we didn't agree with

to the prairies,   them. Because we demanded

to the ocean...   freedom. But it's guys like

wide with foam...   you who don't even listen to

(INCREASES IN VOLUME) reason...

        (MORE)   (MORE)

Season 2, Episode 5

"FLASHBACK: MIKE MEETS ARCHIE"

ON THEIR FIRST WEDDING ANNIVERSARY, THE STIVICS REMINISCE ABOUT THE FIRST TIME GLORIA BROUGHT MIKE HOME TO MEET THE FUTURE FATHER-IN-LAW WHO WOULD DUB HIM "MEATHEAD."

WRITTEN BY: **Phil Mishkin** and **Rob Reiner** ● DIRECTED BY: **John Rich**

ORIGINAL AIR DATE: **October 16, 1971**

NORMAN LEAR: Rob Reiner and Phil Mishkin were writing partners before *All in the Family*, so when the show started, they wrote a few episodes, such as this one. But eventually it made for some difficulty for Rob, because the role of Mike is so important to the show, and the idea of both writing and performing the character became overwhelming. So Phil continued writing, but when Rob got so entrenched in the character, he leaned 100 percent into the performance side. But of course that didn't mean he stopped contributing ideas. Rob and Carroll were a great comedy team and would often come up with suggestions for moments between the characters. The entire cast contributed very much to the content of the show throughout the rehearsal process.

PHIL MISHKIN: The idea for this episode came from Norman, who thought this would be a great time for us, with this relationship between Mike and Archie that had already been established, to see how it all began.

The episode has what I think is the greatest act break after Act One, and it was Rob's idea. As Mike tries to reason with Archie, Archie drowns him out by reciting the lyrics to, and then singing, "God Bless America." In our original draft, there was some dialogue following Archie's singing. But then Rob said to me, you know, we don't need the dialogue. I wasn't sure; how do you "button"

that argument before going to the commercial break? Rob always wanted to direct, and he's always been a great editor. Maybe it's breeding; he was terrific at knowing what would work and what's too much. I used to call him "the Sultan of Slice." And Norman agreed with him; you can't top the song. It made for a great first-act curtain.

The irony is that for a few minutes in the episode, Mike and Archie started getting along, when they realized that they had something they liked in common: baseball. That's why to me, these first moments when they met really did set the tone for their relationship. They never really liked each other, but they loved each other. It makes me sad just to think about it.

Season 2, Episode 7

"EDITH'S ACCIDENT"

EDITH ACCIDENTALLY DENTS A CAR PARKED IN THE SUPERMARKET PARKING LOT WITH HER SHOPPING
CART AND LEAVES A NOTE FOR THE CAR'S OWNER, WHO TURNS OUT TO BE A CATHOLIC PRIEST.

STORY BY: **Tom** and **Helen August** • TELEPLAY BY: **Michael Ross** and **Bernie West** • DIRECTED BY: **John Rich**

GUEST STAR: **Barnard Hughes** as **Father John Majeski**

ORIGINAL AIR DATE: **November 6, 1971**

NORMAN LEAR: I love the sound of the words "cling peaches," especially the way Jean Stapleton said them. And in the course of rehearsal, the more she said them, the funnier they became. Add to that the image that came with them, suggesting a push-cart full of cling peaches, and Edith taking her hands off it for just a moment and losing control, with a can jumping out and denting the priest's car. Actually, when we first came up with the story, it was going to be a station wagon full of nuns. But then it became a priest, because one nun coming to the house, representing a dozen nuns, wasn't going to be as funny as the reaction we would get from Archie over a priest. And the priest could be played by Barnard Hughes,

with whom I'd worked in the summer of 1970 on the film *Cold Turkey*, which we shot—along with Jean Stapleton—on location in Iowa. I adored that film, and working with such a glorious actor and lovely man as Barney. In the end, we were able to save the "station wagon full of nuns" idea for *Mary Hartman, Mary Hartman* instead.

I was thinking back on this recently, about what Archie's problem was with the Catholic church as represented by this priest. Obviously, Archie had problems with people from any group that he didn't understand. But in this case, I think it's more Archie bristling at the idea of the automatic authority conveyed by the priesthood. Archie's reaction, and the distrust he showed over the car accident and the bill, would come foremost from his attitude of "Who do you think you are?" rather than simply the man's being Catholic. That distrust is actually something that goes all the way back to the pilot, when Archie and Edith have left church early because he hated the sermon and didn't like the minister.

ROB REINER: This episode has the comedy bit about the "cling peaches in heavy syrup," part of the reason why Edith had her car accident. It was hysterical, and Jean had perfect timing and knew just how to do it. Anytime they gave Jean anything really funny like that, she was going to find a way to get every ounce of comedy out of it.

                                    EDITH

You told me never to say those two words.

                                   ARCHIE
              or what
Edith, are you trying to tell me, ~~that~~

you hit a car with a can of cling

peaches!

                                   EDITH
                  Ya see
That's right / I was coming out of the

market with my shopping basket full of

hmm hm-hm, and there was Mrs. Duncan

with her new baby. I took a peek in

the carriage -- but I couldn't see the

baby too well, '~~cause~~ he was all squinged
                 his
up with ~~the~~ pillow ~~and the blanket~~ --

                                   ARCHIE
will you
Get on with ~~it~~ *the story.*

                                   EDITH
                 knew   *had*
Well, anyway, I ~~thought~~ I ~~ought~~ to say

something nice about the baby, so I

went --

(CLAPS HAND TOGETHER)

   "Oh! Isn't that a beautiful baby!"

   And when I went...

(CLAPS HAND TOGETHER)
                         basket
   "Oh!" The shopping ~~cart~~ got away from
           rolled
me, ~~and ran~~ down the hill and smashed

into this parked car, and scratched the

fender...

   ... and then this can of hmm hm-hm, in

heavy syrup, jumped out and made a big

dent in the hood!!

(BEAT)

It was a freak accident.

                    HENRY

What's up?

                    ARCHIE

This is kinda private and ~~very~~ *it's a little bit* delicate

... I got this friend of mine ~~who's run~~ *see & he's havin'*

~~into some,~~ what you call, connubible

difficulties.

                    HENRY

Huh!

                    ARCHIE

That means he's a married man, but the

trouble *with him* is he can't -- uhhh -- *he's stuck in neutral.*

                    HENRY

I Got ya!

                    ARCHIE

Well ~~Good.~~ Now, ~~Jefferson~~ -- it's a well

known fact that youse people... I mean,

the men... when it comes to the members

of the opposite there -- ~~you're~~

~~champeens.~~

                    ~~HENRY~~

~~Huh!~~

                    ARCHIE

~~It's a fact~~ you got a kind of ~~special~~ *special*

stanima... along 'em lines.

                    HENRY

Oh, ~~yes.~~ *Yeh* I hear we're ~~quite~~ *very* advanced in

that department.

                    ARCHIE

Right, ~~right.~~ *Yeh well* And that's why I'm ~~coming~~

to you for help. *see*

(QUICKLY)

~~Not for me... for my friend.~~

                    HENRY

Oh, I don't know, Bunker. ~~I mean if it~~ *I don't know if-*

I can tell you that ~~was for you, okay...~~ but it's such a

well-guarded racial secret.

"MIKE'S PROBLEM"

MIKE ASKS ARCHIE FOR ADVICE AFTER HIS ANXIETY OVER FINAL EXAMS RENDERS HIM IMPOTENT.

STORY BY: **Alan J. Levitt** • TELEPLAY BY: **Alan J. Levitt** and **Phil Mishkin** • DIRECTED BY: **John Rich**

GUEST STARS: **Mel Stewart** as **Henry Jefferson** • **Brendan Dillon** as **Tommy Kelcy**

ORIGINAL AIR DATE: **November 20, 1971**

NORMAN LEAR: This episode saw another of our biggest conflicts with CBS's Program Practices department. CBS wanted no part of anything to do with impotence. CBS President Bob Wood even flew out to California to discuss the episode. I was working seven-day weeks, so we had to meet on a Sunday, at 8 in the morning. He said, "You're doing a show, a family show, on television, about how he can't get it up?" We'd heard that CBS founder and Chairman William Paley found the show "unattractive," but I felt sure that high ratings would change his mind.

I asked Bob if he'd like to see the script. We sat there and read this first-draft script aloud line by line. He and I played every character. Bob and I howled, and he had his handkerchief out, wiping his eyes. Bob saw that the big laughs came from the family's inability to discuss sexual matters, and not from Mike and Gloria's attempts to deal with the problem. The script had Archie approaching Henry Jefferson in Kelcy's Bar for his advice. And when Henry told Archie that the secret was hog jowls, and then whispered to Archie to tell his friend to be careful—too many of those jowls and he'll start wanting to shine shoes—Bob lost it. So did the audience who came to see it when it was taped a few weeks later with his blessing.

ROB REINER: I think the two longest laughs we ever had were when Sammy Davis Jr. kissed Archie on the cheek, and the moment in this episode when Archie is talking about Mike with Henry Jefferson at Kelcy's Bar. Archie's already assuming that Black people know a lot

about sex, and now he's unable even to state the problem, saying his son-in-law is "stuck in neutral." That line got what had to be an eleven- or twelve-second laugh—it seemed like it went on forever.

This was one of those shows about taboo topics where CBS said they weren't going to air it. And then this is why I love Norman so much—he's got such balls. If the network didn't want to air an episode, he'd say, "Okay, well, we don't have to air it. But then I'm quitting. And we're not going to do the show anymore. If you want me, I'm going to be in the Fiji islands. And I'm leaving now. You can just call me if you want me to do more shows." He had the strength to tell them, "This is the show we're making."

PHIL MISHKIN: This story had been pitched and written by Alan Levitt, and then Norman asked me to work on the teleplay as well. Some of the new material I added was in the bar scene with Archie talking with Henry, like Henry's recommendation of hog jowls as an aphrodisiac, but with the warning that "you start in with them jowls, and you might develop a sudden craving to shine shoes." And that whole run of jokes led to Carroll ad-libbing a great line, which has become a classic, about Mike being "stuck in neutral." It was something he improv'd in rehearsal—I don't know if he thought it up right there and then, or if he had come up with it earlier and brought it to rehearsal. Alan Levitt and I got an Emmy nomination for this episode. But it was Carroll's line, and I still get credit for it. And I take it.

"COUSIN MAUDE'S VISIT"

WHEN EVERYONE COMES DOWN WITH THE FLU, EDITH'S COUSIN MAUDE COMES TO THE
HOUSE TO HELP, AND IMMEDIATELY CLASHES WITH ARCHIE OVER OLD RESENTMENTS.

STORY BY: **Phil Mishkin** • TELEPLAY BY: **Phil Mishkin, Michael Ross** and **Bernie West** • DIRECTED BY: **John Rich**

GUEST STARS: **Bea Arthur** as **Maude Findlay**

ORIGINAL AIR DATE: **December 11, 1971**

NORMAN LEAR: People remember the character of Maude Findlay being as liberal as Archie was conservative, but actually that came later, on the show *Maude*. There wasn't a trace of that in her appearance on *All in the Family*; she clashed with Archie purely over what happened back when.

This episode was based on my experience in my family, who lived at the top of their lungs. Then, when somebody would come to visit—a cousin or someone who could be close to a relative, but definitely someone who hasn't seen another member of the family for a number of years—they'd be bearing an ancient grudge. So they'd be carrying a hundred pounds of grudge all the way from Boston, and when they'd get into the argument, all those years of holding that grudge would give them a vocal and emotional advantage. And they used it; they slugged with it. That's what I wanted to

do with Archie. I wanted somebody who knew him not necessarily that well, but well enough to have carried such a grudge over all the years. And as soon as I knew I wanted to do that character, Bea Arthur came to mind, because I knew her work well, and we were friends. It was the kick of kicks being able to invite her to come out and play that role. If you needed a relative to slug a relative, there was nobody like Bea Arthur!

When you have a show on the air, and you come across a performer where you think, "Holy shit—that's somebody who could hold their own show," you cast them quite deliberately in a role on your show that's already going, to see if the audience doesn't believe you're right. And that's exactly what happened with Bea Arthur. We put her on *All in the Family* knowing she would kill. And indeed, before the East Coast feed of the show was off the air, I got a call from CBS president Fred Silverman, saying, "There's a show in that woman!"

PHIL MISHKIN: Norman had told the writers that they needed to find a script that he called an "in house," which relied on just the four main characters, only at home. I had just gone through an experience where my wife, my kids, and I had all gotten a winter cold. And when that happens, who does for who, when everybody's sick? So I had brought that up and then got to write it as an episode.

I thought it had some funny scenes in it, but Norman noted that really, nothing happened—and he

---

ARCHIE: Let her go!
I've got my chair back!

MAUDE: Archie, you
can have your chair.
Only don't move around
too much or you'll crush
your brains!

---

was right. And then I remember his face as he had a eureka moment. The next thing I know, he's talking about a character from the British series that he wanted to modify and create for Bea Arthur. And the next thing I wind up having to do is add this new character, Maude.

SALLY STRUTHERS: Every Wednesday, two guys from Program Practices—the censors—would sit in our rehearsal hall with the script on their laps and their pencils out, and we would do a run-through. They wouldn't look at us but would be listening and following along in their scripts, marking them up for meetings later with Norman and the writers with things like "You let Archie say 'Jeez' twice in this episode. And we only allow once, because everyone knows that's short

for 'Jesus,' and that's swearing. So we'll let you have one 'Jeez.' " The conversations went like that.

But when they brought Bea Arthur in to play Cousin Maude, Bea knew this already about Program Practices. And she had zero respect for that part of the process. She laced every single line she had in that run-through that Wednesday with foul, sailor-on-shore-leave language. The Program Practices guys were turning purple, thumbing back and forth in their scripts and filling them with notes. We were all dying with laughter, because Bea was being intentionally, completely foul-mouthed and adding "f-ing" swear words into every line she said to Archie. Program Practices didn't know what to do. I think they both pooped in their pants. It was one of the finest moments in rehearsal hall.

                        ARCHIE

        Will youse two pipe down -- my head's

        killin' me!

(EDITH TRIES TO KEEP THE PEACE)

SOUND: DOORBELL

(ARCHIE TRIES TO GET EVERYBODY'S ATTENTION.

HE GETS UP TO ANSWER THE DOOR)

                        ARCHIE

        Shut up all of youse -- Shush!!! -- There's

        a person at the door.

(HE OPENS THE DOOR ON A TALL, GRIM-FACED WOMAN

CARRYING AN OVERNIGHT BAG)

                        ARCHIE

        Huh? What are you doing here?

                        EDITH

        Maude!

                        MAUDE

        Edith!

(SHE HANDS ARCHIE HER OVERNIGHT BAG)

                        ARCHIE

        Wait a minute, Maude, didn't you get my

        telegram to stay the hell away?

                        MAUDE

        Listen, dum-dum! I've always ignored

        everything you've said, why should I pay

        attention to anything you write?

                        (MORE)

                    MAUDE

     Edith!! Honey-lamb! You can rest easy

     now. Maudie's here.

                    ARCHIE

     Oh, geez --!

FADE OUT.

END OF ACT ONE

"THE ELEVATOR STORY"

ARCHIE GETS STUCK IN AN ELEVATOR WITH A BLACK LAWYER, A NEUROTIC SECRETARY,
A PUERTO RICAN JANITOR, AND HIS HEAVILY PREGNANT WIFE. WHEN THE MOTHER-TO-BE GOES
INTO LABOR, THE GROUP MUST HELP HER DELIVER THE BABY.

WRITTEN BY: **Alan J. Levitt** • DIRECTED BY: **John Rich**

GUEST STARS: **Roscoe Lee Browne** as **Hugh Victor Thompson III** • **Hector Elizondo** as **Carlos Mendoza**
Eileen Brennan as **Angelique McCarthy** • **Edith Diaz** as **Serafina Mendoza**

ORIGINAL AIR DATE: **January 1, 1972**

NORMAN LEAR: Carroll and I had some difficulty in that we didn't agree on everything. He was a very obstinate guy—whose work was fabulous. Working with him through any differences just was part of my day's work; I didn't take it personally at all. But this episode started off with our biggest disagreement.

Most of the episode took place in the cramped quarters of an on-screen elevator. After the first table reading, which seemed an agony for Carroll, he said there was no way in the world he would do this show, as five people in an elevator for practically the whole half-hour would be impossible to shoot. Director John Rich said he could make it work. Carroll disagreed. I think Carroll was concerned with the difficulty of pulling it off, of holding the audience without any movement at all in a cramped elevator—and particularly in the climactic moment, where the script called for just a close-up on Archie. In fact, as I think of it right now, I realize that's a major challenge for any actor. Only the rarest of actors could pull it off, which is why I wanted it for Carroll. I had to have it.

Our schedule called for us to work Monday through Friday and do a dress rehearsal without cameras late Friday. We would take the weekend off, then start to put the show on camera the following Monday morning. We'd have an on-camera dress rehearsal Tuesday afternoon, then shoot two shows before a live audience Tuesday night. We went all the way to Friday

fighting about the episode, with Carroll insisting he couldn't do it.

On Friday afternoon, there was a meeting with his attorney, his agent and his manager, my partner and my attorney, and CBS. It was a big deal. I was simply in love with the idea of that baby being born shown on Carroll's face. The camera was not going to go down to the floor of the elevator and see the woman giving birth; the camera was going to be on Archie, when he first hears the cry of that newborn infant.

After it was eventually settled, we worked on Saturday and taped on Tuesday. The audience cheered. Some cried. Carroll O'Connor's Archie was stunning. The scene was even better than I imagined. The essence of Archie's humanity is right there on his face.

HECTOR ELIZONDO: I noticed that there was some kind of consternation on Carroll's part after the table read, but any other argument about it must have happened while I was just doing the work. That cast was so terrific, theater-trained. Carroll was just a wonderful fellow, so bright and so opposite of his character—and yet he understood the character deeply, and that's what made it such a wonderful work of art. Carroll himself was a writer, and he knew what shaped a scene. He had a great sense of what did and didn't sound like his character, or what was a gratuitous joke. I remember how surprised I was that as they rewrote, the writers took out what they realized were gratuitous jokes—sitcoms often keep in any jokes they can. But *All in the Family* wasn't a jokey show. It was driven by all those indelible characters. That's why the audience started to laugh as soon as a situation came up. They were waiting for the reaction, not the funny line.

The show was talking about things that were relevant right at that moment—and TV was not known for being good at being at-the-moment relevant. There were words you would never say, and now you were hearing them coming out of Archie's mouth. And the artful thing was that people came to love Archie, because they knew deep down he was a decent guy. That's what this episode showed so well. After all the ignorant things he says in that elevator, when that camera pushes in on his face and Archie asks, "A little boy, huh?"—he himself looks like a little boy, with tears in his eyes. That's it—Emmy! Thank you very much!

CARLOS: Let me 'splain something to you, mister. One: How many children we have is 'cause we love each other very much. Two: You talk very intelligent, mister, but you not so smart. Three: Shut up you face.

Season 2, Episode 15

"EDITH'S PROBLEM"

EDITH BEGINS MENOPAUSE, UPSETTING THE BALANCE OF THE BUNKER HOUSEHOLD
AND CALLING ARCHIE'S ABILITY TO BE UNDERSTANDING INTO QUESTION.

STORY BY: **Steve Zacharias** ● TELEPLAY BY: **Burt Styler** ● DIRECTED BY: **John Rich**

★ EMMY AWARD: *Outstanding Writing Achievement in Comedy* ★

GUEST STARS: **Jeannie Linero** as **Waitress**

ORIGINAL AIR DATE: **January 8, 1972**

NORMAN LEAR: In the 1970s, menopause was not a subject that came up on television. But it was perfect for our show, because it was the stuff of family. The show's writers were mostly men, so when we were working on this episode, we were glad that the women within the company were there for advice. And when we wanted more determinative, professional advice—because we really wanted to get this right—we often reached out to the medical staff at UCLA.

We were glad that when this episode aired, the feedback we got was more positive than negative, more applause than criticism. Today, it doesn't seem like depicting menopause would upset anyone, but those were definitely more conservative times.

BOB LAHENDRO, *Associate Producer*: CBS was always wary and sensitive about every show we did. You had to imply a lot, and use other words to say what

> ARCHIE: Edith…If you're going to have the change of life, you've got to do it right now! I'm giving ya just thirty seconds. Now c'mon, change!
>
> EDITH: Can I finish my soup first?

you really wanted to say. You had to beat around the bush—but in doing so, it became funny. Because Edith had a tough time talking about anything that sensitive, she was always beating around the bush when it came to anything sexual. And that was comedy gold.

SALLY STRUTHERS: Jean Stapleton played Edith's personality changes beautifully, and it was so sweet when Archie went out at the end and got her one of those little battery-operated fans. It was always fun to see when Archie would try to be tender to Edith and would usually fail, in his own clumsy way—and yet she appreciated any kernel of kindness he ever threw at her. And I also love the moment where Archie is finally fed up with trying to be nice to Edith, and yells at her: "I'm going to give you thirty seconds! Now come on…change!"

STEVE ZACHARIAS: I had been with my parents in Palm Springs, and my mother had a little battery-powered fan. When I asked her about it, she said it was her "menopause fan." I was just starting out as a writer, and had a meeting to pitch ideas to *All in the Family*—and now I realized that menopause would be a good story for Edith.

When I went in to meet with one of the senior writers, I brought eighteen ideas, and my mother's fan. I used to bring all kinds of props to pitch meetings; I once brought a raw fish and vodka. When I got to the Edith menopause story, I showed him the fan. He stopped me and asked if he could bring it over to show Norman.

A short while later, I was still running through my list when we were interrupted by a phone call: Norman would like to see me. It was a surreal experience to get to go into Norman's office—and when I did, he was fanning himself with my mother's fan. He said, "Steve, we're going to buy your show."

Norman explained that they didn't want me to be the one to write the script, because they thought I was too young, and that a middle-aged person should do it. I couldn't disagree with that, really. So Burt Styler wrote a draft—but then Don Nicholl, one of Norman's most trusted writers and someone I think is one of the greatest writers in the history of television, did the rewrite.

The end result was like a Broadway play. I looked at it and thought I couldn't complain, because I couldn't have written that. It was sensational. Then, just as they were about to shoot "Edith's Problem," I got a call from Norman's office. They said, "Steve, we hate to bother you—but we've looked all over, and we can't find another fan like that. Can we use yours?" So I brought it down to the studio again, and that's the one that Archie gives Edith.

That was the end of the story—until the episode won the Emmy. When you get only a "Story By" credit, you don't get an Emmy trophy. I got a certificate but wasn't invited to the Emmys. I was in my bed, in my boxer underwear, watching the ceremony with my wife, as Burt Styler accepted the award. It was a good first lesson about how things can work in Hollywood—but on the other hand, I had won an Emmy and I was twenty-three years old. So I was a pretty happy guy.

ARCHIE

Well, you ain't long out of the trees...

(THE FRONT DOOR BURSTS OPEN AND IN STORMS EDITH.

BUT THIS IS AN EDITH WE HAVE NEVER SEEN BEFORE.

SHE'S IN A FOUL, BAD-TEMPERED MOOD. SHE

CARRIES BAGS OF GROCERIES)

ARCHIE

Oh, there you are, Edith. We're starvin'

here.

EDITH

(SNAPS AT HIM)

Don't rush me, Archie Bunker! Your

dinner will be ready on time! It's

always ready on time.

(AS SHE HEADS FOR THE KITCHEN)

GLORIA

Let me help you with those bags, Ma.

EDITH

Leave me alone!

(SHE BRUSHES GLORIA ASIDE AND EXITS TO KITCHEN)

GLORIA

What's the matter with Ma?

ARCHIE

I was gonna ask you.

(EDITH STORMS OUT OF KITCHEN AND GOES TO HANG

UP HER COAT.)

EDITH

Get out of the way, Gloria.

(ARCHIE GOES TO HER)

ARCHIE

Hey, Edith there, is there something

wrong?

EDITH

No!

ARCHIE

Then why are you actin'...?

EDITH

Don't argue with me!

ARCHIE

I ain't arguing! All I'm doin' is

asking...

EDITH

If you're asking for a fight, you're

gonna get one!

MIKE

(ANXIOUSLY)

Can I do anything for you, Ma?

EDITH

You can all leave me alone... Dammit!!

(EDITH SLAMS INTO THE KITCHEN AGAIN. MIKE,

ARCHIE AND GLORIA EXCHANGE STUNNED LOOKS)

ARCHIE

Did she really say that?

MIKE

If I didn't hear it with my own ears, I

wouldn't believe it!

"SAMMY'S VISIT"

LEGENDARY ACTOR AND SINGER SAMMY DAVIS JR. VISITS THE BUNKERS TO
RETRIEVE THE BRIEFCASE HE ACCIDENTALLY LEFT IN ARCHIE'S CAB.

WRITTEN BY: **Bill Dana** ● DIRECTED BY: **John Rich**

★ EMMY AWARD: Outstanding Directorial Achievement in Comedy ★

GUEST STARS: **Sammy Davis Jr.** as **Himself** ● **Mike Evans** as **Lionel Jefferson**
Isabel Sanford as **Louise Jefferson** ● **Allan Melvin** as **Barney Hefner** ● **Fay DeWitt** as **Mrs. Haskell**
Keri Shuttleton as **Clarissa Haskell** ● **Billy Halop** as **Bert Munson**

ORIGINAL AIR DATE: **February 19, 1972**

NORMAN LEAR: Sammy Davis was a close personal friend, whom I knew from when I wrote for the Dean Martin and Jerry Lewis *Colgate Comedy Hour* in the early 1950s. He was a very early fan of *All in the Family*. In fact, when we had aired only three episodes, Sammy started to call me to say that he just had to be on the show.

I told him that we were never going to use big-name guest stars, because we wanted to keep the conceit that the Bunkers were an average family living somewhere in Queens. But he pestered me so much—with emphasis on the word *pestered*—that we finally thought it over. By then, Archie was driving a cab as a second job. So we realized we could have Sammy be a passenger in the cab.

SAMMY DAVIS JR.: And if you were prejudiced,
you'd walk around thinking that you're better than anybody else
in the world. But I can honestly say, after spending these
marvelous moments with you, you ain't better than anybody.

ARCHIE: Can I have your hand on that, Sammy?

It ended up being a perfect fit for the show because Sammy was African-American, and because Archie was always talking about Black people as he did. Sammy saw this episode as a great chance to give back as good as he got.

It was wonderfully written by Bill Dana, and it turned out to be a great episode. Once we taped it, we knew it was going to contain a moment that nobody would easily forget.

That, of course, was the kiss, that moment at the end when, as Archie and Sammy take a photo together, Sammy kisses Archie on the cheek. It hadn't been in the script. I first saw it when I walked into rehearsal, when the director, John Rich, told me it had been Sammy's idea. It was very shocking to people back then to see a Black man kiss a White man, but by the time it happened, the three hundred people sitting in that live audience, who experienced that kiss first, cared deeply

about each of those characters. After all, everybody loved Archie, whether they disagreed with him or not. You couldn't not love the brilliant Carroll O'Connor in that role, and it was the same with Sammy. And so that live audience went wild, in the best possible way.

In my experience, people remember two episodes of *All in the Family* the most. People talk to me about that kiss more than anything, and the next most beloved moment is what has come to be called the "Sock and a Sock, Shoe and a Shoe" routine [in Season 4, episode 22, "Gloria Sings the Blues"], with Archie and Mike debating on the order of putting on footwear. But the Sammy kiss is definitely number one.

Sammy loved the finished episode, too. He sent a note to everybody connected with the show, and he sent flowers to the crew. Sammy wanted to be in a classic episode of *All in the Family*, and he sure got his wish. And he's the one who made it a classic.

                         LIONEL
      LISTEN,
      ~~Excuse~~ me, Mr. Davis, I gotta tell my

      mother you're here. She's crazy about

      you. I'll be back.

(HE RUNS OUT FRONT DOOR)

                         ARCHIE

(CALLING AFTER HIM)

      Wait! Don't be blabbin' --

(LIONEL IS GONE)
      COME ON, YOUSE TWO, GET OVER HERE.
      ~~Ah, Gheez! -- Edith, you pour the coffee.~~
      EDITH, MAKE THE COFFEE.
      ~~Come on, you kids, sit down over here.~~

(MIKE AND GLORIA SIT ON COUCH)

(ASIDE TO EDITH)
      EXCUSE ME, MR. DAVIS. EDITH, REMEMBER HIM, NOTHIN' ABOUT...
      ~~For God's sake, button~~ up and don't

      ~~make~~ no slip ups.   ~~especially with his~~

      ~~eye.~~

(HE WINKS ONE EYE)
      WELL   *WANNA*   *IT'S A REAL*
      ~~Now~~, Mr. Davis, I ~~can't~~ tell you ~~what an~~
                             IN OUR HOME
      honor ~~it is~~ to have you ~~come here and~~
           in'   *THIS WAY.*   *I WAS JUST*
      break bread with us ~~in our house.~~ You
      SAYIN' TO MY FAMILY BEFORE YOU CAME IN...
      ~~can ask any of my family here...~~ I SAYS, SAMMY DAVIS, JR.
      IS MAYBE THE GREATEST   *HIS*
      ~~always considered you a~~ credit to ~~your~~

      race.

                         SAMMY
                   VERY MUCH.
      Well, thank you. ~~I bet~~ you've done
                      I'M SURE
      good for yours, too.

                         ARCHIE

      ~~Well, you know~~, I try.

Prod. #0221   17.

                    EDITH

(BRINGS THE COFFEE)

    Here we are.
                                          ← SAMMY:
                    ARCHIE   OH, THANK YOU, MRS. BUNKER

THANKS, EDITH. NO, THAT'S All RIGHT, I CAN SERVE
~~I'll serve it~~. Get out of here.
MR DAVIS.
(ARCHIE TAKES CREAMER)

                              NOW,
    ~~Let me help you here~~, Mr. Davis, do

    you take ~~any~~ cream and sugar in your

    eye?

(FADE, MERCIFULLY)

END OF ACT ONE

BILL DANA: Norman Lear requested for me to write this episode, which remains one of the joys of my writing career. We all knew that the interracial element of the story would have an impact. But that the episode would become the heavenly gift which evolved, that's another matter.

As an extra bonus, my first draft contained what Norman calls one of his all-time favorite lines, the "curtain line" of Act One, where Archie stumbles after his own admonition for everyone to avoid mention of Sammy's visual aid. "Mr. Davis, do you take cream and sugar in your eye?"

Sammy shared with me that it was the words of the script—and of course with all credit to Norman, too—that gave him the comfort to improvise the show's most famous moment, his planting a kiss on Archie's cheek. It had also been such a great boost to me personally when Sammy called after the first reading of the script to say, "Prepare your acceptance speech, pal." But ironically, later, my manager's secretary mishandled the nomination papers, thus costing me a possible Emmy.

Season 3, Episode 4

"GLORIA AND THE RIDDLE"

GLORIA PRESENTS A RIDDLE TO ARCHIE AND MIKE, WHICH NOT ONLY PROVES THEIR
MALE CHAUVINISM BUT ALSO SPARKS A DEBATE ABOUT WOMEN'S LIBERATION. DESPITE THEIR BEST
EFFORTS, THE MEN ARE, OF COURSE, ULTIMATELY BESTED BY EDITH.

WRITTEN BY: **Don Nicholl**   •   DIRECTED BY: **Bob LaHendro** and **Robert H. Livingston**

GUEST STARS: **Patricia Stich** as **Tammy Robinson**   •   **Allan Melvin** as **Barney Hefner**
Brendan Dillon as **Tommy Kelcy**   •   **Billy Sands** as **Nick**

ORIGINAL AIR DATE: **October 7, 1972**

NORMAN LEAR: The riddle at the center of this episode is something that was going around at the time. When I heard it, I thought it was the essence of a really good episode for a show.

We know Archie won't be the one to solve the riddle, and what does it say about Mike that he doesn't, either? Well, what does it say about human nature? What does it say about the world all these characters were raised in that it takes so long to find the answer? On some level, there may just be a touch of the same prejudice in all of us.

BOB LAHENDRO: There were female surgeons and doctors back then, but not like there are today, fifty years later. So I think for most people, that was kind of a new thought, that women could be surgeons, too. And once again, the show was breaking new ground, opening up the horizon for people to see beyond what they knew. That was part of the joy of it. I felt like we were being pioneers.

ROB REINER: It's interesting that Edith is the one to solve the riddle, because it shows the evolution that Edith went through. She was somebody who was raised a certain way, and then was introduced to feminism through her daughter and started to change, to think about a woman's role in the world differently than she did when the series first started. It was a similar evolution for Jean, I think. Being introduced to all these crazy liberals in Hollywood changed her politics and her way of thinking about women. Her own life mirrored the evolution that her character was going through.

In her oral history for The Interviews, **JEAN STAPLETON** *remembered:* Before *All in the Family* I had been quite an apolitical person, but I found myself in this nest of activists in L.A., and began to get a little educated about things. Activists for the Equal Rights Amendment asked if they could use the image of Edith Bunker as a "second-class citizen" in magazine ads and I said it's fine with me. I was appointed to a commission that was formed to produce the second conference on women's rights. The first one was in 1848, in New York State. And this was held in Houston in 1977. I had several trips to Washington. It was like going to university to learn this whole political sense of things. I appeared at rallies here and there and in Houston. And of course I didn't appear as Edith Bunker, but I played the role, so that was a big part of my welcome there. It was quite an experience, and of course that awakened me a great deal to the political scene and also to the support of the ERA and a certain degree of activism.

A father and his son are in a car accident.
The father dies immediately, but the son gets taken to the
hospital for surgery. Once in the operating room,
the surgeon takes one look at the boy and says,
"I can't operate on him. He's my son." Who is the surgeon?

"THE BUNKERS AND THE SWINGERS"

EDITH UNWITTINGLY ANSWERS AN AD PLACED BY THE REMPLEYS,
A NEW JERSEY COUPLE INTERESTED IN WIFE-SWAPPING.

STORY BY: **Norman Lear** ● TELEPLAY BY: **Michael Ross**, **Bernie West**, and **Lee Kalcheim**
DIRECTED BY: **Bob LaHendro** and **John Rich**

★ EMMY AWARD: Outstanding Writing Achievement in Comedy ★

GUEST STARS: **Vincent Gardenia** as **Curtis Rempley** ● **Rue McClanahan** as **Ruth Rempley**
Isabel Sanford as **Louise Jefferson**

ORIGINAL AIR DATE: **October 28, 1972**

NORMAN LEAR: I swear it gives me a few extra weeks of life when I remember the pleasure of working with Rue McClanahan and Vincent Gardenia. They were lovely people, and I had been knocked out by them in earlier performances elsewhere. Now, to walk into a room knowing you will hear words you'll like is one thing—but then to hear an actor pick up those words and deliver something you could never have imagined is amazing. It's hard to believe, when that happens, that it's your work.

Isabel Sanford, as Louise, brought something special to this episode, too, in the way she reacts when she and Edith realize what's going on. Her exit, during that "block comedy" scene—that wasn't from the director. That exploded from the actress.

What I loved about all these actors is the way they brought humanity to this story. No matter what the audience felt about swinging itself, we are reminded, as we hear Rue's character talk about it, and watch Archie and Edith's reaction, of their humanity. We were always aiming to portray as close as we could get to 360 degrees of our characters' humanity, and this was another way to explore what each of them would make of a new situation.

In her oral history for The Interviews, **RUE McCLANAHAN** *recalled:* In 1965, Vincent and I had played husband and wife Willy and Linda Loman in *Death of a Salesman* at the Moorestown Theater in New Jersey, and we had become good friends. So it was just lovely casting.

Jean Stapleton, I've always said, was like a hearth—just wonderful and warm. And Carroll O'Connor behaved himself completely. I'd been told that he was a mess to work with, that he threw scripts in the air and stormed. Boy, the week I was there, he was a perfect angel. We all got along great. I think maybe Vincent and I were good influences, because we weren't temperamental. And we delivered. We were really professional actors, and that probably made Carroll happy, because he was a professional actor.

RUTH: There was a time when our marriage got a little boring, a little humdrum, a little…

CURTIS: Tedious.

RUTH: Then we discovered swinging.

ARCHIE: Swinging? Is that what you call it?

CURTIS: Yeah, why? What do you call it?

ARCHIE: Communism!

May 15, 1973

Dear Sirs:

Our family is quite selective about our choices of television programs. We have always enjoyed "All in the Family", because it was cleverly done, good humor, and usually a good moral – plus excellent acting. It has been a show where our children, 10, 11, and 13 and my husband and I could all enjoy together.

It has been going down hill a bit in our estimation lately and last Saturday night, the swinger show was in-excusable. To take a prime time,

8 PM on a Saturday night, and to scrape the bottom of the barrel with that was disgusting. I believe you have exhausted your talent of good humor and imagination to resort to this sort of subject.

This letter will probably accomplish nothing, and I imagine I will receive no reply, but I did want you to know how one family feels about your fallen sense of humor. You have shown in the past humor can be terribly funny without being so crude.

Portland, Ore.

Dear Sirs   Oct 28, 1972

My husband & I just finished watching "All in a Family." This was the episode about the "Swingers," and we want to protest against having this type of dialogue & circumstance on a time when children as young as 10 & 14 would be watching.

We did not object to Edith's menopause – or the time the young man was having trouble with relating to his wife. Those are normal, healthy human experiences.

Wife swapping is a perversion, and not something to laugh about.

Sincerely

P.S. Please do not allow any stripping of clothes like was done in one episode of Maude. We watched that once & never again.

"FLASHBACK: MIKE AND GLORIA'S WEDDING"

ON THE STIVICS' SECOND WEDDING ANNIVERSARY, THE FAMILY REMINISCES
ABOUT HOW ARCHIE CLASHED WITH MIKE'S UNCLE CASIMIR.

WRITTEN BY: **Phil Mishkin** and **Rob Reiner** ● DIRECTED BY: **Bob LaHendro** and **John Rich**

GUEST STARS: **Mike Evans** as **Lionel Jefferson** ● **Michael Conrad** as **Uncle Casimir Stivic**
Peter Hobbs as **Judge Francis J. Polanski**

ORIGINAL AIR DATES: **November 11** and **November 18, 1972**

NORMAN LEAR: This episode has one of the great flush jokes we ever did on *All in the Family*, when Edith starts playing the piano at the wedding, and there's a delay: "Where's Archie?" And then SFX: FLUSH.

When the network saw the first toilet flushes in an *All in the Family* script, they didn't say anything, because they thought we were putting them on. They believed that we didn't mean it. Then, when they heard it in the rehearsal hall the first time, they said, "You don't mean you're really going to do that?" We said, "Of course we're going to do that. That's a little house. You hear the bathrooms."

We enjoyed the toilet jokes on the show. Not because we have a predilection for bathroom humor, but as a group we've always felt that American humor has its roots in bawdiness. It's part of our heritage, and we never had any business leaving that heritage. And the first joke that ever passes between a parent and a child is a joke related to bodily functions and private parts. It is always the first smile. That first joke is inevitably a bathroom joke, so how could it be anything but lovely and funny?

BOB LAHENDRO: Whenever we used a toilet flush on *All in the Family*, the stage direction in the script would just say "toilet flush." But John Rich would say it's got to be a funny toilet flush. It can't just be a run-of-the-mill flush, but a huge plunging sound that the old-fashioned kind of toilet would make, the kind with the tank up near the ceiling and a pull-chain. As John said, the Bunker house was an old house, and a bigger sound effect would be funnier, and more Archie's style.

SALLY STRUTHERS: I think one of the show's most memorable moments for the audience, and for me as an actress, was the advice scene in this episode

MIKE: Archie, whether you like it or not, people do make love every now and then.

EDITH: More then than now.

with Jean. We're sitting on the edge of my bed on my wedding day, with people waiting downstairs, and Edith is telling Gloria about the wedding night as best she can. It was all skirting the issue—Edith couldn't say it. Gloria was like the adult, and Edith the child. Whenever we talked, Edith couldn't say "sex," which was so funny.

PHIL MISHKIN: Rob and I wrote our first draft for the first of these two episodes—and then I lost it somewhere in my office. This was before we worked on computers, and I just could never find the paper script again. We had loved what we'd written, some great scenes. But then we had to rewrite it all from memory. Of course, usually when you do that, it comes out better the second time, because you revise and refine it. But I don't know if Rob has to this day forgiven me for having lost that script!

Rob and I didn't come up with this idea, but we loved it, and the relationship with Mike's Uncle Casimir. There were a few scenes I'm very proud of, one of which came directly from my life. I love the sweet scene where Edith talks to Gloria about the wedding night; Rob and I had a whole run of dialogue in there that stayed intact. And in the scene where Archie talks to Gloria and he reminisces about picking her up from camp one summer when she got homesick—that was actually something my dad did for me. A lot of people have told me that was memorable for them.

In this second episode here, I got to be part of it. I'm the curly-haired guy standing with the group of people in the living room who react to hearing the toilet flush when Archie is delayed coming down the stairs with Gloria. I react with a frown or something—I definitely milked my one moment.

Season 3, Episode 15

"ARCHIE IN THE HOSPITAL"

ARCHIE GOES TO THE HOSPITAL AND MAKES FRIENDS WITH A PATIENT ON THE
OTHER SIDE OF THE CURTAIN IN HIS ROOM WHO, UNBEKNOWNST TO HIM, IS BLACK.

STORY BY: **Martin Cohan** and **Stanley Ralph Ross** ● TELEPLAY BY: **Don Nicholl**
DIRECTED BY: **Bob LaHendro** and **John Rich**

GUEST STARS: **Mike Evans** as **Lionel Jefferson** ● **Isabel Sanford** as **Louise Jefferson**
Roscoe Lee Browne as **Jean Duval** ● **John Heffernan** as **Dr. Spence** ● **Priscilla Morrill** as **Nurse**

ORIGINAL AIR DATE: **January 6, 1973**

ARCHIE: Hey! You didn't tell me you was black!

JEAN: You did not tell me you was white!

NORMAN LEAR: The whole purpose of this episode was to examine what meeting someone blindly has to say about all of us. Would we know he is of a different race? Would we even be thinking about that?

Roscoe Lee Browne had previously appeared in the episode "The Elevator Story" in season 2, and I thought he was a lovely actor, and very funny in both of these roles. He had such a mellifluous voice, which is one of the reasons he was so great for this role. I wanted the Black guy in the next hospital bed to sound like the intellectual he was, as opposed to another Archie Bunker type.

BOB LAHENDRO: Working with Roscoe Lee Browne was a joy, because he was such a consummate actor, with such class about him. He had such a precise diction that made him perfect for this role, as someone who didn't fit Archie's stereotype of a Black person.

But what I also remember about this episode is that we had to tape it during a strike of the engineering union, the IBEW. We who were in other unions like the Directors Guild and the Screen Actors Guild were forbidden by our union contracts to walk out in support. Carroll in particular hated that we had to keep working, because none of us wanted to hurt the cause of all these people we enjoyed working with.

Production did eventually stop for a bit while the strike was resolved, but at this point everyone was focused on having to deliver a certain number of shows, ready for air at a certain time. And so instead of our regular crew, we used the people from the offices upstairs. They took a quick class in running a camera or a boom, and I kept the blocking simple, so they didn't have any big camera moves. Luckily, the hospital scenes were perfect for that, because both actors were in bed for the most part. That helped a lot, because the hardest thing about running a camera is staying in focus when you're following somebody across the room.

We shot it almost like a radio show, because we deemphasized movement, and the words were so good. The script was so strong, we didn't need to do much to embellish it. I made it simple for the substitute technicians, and we got through it.

IN SOME WAYS THE TELEVISION I CREATE is nothing like what Norman did. I stay away from social issues. Not my thing. And honestly, I am too intimidated by what Norman accomplished to compete. But his characters and dialogue and plotting! That's what I learned from watching Norman's shows. And the fact he was able to turn a bigot into the most beloved TV character of all time...well, it's a demonstration of skill that I continually seek to acquire, all the while knowing I never will.

All in the Family could not be written today anyway. The freedom Norman had in post-Vietnam America has disappeared. We wanted to be challenged back then. We knew, as a nation, we needed to be shaken up. But now? We've become a nation of PC victims looking to be offended by every word and idea that doesn't fit into our narrow worldview. No one can challenge the groupthink that pervades our industry. No one can change it.

Well, maybe Norman could. We should check to see if he'll stick around for another few decades and change the world again. I'll bet he would if we asked nicely.

—*DESPERATE HOUSEWIVES* AND *WHY WOMEN KILL* CREATOR MARC CHERRY

"ARCHIE IS BRANDED"

WHEN ARCHIE DISCOVERS A SWASTIKA PAINTED ON THE FRONT DOOR, HE CLASHES
WITH MIKE OVER WHETHER OR NOT TO ACCEPT PROTECTION FROM A VIGILANTE GROUP.

WRITTEN BY: **Vincent Bogert** ● DIRECTED BY: **Bob LaHendro** and **John Rich**

GUEST STARS: **Gregory Sierra** as **Paul Benjamin** ● **Billy Halop** as **Bert Munson** ● **Michael Gregory** as **Jerry**
John Putch as **Boy Scout** ● **Patrick Campbell** as **Mailman**

ORIGINAL AIR DATE: **February 24, 1973**

NORMAN LEAR: This episode may be from 1973, but I wasn't surprised that in recent months, here it was again: vigilantism. Human nature doesn't change. You pray that it might slowly evolve and arrive at a better degree of sanity at some point—but it doesn't change.

I like to think that I agree with Mike, and that most people would, about not engaging in the violence the man from the Hebrew Defense Association advocates. But Archie wouldn't have been as interesting a character if it weren't true that a good percentage of the population, whether they expressed it or acted upon it or not, understood him, and related to his point of view. So much of what motivated Archie, which he didn't understand, was fear: the fear of what he didn't know, which was going to teach him something he didn't know he needed to be taught. And that's a serious element in human nature, too.

Even though the Bunkers ultimately didn't engage in the fight on their street, the episode ends with a

April 4, 1973

Your letter to Mr. Lear was referred to me for answer, but he wants to tell you how much he appreciated your taking the time to share your opinions of the "swastika" episode with him.

Resistance is a philosophical concept and the pros and cons have been argued since before Buddha.

However, we are glad that our minds met on some aspects of this problem, if not all. And want to thank you again for your comments on the show.

Sincerely,

S'halom!

moment of violence nonetheless. The defense league guy, played by the brilliant Gregory Sierra, loses his life at the end. The camera is on the Bunkers, looking out their front door after they hear the explosion. That was what I think of as "audible silence." There are some times when silence can be so loud, and more effective than anything anyone could have said at that moment.

ROB REINER: The ending, with the man from the defense league getting blown up, was such a powerful moment. The Bunkers opened the door to learn what had happened, and then the show faded to black. It was powerful to talk about vigilantism, and it's horrible that it is something happening again today.

JOHN PUTCH: My parents, William Putch and Jean Stapleton, waited until the show really seemed like it would keep going before my dad, my sister, Pam, and I moved out to California. I had been a child actor at my father's theater, the Totem Pole Playhouse in Fayetteville, Pennsylvania. And when we moved to L.A., there was a concerted effort to get me auditions for shows. But you know, the best way to get jobs is to already be there. For the role of the Boy Scout, I was already in the building, and the producers saw me and said, "Hey, do you want to read for the part next week, of the Boy Scout?" I looked at my mom, and she nodded.

I was raised in the theater, where you play everything big. And you did on sitcoms, too. Still, even though I'd been onstage in front of four hundred people, I'd never been on a soundstage with artificial lights like that. The stage was kept cold, and there were giant video cameras pointing at me, so I was nervous. The actual character didn't unnerve me, because I had played the same thing before, the fat wise-guy kid. The only problem I remember having was that Carroll O'Connor was so funny that I had to work really hard not to laugh when he chases my character away.

BENJAMIN

I know that -- but they don't!

JERRY

They do now! We just got word they're

on their way to Bloom's place.

BENJAMIN

All right
~~Well~~ we'll be ready for 'em. *Look, why don't* You go on

ahead. I'll drive on up and meet ya there.

JERRY

Right.

(JERRY EXITS)

BENJAMIN

Well I guess you folks are off the hook!

.... So long, everybody! _____ *Archie*
                                 So long there chubby.

(HE SHAKES MIKE'S HAND WARMLY)

You too, friend. I don't agree with

                      chutzpah
what you say but I like your ~~style~~, but one

of these days you're gonna find out that

this....

(HE CLENCHES MIKE'S FIST)

is the only answer. *Right there* .

MIKE

                                    this
~~And~~ I still think you're wrong, because ~~that~~

(HE HOLDS UP THE OTHER FIST CLENCHED)

only gets ~~that!~~ *you this* .

BENJAMIN

Okay Friend. You keep talking. I'll do

what I have to do! Shalom, ~~everybody~~!

(HE WAVES - AND EXITS)

EDITH

'Shalom'? What does that mean?

MIKE

Believe it or not ma — it
~~You're not gonna believe it ma, it~~

means 'peace'!

GLORIA

Jewish people also use it ~~for~~ *to say* 'hello'

or 'goodbye.'

EDITH

But how do you know which one they mean?

ARCHIE

Why don't you use your common sense, Edith.
~~That's easy, Edith.~~ If a Jewish guy

is comin' at ya it's 'hello.' If he's

goin' away from you it's 'goodbye.'

EDITH

But when does it mean peace?

ARCHIE

In between 'hello' and 'goodbye'!

SOUND: A LOUD EXPLOSION

(THE FAMILY REACTS - STUNNED BY THE EXPLOSION

IN THE STREET. ARCHIE LOOKS OUT THE DOOR.

EDITH AND GLORIA GET UP - MIKE STOPS THEM.

ARCHIE TURNS BACK INTO THE ROOM WITH AN

EXPRESSION OF SHOCK AND HORROR)

ARCHIE

Oh, gees
That's ~~was~~ Paul. They blew him up in his

car.

(AS THEY STARE AT EACH OTHER)

FADE OUT:

END OF ACT TWO

"GLORIA THE VICTIM"

GLORIA WEIGHS THE PROS AND CONS OF FILING A COMPLAINT WITH THE POLICE ABOUT HER SEXUAL ASSAULT.

WRITTEN BY: **Austin Kalish**, **Irma Kalish** and **Don Nicholl** • DIRECTED BY: **Bob LaHendro** and **John Rich**

GUEST STARS: **Mike Evans** as **Lionel Jefferson** • **Mel Stewart** as **Henry Jefferson** • **Charles Durning** as **Detective**

ORIGINAL AIR DATE: **March 17, 1973**

NORMAN LEAR: The germ of this idea came from something I noticed at a construction site on a New York street, where some guys, with their heads just above the sidewalk as they worked, were commenting on the pretty legs walking by.

Particularly back then, there was the problem for victims of rape that they would not be believed, or they would be portrayed as horrible people on the witness stand if they testified. It was a problem well-known enough for us to have heard about it, and I always found it tremendously satisfying to be able to shed light on situations that weren't often discussed.

In the writers' room, there was a lot of discussion about how this episode would end, whether or not Gloria would report the attack. But thinking about this again, I wonder if I would still end it the same way if I had done this episode last week. In my mind, I'm thinking maybe not.

Still, we got the opportunity to address a very similar situation later in the show, in season 8, in the episodes of "Edith's 50th Birthday." At the end of that second episode, Edith does report her attacker. I don't remember us thinking of the Edith episodes as a chance for a "do-over" in terms of the decision to report the attack, but I recognize it could have been.

SALLY STRUTHERS: A few years before I landed the role on *All in the Family*, I had been held captive by a neighbor across the street from the apartment I was sharing with my friend in Hollywood. And I knew what it felt like to lose the ability to protect yourself. So all those feelings came immediately to the surface when they wrote this script. Although it wasn't one of my idiosyncrasies that happened afterward, when Gloria couldn't stop washing her hands, it made perfect sense to me.

Doing this episode was both good and bad for me. It was good to present yet another episode that was educational, and show the emotions of someone who's gone through this trauma, especially because she was a character whom people loved. At the same time, it was close to the surface for me, and I don't think I had completely dealt with all the baggage that came with that.

Just like Gloria, I didn't report my attacker to the police, and he really should have been arrested. And there's so much regret in that. I was so ashamed that I had been lured into his apartment. I'm glad that in the second episode of "Edith's 50th Birthday," the storyline ends where Edith does report the attacker. Times have changed so much since then—look at the #MeToo movement. Women are finding their voices.

March 17, 1973

Norman Lear and company
"All in the Family"
CBS
51 West 52 St.

Dear People:

I am writing in response to your program on rape which I just viewed. I am pleased to see finally the treatment of the "real" issue of rape: that of "victim as criminal".

As an active, full-time feminist, I have often been disappointed by your programs, usually for not being all I'd want them to be, for not making as strong a point as I wish you would.

But this particular segment, I felt was sensitive and direct and I also must comment that I thought it was Sally Struthers' best, most effective performance.

It helped, I'm sure. Keep it up, we need the clear, strong comments, if we're ever going to reach people.

Sincerely,

c: FCC
NOW

Aug. 26th

Dear Sir,

I'd like to personally thank you for doing that program of _All in the Family_ dealing with Gloria being accosted. A dear friend of mine recently went through a grueling ordeal of rape & she now faces court & possibly being slandered while trying to prosecute the man who abducted her. Fortunately her family and friends are 100% behind her, but your show showed the way everyone tries to "protect their own." Again, I'd like to thank you so much because your program dealt with a very real problem which faces many women every day.

GLORIA

Michael, are you sure we did the right

thing?

MIKE

No, I'm not sure. /we're doing the right thing Gloria, ~~I don't know what the~~

I don't know what ^the right thing is. All I know is I'm trying

to do the right thing for you. You ~~didn't~~ should have

hear some of the things that guy said.

ARCHIE

Yeah. Some of the things that guy said, it ~~You didn't hear what he said. It~~

would make your flesh stand on end.

GLORIA

But, daddy, that meniac is still out there

on
~~in~~ the streets/ somewhere and so are a lot of innocent

girls. What about them?

ARCHIE

bring him into court if they wanna.

Let them ~~take the guy to court.~~ He ain't

girls
responsible for all the ~~women~~ in New York.

MIKE

Gloria. All I care about is you.

ARCHIE

what he
That's right. ~~And~~ That's ~~all you~~ should, care about his own wife

his
~~Your wife~~ and the women under ~~your~~ own

roof.

MIKE

All right, Arch. I've said ~~that~~ its, okay!

ARCHIE

Well. I wanna It's everybody
~~And I'll~~ say~~s~~' it again. ~~You look out~~ for

~~your own.~~ himself in this world.

(MORE)

ARCHIE (CONT'D)

~~That's the way it oughta be.~~ As *our President said... in his renaugural address* ~~Richard E. Nixon made it perfectly~~ *Youre on your own.* ~~clear in his~~ *renaugural* ~~renaugural address.~~ *No that's a fact,* ~~Don't expect nobody to do nothing~~ *nothin' from nobody.* ~~for you. If you expect the government~~ *And especially* ~~to do something for you - you're nuts.~~ *from the government.*

Sit down and ask yourself. 'What can

I do for myself'/ and then go out

and do it for youself. ~~We done the~~

~~right thing here today.~~ If more

done that

people ~~took care of their own,~~ this

in which to

would be a better country ~~for us to~~

Do it for your own,

live in. ~~And, that's what we done~~

to

~~here today,~~ we took care of our own. *That's the rule. That's what we done here today. We took care of our own.*

and find out what you can do for yourself.

(AS ARCHIE IS DOING HIS MONOLOGUE, THE CAMERA

MOVES IN ON GLORIA'S LONELY FACE. SHE HAS

TEARS IN HER EYES.)

FADE OUT.

END OF ACT TWO

ALL OF *ALL IN THE FAMILY*
Seasons 2 and 3

Season 2
1971–72

Episode 1

"The Saga of Cousin Oscar"

WRITERS: **Norman Lear, Burt Styler**
DIRECTOR: **John Rich**
AIR DATE: **September 18, 1971**

★

Episode 2

"Gloria Poses in the Nude"

WRITERS: **Michael Ross, Bernie West, Norman Lear**
DIRECTOR: **John Rich**
AIR DATE: **September 25, 1971**

★

Episode 3

"Archie and the Lock-up"

WRITERS: **Michael Ross, Bernie West, Paul Wayne**
DIRECTOR: **John Rich**
AIR DATE: **October 2, 1971**

★

Episode 4

"Edith Writes a Song"

WRITER: **Lee Kalcheim**
DIRECTOR: **John Rich**
AIR DATE: **October 9, 1971**

★

Episode 5

"Flashback: Mike Meets Archie"

WRITERS: **Phil Mishkin, Rob Reiner**
DIRECTOR: **John Rich**
AIR DATE: **October 16, 1971**

★

Episode 6

"The Election Story"

WRITERS: **Michael Ross, Bernie West**
DIRECTOR: **John Rich**
AIR DATE: **October 30, 1971**

★

Episode 7

"Edith's Accident"

WRITERS: **Tom & Helen August, Michael Ross, Bernie West**
DIRECTOR: **John Rich**
AIR DATE: **November 6, 1971**

★

Episode 8

"The Blockbuster"

WRITERS: **Phil Mishkin, Alan J. Levitt**
DIRECTOR: **John Rich**
AIR DATE: **November 13, 1971**

★

Episode 9

"Mike's Problem"

WRITERS: **Alan J. Levitt, Phil Mishkin**
DIRECTOR: **John Rich**
AIR DATE: **November 20, 1971**

★

Episode 10

"The Insurance Is Canceled"

WRITER: **Lee Kalcheim**
DIRECTOR: **John Rich**
AIR DATE: **November 27, 1971**

★

Episode 11

"The Man in the Street"

WRITERS: **Don Nicholl, Paul Harrison, Lennie Weinrib**
DIRECTOR: **John Rich**
AIR DATE: **December 4, 1971**

★

Episode 12

"Cousin Maude's Visit"

DIRECTOR: **John Rich**
WRITERS: **Phil Mishkin, Michael Ross, Bernie West**
AIR DATE: **December 11, 1971**

★

Episode 13

"Christmas Day at the Bunkers'"

WRITER: **Don Nicholl**
DIRECTOR: **John Rich**
AIR DATE: **December 18, 1971**

★

Episode 14

"The Elevator Story"

WRITER: **Alan J. Levitt**
DIRECTOR: **John Rich**
AIR DATE: **January 1, 1972**

★

Episode 15

"Edith's Problem"

WRITERS: **Steve Zacharias, Burt Styler**
DIRECTOR: **John Rich**
AIR DATE: **January 8, 1972**

★

Episode 16

"Archie and the FBI"

WRITERS: **Michael Ross, Bernie West, Susan Harris**
DIRECTOR: **John Rich**
AIR DATE: **January 15, 1972**

★

Episode 17

"Mike's Mysterious Son"

WRITER: **Warren S. Murray**
DIRECTOR: **John Rich**
AIR DATE: **January 22, 1972**

★

Episode 18

"Archie Sees a Mugging"

WRITERS: **Henry Garson, Phil Mishkin, Don Nicholl**
DIRECTOR: **John Rich**
AIR DATE: **January 29, 1972**

★

Episode 19

"Archie and Edith, Alone"

WRITERS: **Tina & Les Pine, Lee Kalcheim, Michael Ross, Bernie West**
DIRECTOR: **John Rich**
AIR DATE: **February 5, 1972**

★

Episode 20

"Edith Gets a Mink"

WRITERS: **Don Nicholl, David Pollock, Elias Davis**
DIRECTOR: **John Rich**
AIR DATE: **February 12, 1972**

★

Episode 21

"Sammy's Visit"

WRITER: **Bill Dana**
DIRECTOR: **John Rich**
AIR DATE: **February 19, 1972**

★

Episode 22

"Edith the Judge"

WRITER: **Lee Kalcheim**
DIRECTOR: **John Rich**
AIR DATE: **February 26, 1972**

★

Episode 23

"Archie Is Jealous"

WRITER: **Rod Parker**
DIRECTOR: **John Rich**
AIR DATE: **March 4, 1972**

★

Episode 24

"Maude"

WRITER: **Rod Parker**
DIRECTOR: **John Rich**
AIR DATE: **March 11, 1972**

Season 3
1972–73

Episode 1

"Archie and the Editorial"

WRITERS: **Don Nicholl, George Bloom**
DIRECTOR: **Norman Campbell**
AIR DATE: **September 16, 1972**

★

Episode 2

"Archie's Fraud"

WRITERS: **Michael Ross, Bernie West**
DIRECTOR: **Norman Campbell**
AIR DATE: **September 23, 1972**

★

Episode 3

"The Threat"

WRITERS: **Bill Manhoff, Lila Garrett, Michael Elias**
DIRECTOR: **John Rich**
AIR DATE: **September 30, 1972**

★

Episode 4

"Gloria and the Riddle"

WRITER: **Don Nicholl**
DIRECTORS: **Bob LaHendro, Robert H. Livingston**
AIR DATE: **October 7, 1972**

★

Episode 5

"Lionel Steps Out"

WRITERS: **Terry Ryan, Michael Ross, Bernie West**
DIRECTOR: **John Rich**
AIR DATE: **October 14, 1972**

★

Episode 6

"Edith Flips Her Wig"

WRITERS: **Sam Locke, Olga Vallance, Don Nicholl**
DIRECTOR: **Hal Cooper**
AIR DATE: **October 21, 1972**

★

Episode 7

"The Bunkers and the Swingers"

WRITERS: **Norman Lear, Michael Ross, Bernie West, Lee Kalcheim**
DIRECTORS: **John Rich, Bob LaHendro**
AIR DATE: **October 28, 1972**

★

Episode 8

"Mike Comes Into Money"

WRITERS: **Michael Ross, Bernie West**
DIRECTOR: **John Rich**
AIR DATE: **November 4, 1972**

★

Episode 9

"Flashback: Mike and Gloria's Wedding - Part 1"

WRITERS: **Rob Reiner, Phil Mishkin**
DIRECTORS: **John Rich, Bob LaHendro**
AIR DATE: **November 11, 1972**

★

Episode 10

"Flashback: Mike and Gloria's Wedding - Part 2"

WRITERS: **Rob Reiner, Phil Mishkin**
DIRECTORS: **John Rich, Bob LaHendro**
AIR DATE: **November 18, 1972**

★

Episode 11

"Mike's Appendix"

WRITERS: **Michael Ross, Bernie West**

DIRECTORS: **John Rich, Bob LaHendro**
AIR DATE: **December 2, 1972**

★

Episode 12

"Edith's Winning Ticket"

WRITER: **Don Nicholl**
DIRECTORS: **John Rich, Bob LaHendro**
AIR DATE: **December 9, 1972**

★

Episode 13

"Archie and the Bowling Team"

WRITERS: **Don Nicholl, Allan Katz, Don Reo**
DIRECTORS: **John Rich, Bob LaHendro**
AIR DATE: **December 16, 1972**

★

Episode 14

"The Locket"

WRITERS: **Robert Fisher, Arthur Marx**
DIRECTOR: **Hal Cooper**
AIR DATE: **December 23, 1972**

★

Episode 15

"Archie in the Hospital"

WRITERS: **Stanley Ralph Ross, Martin Cohan, Don Nicholl**
DIRECTORS: **John Rich, Bob LaHendro**
AIR DATE: **January 6, 1973**

★

Episode 16

"Oh Say Can You See"

WRITERS: **Jess Oppenheimer (credited as Joe Kerr), Michael Ross, Bernie West**
DIRECTORS: **John Rich, Bob LaHendro**
AIR DATE: **January 20, 1973**

★

Episode 17

"Archie Goes Too Far"

WRITERS: **Austin and Irma Kalish**
DIRECTORS: **John Rich, Bob LaHendro**
AIR DATE: **January 27, 1973**

★

Episode 18

"Class Reunion"

WRITERS: **Stanley Ralph Ross, Don Nicholl**
DIRECTORS: **John Rich, Bob LaHendro**
AIR DATE: **February 10, 1973**

★

Episode 19

"Hot Watch"

WRITERS: **Sam Locke, Olga Vallance**
DIRECTORS: **John Rich, Bob LaHendro**
AIR DATE: **February 17, 1973**

★

Episode 20

"Archie Is Branded"

WRITER: **Vincent Bogert**
DIRECTORS: **John Rich, Bob LaHendro**
AIR DATE: **February 24, 1973**

★

Episode 21

"Everybody Tells the Truth"

WRITER: **Don Nicholl**
DIRECTORS: **John Rich, Bob LaHendro**
AIR DATE: **March 3, 1973**

★

Episode 22

"Archie Learns His Lesson"

WRITERS: **John Christopher Strong III, Michael R. Stein, Michael Ross, Bernie West**
DIRECTORS: **John Rich, Bob LaHendro**
AIR DATE: **March 10, 1973**

★

Episode 23

"Gloria the Victim"

WRITERS: **Austin and Irma Kalish, Don Nicholl**
DIRECTORS: **John Rich, Bob LaHendro**
AIR DATE: **March 17, 1973**

★

Episode 24

"The Battle of the Month"

WRITERS: **Michael Ross, Bernie West**
DIRECTORS: **John Rich, Bob LaHendro**
AIR DATE: **March 24, 1973**

EMMYS
1972

Outstanding Series - Comedy
NORMAN LEAR, PRODUCER

★

Outstanding Continued Performance by an Actor in a Comedy Series
CARROLL O'CONNOR

★

Outstanding Performance by an Actress in a Supporting Role
SALLY STRUTHERS

★

Outstanding Continued Performance by an Actress in a Leading Role
JEAN STAPLETON

★

Outstanding Directorial Achievement in Comedy
JOHN RICH – "SAMMY'S VISIT"

★

Outstanding Writing Achievement in Comedy
BURT STYLER – "EDITH'S PROBLEM"

EMMYS
1973

Outstanding Comedy Series
NORMAN LEAR, EXECUTIVE PRODUCER, JOHN RICH, PRODUCER

★

Outstanding Writing Achievement in Comedy
MICHAEL ROSS, BERNIE WEST, LEE KALCHEIM – "THE BUNKERS AND THE SWINGERS"

THE SCRIPT

ROB REINER: On day 1, we'd read the script around the table, then suggest or make changes. Either that afternoon or the next morning, we would put the show up on its feet and start blocking it in the rehearsal hall, improvising and getting the show down. We'd rehearse again all through day 3; that afternoon, we'd have a run-through for the producers, writers, and director, keeping an eye out for any fixes or changes that needed to be made. Then, on the morning of day 4, we'd go down to the stage and block the show with the cameras. On tape day, day 5, we'd block it again in the morning and then shoot two shows in front of two different live audiences: the dress rehearsal at 5:30, and then the "air show" at 8 p.m.

IT ALL STARTS WITH THE WRITERS

In his oral history for The Interviews, Associate Producer **GEORGE SUNGA** *remembered:* The *All in the Family* writers came out of vaudeville and all the proving grounds of the East Coast, such as the Catskills and radio. So they knew what worked.... Don Nicholl had been a newspaper writer in London. He was the backbone of the show. Mickey Ross had staged grand opera on the East Coast, and interpreted and translated operas. Bernie West was a performer. And they all had something to contribute. Now, you wanted ten lines? Give it to Bernie. Bernie would go *zap zap zap zap*, then look them over and say, "I like that one." They'd use that line. They were a great team, and the first three-member writing team that the Writers Guild allowed.

In his oral history for The Interviews, director **JOHN RICH** *remembered:* One of the rules of the show was that every Black man was smarter than Archie Bunker, every Jewish character was smarter, every nun, every minority. Whoever it was who came to grips with Bunker always bested him, because Bunker was wrong.

GARY SHIMOKAWA, *Associate Director*: There were very few series that grew the way *All in the Family* grew. It wasn't just episodic; it wasn't just season to season. It wasn't basically the same show across nine years. Every season was a new year, and the growth that took place

with all the characters was really established inside that season. The characters change, which is very smart writing, and exactly the way it is in real life.

DAY 1: The Table Read

BOB LAHENDRO, *Assistant Director/Director*: At the table reading, on day 1 of production for an episode, everyone would get a sense of what the words sounded like from the mouths of the actors, because that added so much color to what had been written.

DAYS 2–3: Rehearsal Hall 5, 2nd floor

BOB LAHENDRO: Every day there would be rewrites, and the writers would be fine-tuning the script all the way up until the final taping. The actors would perform run-throughs, where the writers and producers would come in. They'd take notes, they'd give their notes, and the next day the actors would have new pages reflecting changes. It was an evolution, and sometimes the show that we ended up with was very different from the one we started with, because it became so much better with all the input.

In rehearsal hall, Carroll would come up with a malapropism or something, and I'd say, "Damn, that's funny!" I'd tell the script coordinator, "Hey, put that in, and we'll show it to Norman. Don't tell anybody about it—we'll surprise them with it when they come for the run-through." That way they could hear something that they didn't write, and we could see how they'd react.

ROB REINER: When I made *This Is Spinal Tap*, people said, "I can't believe for your first film, you made it without a script!" I said it was because I knew I had people who knew how to do that. I remember one year, when our head writer, Mort Lachman, accepted a Golden Globe for best writing. He said, "I want to thank..." and listed everyone on the writing staff. And then he added, "And Carroll O'Connor and Jean Stapleton, Rob Reiner and Sally Struthers." He listed us as if we were writers on the show, because all of us contributed dialogue and ideas.

"ALL IN THE FAMILY" #0617

REHEARSAL & TAPE SCHEDULE

TENTATIVE

THURSDAY, 12/11/75   STUDIO #6

REHEARSAL W/PROPS (REHEARSAL HALL A)
E.S.U.   9:00AM - 11:00AM
FAX   10:00AM - 11:00AM
LUNCH   11:00AM - 1:00PM
FAX   2:00PM - 4:00PM
RUN THRU W/COMPLETE WARDROBE   4:00PM - 4:30PM
DIRECTOR'S NOTES W/CAST   4:30PM -

FRIDAY, 12/12/75   STUDIO #6

DIRECTOR'S NOTES W/CAST
E.S.U.   1:30PM - 2:00PM
FAX   1:30PM - 2:30PM
BREAK FOR CAST NOTES, MAKEUP & WARDROBE   2:30PM - 4:30PM
2 VTR/FAX (DRESS W/AUDIENCE)   4:30PM - 5:30PM
MEAL BREAK. NOTES IN DRESSING ROOM   5:30PM - 6:30PM
VT CHECK-IN   6:30PM - 7:30PM
2 VTR/FAX   7:30PM - 8:00PM
PICK UPS   8:00PM - 9:00PM
                                                             9:00PM -

"ALL IN THE FAMILY" #0323

REHEARSAL & TAPE SCHEDULE

WEDNESDAY, 2/21/73　　　　　　　　　　　　　　**REH. HALL C-2**

READ & DISCUSS SCRIPT	10:30AM - 3:00PM
LUNCH (served in rehearsal hall)	1:00PM - 2:00PM
BEGIN ROUGH STAGING	3:00PM - 6:30PM

THURSDAY, 2/22/73　　　　　　　　　　　　　　**REH. HALL C-2**

CONTINUE STAGING	9:30AM - 1:00PM
LUNCH	1:00PM - 2:00PM
CONTINUE STAGING	2:00PM - 6:00PM

FRIDAY, 2/23/73　　　　　　　　　　　　　　**REH. HALL C-2**

REHEARSE W/PROPS	9:30AM - 1:00PM
LUNCH	1:00PM - 2:00PM
REHEARSE	2:00PM - 3:30PM
LINE REHEARSAL	3:30PM - 4:30PM
RUN THRU	4:30PM - 5:00PM
NOTES W/CAST	5:00PM

MONDAY, 2/26/73　　　　　　　　　　　　　　**STUDIO #31**

DRY BLOCK IN SET W/ALL PROPS	9:30AM - 11:00AM
E.S.U.	10:00AM - 11:00AM
FAX	11:00AM - 1:00PM
LUNCH	1:00PM - 2:00PM
FAX	2:00PM - 4:30PM
RUN THRU W/COMPLETE WARDROBE	4:30PM - 5:00PM
DISMISS CREW. DIRECTOR NOTES W/CAST	5:00PM

NOTE: Cast please rehearse in color compatible
　　　　clothes. (No whites, bright yellows, or
　　　　exceptionally busy patterns)

TUESDAY, 2/27/73　　　　　　　　　　　　　　**STUDIO #31**

DIRECTOR'S NOTES W/CAST IN CARROLL O'CONNOR'S 　　DRESSING ROOM	1:00PM - 2:00PM
E.S.U.	1:30PM - 2:30PM
FAX	2:30PM - 4:30PM
BREAK FOR CAST NOTES, MAKEUP & WARDROBE	4:30PM - 5:30PM
2 VTR/FAX (DRESS) W/AUDIENCE	5:30PM - 6:30PM
MEAL BREAK. NOTES IN CARROLL O'CONNOR'S 　　DRESSING ROOM	6:30PM - 7:30PM
VT CHECK IN	7:30PM - 8:00PM
2 VTR/FAX (AIR) W/AUDIENCE	8:00PM - 9:00PM
PICK UPS	9:00PM

SALLY STRUTHERS: Jean would always be the voice of reason. If something was up for discussion, she would say something so cleanly and so simply that it left us all back on our heels, having to think. Because she didn't just yell and throw things in like Rob Reiner. And she didn't go home and rewrite things all night like Carroll O'Connor. But when she had something to say, everybody listened.

In her oral history for The Interviews, **JEAN STAPLETON** *remembered:* They were marvelous, our writers. They let us participate by guarding our characters. And if something was not in character, we were allowed to discuss it and then go back and fix it. Our director, John Rich, and then later Paul Bogart, said, "You are in a free theater; enjoy it and relish it while you have it." It really was a marvelous collaboration, and I respect the writers who were so brilliant for allowing that to take place.

BRIGIT JENSEN-DRAKE, *Associate Producer***:** That was one remarkable thing about the *All in the Family* cast—they never argued about who should have the laugh. I remember watching a whole scene with Rob and Carroll where they realized it was totally wrong. One of them said, "Why don't you do my lines, and I'll do your lines." They did, and it worked.

In his oral history for The Interviews, **PAUL BOGART** *remembered:* Norman would come in with the writers and producers on day 3 to see a run-through of the new episode. Then we would have a notes session where we would all sit around and talk about what was wrong, what could be done better. . . . The next day, day 4, we were in the studio, and we would incorporate any newer material then. Norman would be there that day; he would watch the dress rehearsal, make his notes, and at dinner, we would hear his notes and deal with them, and then incorporate them, or not.

SALLY STRUTHERS: When my sister and I were growing up in Portland, Oregon, we were taught to share and love everybody. So it was a shock to me to show up in this rehearsal hall and hear all these words. I kept leaning over to Betty Garrett and whispering, "What does that mean?" She'd say, "That's a slur. That means a Jewish person." And I'd say, "That's terrible!" And she'd say, "Yeah—that's why we're making the show!"

IT'S SHOWTIME

GEORGE SUNGA: Norman was there at every taping. So we were all counting on his eye, his point of view, and recommendations if we needed to do a fix.

BRIGIT JENSEN-DRAKE: Today, sitcom tapings last for hours, especially for shows shot on film. "Okay, now let's do it from another angle." "Now, you do your line." It takes forever, and I think they lose the momentum of the comedy. *All in the Family* shot like a play, from start to finish in usually less than forty minutes. It would really only take however long the show actually was unless they had dress changes or had to reset the set for something. If someone did flub a line and they had to do a "pickup" to get it again, they would wait and do it after the audience left. They would never stop the show to do it.

ROB REINER: This is how tight we were as a unit at a certain point. We'd do the show in front of a live audience, taping at 5:30. Then we'd go and have dinner and do notes. And then we'd do it again at 8 o'clock for a second, brand-new audience. And they would cut the best of both shows together. But on one show, the second act just didn't work at all. We got laughs in the first act, and then the second act was just lying there. So between the 5:30 taping and the 8 o'clock taping, the four of us just started riffing and ad-libbing. The writers were writing it down and throwing in ideas. And so basically we went into the second show with a completely new second act. We were like a machine, all working together. Everybody contributed, and Norman and Carroll set the tone to allow that.

GEORGE SUNGA: After the show was shot, the associate director would do the first rough-cut of the episode. The director, the key writers, and I would go and see that rough cut. When that rough cut is going on, I'm making additional notes on my script, because I know where it's going to need sweetening of the laughs, because sometimes an edit would leave an audio hole. The guys on the creative side are looking to see if we need to make cuts. Very seldom did we have to make cuts. It was just the way it was written, and the way Norman wanted to do the shows.

Seasons 4–6

"YOU CAN'T PUT THAT IN THE SCRIPT!"

12 Episodes about Human Nature

I found myself doing a show for the entire country, with the network blowing down my neck. I had done live shows, with Madison Avenue all over me. But in this, I needed the support of people who would laugh with me in the room while we were developing. We never set out to make *All in the Family* as a classic. I worked hard, as did all of us involved with the show. It was what I got up to do every morning. I was attracted to the real problems of living, and the foolishness of the human condition in the most serious moments.

—NORMAN LEAR

Season 4, Episode 4
"Archie and the Kiss"

———

Season 4, Episode 6
"Henry's Farewell"

———

Season 4, Episode 10
"Archie in the Cellar"

———

Season 4, Episode 15
"Edith's Christmas Story"

———

Season 4, Episode 20
"Lionel's Engagement"

———

Season 4, Episode 22
"Gloria Sings the Blues"

———

Season 5, Episode 7
"Gloria's Shock"

———

Season 5, Episode 11
"Archie and the Miracle"

———

Season 6, Episode 1
"The Very Moving Day"

———

Season 6, Episode 4
"Archie the Hero"

———

Season 6, Episode 11
"The Little Atheist"

———

Season 6, Episode 22
'Joey's Baptism"

———

Season 4, Episode 4
"ARCHIE AND THE KISS"

ARCHIE DECLARES A STATUE OF AUGUSTE RODIN'S *THE KISS*, A GIFT FROM IRENE TO GLORIA, FILTHY.

WRITTEN BY: **John Rappaport** • DIRECTED BY: **Bob LaHendro** and **John Rich**

GUEST STARS: **Betty Garrett** as **Irene Lorenzo** • **Vincent Gardenia** as **Frank Lorenzo**

ORIGINAL AIR DATE: **October 6, 1973**

NORMAN LEAR: When I hear the name Betty Garrett, whom I adored, my mind goes to the end of World War II, my coming home, and Betty was the star of a show on Broadway called *Call Me Mister*. And my God, it touched me so deeply to remember going to that show, and falling in love with her and with it. And then seeing it three or four more times following. When it came time to cast Irene Lorenzo for the opening episodes of season 4, immediately preceding this one, I remembered Betty. It was one of the great thrills of my life getting to work with that woman.

In this episode, Archie hates the statue of Rodin's *The Kiss* that Irene gives to Gloria, because to him it was sexual, and now here it was, in his home. To me, it was also about Archie censoring art—and here we were discussing that on a network that had its Program Practices department reviewing what we could and couldn't say. So with this episode, I was in a way giving them the finger.

MIKE: Who are you to judge what's dirty? Even the
Supreme Court copped out on that! They left the interpretation
of what's obscene up to local standards.

ARCHIE: And they were right! This is my house
and I'm the local standard!

In her oral history for The Interviews, **BETTY GARRETT** *remembered:* The way Irene and Frank Lorenzo were explained to me was that I was adept at mechanical things. I think the idea was to present a male doing domestic things, and a woman doing what is usually considered correct for a male to do. So I was Miss Fix-It, and Vince was a great cook. Norman always tried to get some kind of a little twist on something that he felt was an important point to make. And then there was the element of my being Irish-Catholic, which of course Archie immediately bridled at.

BOB LAHENDRO: Viewers knew *All in the Family* so well by this point that once the studio audience saw the statue of *The Kiss* in the living room, and knew Archie was on his way home—well, that's all they needed to anticipate what his reaction was going to be. It was a perfect setup, and another example of these characters being so rich, and the audience knowing these people so well, they know what they're thinking before they even say it. And they know what their reaction is going to be before they even do it. You knew that Archie was going to have all kinds of things to say about this statue, so it was a perfect visual setup.

ALL IN THE FAMILY **COMPLETELY AND UTTERLY CHANGED** the narrative of what American television was. It was the first show that spoke to what was going on in the changing times we were living in. It was the first show that wasn't afraid to say, "This feels right" and "This feels wrong" and "This is why."

To know Norman is to know that each of his shows, each of his characters, lived inside him or within the world that he occupied—as it should with all writers when we write. That is what Norman does. In each of his characters, there is a little piece of his father, his wife, or his kids—people he grew up with, people he loved, and people he lost. Norman writes from the position of a witness and less so as a researcher, and that's the best place—and my favorite place—to tell stories from.

In December 2019, when ABC aired a live re-creation of the show, I was lucky enough to be there at the taping. I remember I leaned over to Norman and said, "You change a few names and the setting, and this could be television today." It was amazing, but also sad at the same time, that we as a society still need to have the same conversations that Norman first brought to life nearly fifty years ago.

—*BLACK-ISH, GROWN-ISH,* AND *MIXED-ISH* CREATOR KENYA BARRIS

MIKE

Yeah, you shouldn't swear like that!

ARCHIE

(IN ALL INNOCENCE)

Who was swearing?

MIKE

You were swearing.

ARCHIE

I was not swearing.

EDITH

Ever since this Watergate thing,

it's G-D this and G-D that --

ARCHIE

That ain't swearing. G-D when you

say it out! The first word you hear

is God. How can that be swearin' --

the most popular word in the Bible.

And the second word's damned.

That's a perfectly good word. Ya

hear that all the time like they

damned the river to keep it from

flooding. Then even in the Bible

you read where some guy was damned

for stealing or cheating or

committing insects in the family.

And who damned him, huh? God, who

else.

(MORE)

RECEIVED

APR 11 1974

BINA BERNARD

C-lang.

z

Dear,Mr.Lear
My name is James C. Worthington,I would like to talk to you about your show All in the Family . Ithink the program would be just as funny if you would not use such bad words such as Dam and Hell.I am 8 years old and watch All in the Family.

C-lang. no ret. add.

Dear Mr.Director:

References to personal habits like going to the "john" are uncalled for on television. I was shocked; then the script immediately called for Archie to say"what the hell" also superfluous and uncalled for.

Couldn't he say what the heck. There is always a more civilized alternative.

Con-Gen. 10/18/73 Sept 25

Dear Sir

I am getting sick + Tired of being preached to with messages from your show "All in the Family." You are much to Liberal + Left and I resent the fact that you use TV as your medium to get your opinons across to the American public. I especially was upset when Archie took the name of The Lord in vain and I do not plan to watch your show anymore. I hope you will revise your whole format

Most emphatically,

Season 4, Episode 6

"HENRY'S FAREWELL"

ARCHIE INCITES AN ARGUMENT WITH BOTH HENRY AND HIS NEVER-BEFORE-SEEN
BROTHER, GEORGE, DURING A FAREWELL PARTY FOR HENRY JEFFERSON.

WRITTEN BY: **Don Nicholl** • DIRECTED BY: **Bob LaHendro** and **John Rich**

GUEST STARS: **Vincent Gardenia** as **Frank Lorenzo** • **Mike Evans** as **Lionel Jefferson**
Isabel Sanford as **Louise Jefferson** • **Mel Stewart** as **Henry Jefferson** • **Sherman Hemsley** as **George Jefferson**

ORIGINAL AIR DATE: **October 20, 1973**

NORMAN LEAR: When we were trying to find a George Jefferson, out of the blue I remembered having seen Sherman Hemsley on Broadway in *Purlie*. I never forgot that performance. The problem was, we'd lost track of him, and then when we did hear from him, he was tied up doing theater in San Francisco. But we were able to fly him down to meet with us for what was going to be just one episode.

I took such delight about being part of the writing team to come up with these episodes that would finally

100

EDITH: Oh, Archie, Henry Jefferson is gonna be so disappointed if you don't go to his party. Just yesterday, he told me if there was one person he'd be happy to say goodbye to, it was you.

bring these two men, Archie Bunker and now George Jefferson, together. Even the episodes that preceded this were fun, because we knew this was coming, and it would be delicious.

I'll never forget Sherman at the door, not wanting to come into the Bunker house, and then coming in just a few steps. He and Archie were so much alike in their stubbornness. And of course, George's wife, Louise, was 180 degrees in the other direction. She and Edith weren't seeing black and white; they were just two women enjoying each other. I'm not sure I'm qualified to have an opinion that matters, but reflexively I do feel that women can be more understanding and more open to each other than might men be.

In doing this episode, it was clear Sherman and Isabel Sanford had such great chemistry together. So we brought him back. And we began talking with the two of them about doing their own spin-off, *The Jeffersons.*

In his oral history for The Interviews, **JOHN RICH** remembered: Most people don't know that in the original concept, we were never going to see George Jefferson. We always had Mel Stewart, who was the brother, with the idea that George Jefferson was so offended at living in a "honky" neighborhood that he wouldn't be seen. If the families had any kind of dialogue, George would send the brother, who came over with Louise—and Archie first thought he was the husband, and had these fights with Henry.

In his oral history for The Interviews, **SHERMAN HEMSLEY** remembered: They had talked about the character for years, about George not wanting to come into the Bunker house. But no one had ever seen him. I'm glad I didn't know all this. All they told me about

George was that he was "pompous and feisty." All I knew was that I'm here, I'm staying here, and I had to make this entrance into a show that had been a smash for years. I remember standing outside the door waiting for my entrance, and I was like, "Should I run? Do I know these lines?" All this craziness goes through your head. But the cast was all so sweet. I was more worried about messing up because they were trusting me so much. I didn't want to let them down.

When John Rich had first introduced me to Isabel, he said, "Here's your new husband. Show him his dressing room." So she looked me up and down and said, "Come this way." She had expected a big guy—that's what she told me later. She saw me, and at the time I weighed 135 pounds, and she said, "I could wear him around my little finger!"

But we really started clicking as characters, especially in the third show I did, which was "Lionel's Engagement Party." That's when the characters really came together. We had that big fight, and I knew how to argue. That's when John Rich felt comfortable with me. That's when I heard about the idea for a spin-off, *The Jeffersons.*

"ARCHIE IN THE CELLAR"

WHILE THE REST OF THE FAMILY IS AWAY, ARCHIE ACCIDENTALLY LOCKS HIMSELF INSIDE THE CELLAR.

WRITTEN BY: **Don Nicholl** ● DIRECTED BY: **Bob LaHendro** and **John Rich**

GUEST STARS: **Betty Garrett** as **Irene Lorenzo** ● **Juan DeCarlos** as **Oil Man**
Billy Sands as **Stretch Cunningham** (voice)

ORIGINAL AIR DATE: **November 17, 1973**

NORMAN LEAR: My favorite word for thinking about this episode is *stretching*. It's what we did in writing it, and it's what Carroll had to do to make all those moments in it special, whether the physical comedy of trying to break the door down, or later of acting drunk, or the precise timing of the joke when he realizes that apparently God is a Black man: "Forgive me, Lord! The Jeffersons was right!" Carroll had a big appetite for an episode like this, because this was the kind of stretching that he was brilliant at as an actor.

BOB LAHENDRO: When John Rich was moving over to become a producer on the show, I began to share directing duties. This was a somewhat challenging episode, because it involved a video effect, superimposing Archie's interactions with Edith, Mike, and Gloria as his hallucinations. We shot all those scenes live, with the actors against black velour curtains on the sides of the stage. We didn't pre-tape anything like that, because we wanted to time the lines and the laughs just right.

I will always remember this episode, because as with any other, John and Norman and the other producers would sit on tall director's chairs in the control room, from which they could see the console where I was sitting, and the monitors with the feed from each camera. There's the moment near the end where the oil man has come down the stairs, and Archie is about to look up and get a look at him. The audience is antici-

pating this like crazy—you can tell because they're already reacting with every step the guy has taken down the stairs. And then, when he was revealed to them as a Black man, the anticipation increased even more.

After playing being taken aback when he first looked at the man, Carroll sank to his knees and played Archie's drunken stupor, waiting and waiting and waiting for the laugh to die down. He had to wait until exactly the right moment, and didn't know when that moment was going to be, to look up and deliver his line about the Jeffersons having been right.

My cut from the two-shot of the oil man standing over Archie to a close-up of Archie, looking up at him, had to be timed just right. I couldn't be late, I couldn't be early. As Carroll was waiting and waiting through the laugh, I was waiting with him. From behind me, I could hear John starting to get restless. He started groaning, and said, "Now! Don't wait!" But I waited, while Carroll milked the hell out of the moment. And then I cut, just a fraction of a second before Carroll looked up, to show his big blue eyes. It was probably the most perfect cut I've ever made. It was important to see the right moment just a fraction before Carroll did, and I was able to, because by this point in the show I had a real sense of his timing. I was able to feel what his instinct was. Because we had worked on so many shows, I could tell when he was about to go on to the next step.

OIL MAN: Mr. Bunker?

ARCHIE: Here I am, Lord. This is it.
[turns around to see a Black man]

ARCHIE: Forgive me, Lord…the Jeffersons was right.

Season 4, Episode 15

"EDITH'S CHRISTMAS STORY"

EDITH FINDS A LUMP IN HER BREAST, BUT TRIES TO HIDE HER WORRY AND PUT ON A HAPPY FACE FOR CHRISTMAS.

STORY BY: **Austin Kalish** and **Irma Kalish** ● TELEPLAY BY: **Austin Kalish, Irma Kalish,** and **Don Nicholl**
DIRECTED BY: **John Rich**

GUEST STARS: **Betty Garrett** as **Irene Lorenzo** ● **Vincent Gardenia** as **Frank Lorenzo**
Katherine MacGregor as **Nurse**

ORIGINAL AIR DATE: **December 22, 1973**

NORMAN LEAR: This was a special episode for everybody. It was so true to real life and what many of us experienced, or knew someone who did. And yet at that time, it didn't seem like anybody had gone near the subject.

I did hear some people at the time criticizing why a comedy show would have "talked about breast cancer." Well, the "why" of it is that it was done by a lot of grown-up people. The writing staff alone, at any given year, totaled a thousand and fifty years old. We dealt with the things that were closest to us. "How could it be funny?" Well, we never thought any of the tough sub-jects were funny—it's the things that happen in daily life in the course of those subjects that are funny.

We were thrilled to hear from women's groups about their excitement that we were talking about breast cancer. Jean, too, cared deeply about this epi-sode, and was very happy that there were profession-als there to advise her—although her every instinct was always so perfect, from a performance standpoint. Betty Garrett was a standout here, too, in the scene where she reassures Edith in the kitchen, with her very telling delivery of the words "I know." It was a glorious moment between those two women.

In her oral history for The Interviews, **JEAN STAPLETON** *recalled:* At first, I was bothered by this script. I didn't want to dramatize it, to dwell on breast cancer, and I was very concerned about it. And Norman, in his intuitive way, knew that, and so we had a little talk. I said, "I just don't like doing this whole show." And he said, "Well, it's not about breast cancer. It's about love, and how she's providing for the family and comforting them." And I said, "Oh, of course!" And so I was able to do it with pleasure, with ease and peace. I thought it was a wonder-ful suggestion on his part, and that's true. It was about her desire to comfort her loved ones about it.

104

GLORIA

Ma, something's wrong. I know you.

EDITH

Why does everybody around here think
they know me? Remember, Gloria,
deep waters run very still!

GLORIA

But, Ma...

EDITH

... and I've known me a lot longer
than any of you! So don't go around
saying that you know me.

GLORIA

Okay. Okay. I'm sorry. I didn't
mean to upset you.

(SHE STARTS TO GO AWAY)

EDITH

I've got a lump in my breast!

GLORIA

What did you just say?

EDITH

I've got a lump in...

GLORIA

Oh -- Ma.

(SHE HUGS HER)

EDITH

That's the first time I've said
it out loud.

                    IRENE

          What was it you wanted to ask me?

                    EDITH

          I'm afraid if I have this operation,

          Archie won't think of me in the

          same way.

                    IRENE

          Edith! Stop scaring yourself.

          Archie loves you. Nothing's going

          to change that.

                    EDITH

          But I'm gonna change -- a lot.

                    IRENE

          Listen, even if you have to have

          the operation, it's still gonna be

          all right. Believe me!

                    EDITH

          You don't know.

(IRENE IS LOOKING RIGHT INTO
HER EYES)

                    IRENE

          That's just the point, Edith. I

          do know. I know.

                    EDITH

(BEAT)

          You mean... you...?

                    IRENE

(NODS)

          Six years ago. And you see how

          Frank and I get along. It hasn't

          made one bit of difference in our

          marriage.

(EDITH'S EYES AUTOMATICALLY
FLICKER TO IRENE'S CHEST.
IRENE SMILES)

          Don't bother looking, Edith.

                    EDITH

          Oh, I wasn't.

(SHE LOOKS AGAIN)

> "ALL IN THE FAMILY" 6/11/73 Maywood, Ill
>   CBS TV 2   Cm-   5-22-73
>
> After looking at "All in the Family" for 25 times, it is now very clear to me that your _Writers_, _Owners_, producers, _Consultants_, _directors_ and _Actors_ have never met, known, seen, nor understood a real conservative!
>
> "_Archie Bunker_ is your "STRAW MAN" a reverse propagandistic man, which you continually, and commercially hold up as a true representative of a valid intelligent conservative – But your image of a real conservative is false, grotesque and ridiculous in all of its posture, inferences and dialog of profanity! And DISTORTION!
> LIES ARE NOT FUNNY!

SALLY STRUTHERS: I was raised in a household with a mom and a sister, in a tiny house the size of a Triscuit box. We were raised to be so modest—my mom didn't want my sister or me to cross those three feet from our bedroom door to the bathroom without being in bathrobes. We weren't to see each other naked, ever. And we didn't talk about our body parts, ever. So when the words "breast" and "breast cancer" kept being thrown about all that week, I was cringing inside.

But that kind of thing is good for a person, because you need to be desensitized about something you shouldn't actually be embarrassed about. I had aunts on both sides of my family who died of breast cancer, and doing this episode is what made me wind up going to get mammograms every couple of years. I think this was a week of huge growth for me—especially because Jean Stapleton carried the story with such aplomb. I could finally say the word "breast" to my doctor.

EDITH: When they told me everything was all right, I got so excited
I jumped off the examining table . . . and I broke my ankle!

"LIONEL'S ENGAGEMENT"

ARCHIE MEETS LIONEL JEFFERSON'S FUTURE IN-LAWS, A MIXED-RACE COUPLE NAMED LOUIS AND HELEN WILLIS.

WRITTEN BY: **Michael Ross** and **Bernie West** • DIRECTED BY: **John Rich**

GUEST STARS: **Mike Evans** as **Lionel Jefferson** • **Isabel Sanford** as **Louise Jefferson**
Sherman Hemsley as **George Jefferson** • **Lynne Moody** as **Jenny Willis** • **Charles Aidman** as **Louis Willis**
Kim Hamilton as **Helen Willis** • **Zara Cully** as **Mother Jefferson**

ORIGINAL AIR DATE: **February 9, 1974**

NORMAN LEAR: Interracial marriage was something going on in the world around us—a good deal rarer than it became, but it was happening in the culture in the '70s, and yet had not really been seen on the tube. Nobody had dealt with it. And we realized that any issues around interracial marriage could be a premise for a story for us, so we wouldn't have just another engagement but also a set of problems that goes with it.

In the cocktail-party scene, George uses the N-word. For the audience, the actor, Sherman Hemsley, said the word, and it was broadcast that way as well—the first time. They bleeped it later, even in the network reruns. We got mail about it, in both directions. Some people wrote to say it's time we dealt with the word, and others said no, we don't need that in our language.

LYNNE MOODY: This was very early in my career, my first sitcom role. And outside Norman Lear's shows, *Good Times* and *Sanford and Son* and very few others, it wasn't common to have Black people on TV, period, never mind a biracial character like Jenny Willis. Black actors would be frustrated trying just to get an audition, much less a job. And when there was a role for a Black person, we'd laugh about how they'd call everybody from four to forty for it, so all the Black people would be there for this one tiny little carrot.

I remember being scared at the first table read, not wanting to stand out or get fired on the first day. But when I had auditioned, the casting director, Jane Murray, had told me exactly what they wanted, and exactly how to perform the scene where the audience first meets Jenny: "Go from A, to B, to C"—and that was literally part of the lines, where Jenny ticks off her future goals with "A, B and C." So I did it exactly that way at the table read, and John Rich said, "That's fantastic. I don't want you do it every day during rehearsals, because I want you to save it."

Everyone at that time was struggling with issues of race in television. I went on one audition for a commercial, and noticed that there were separate audition sides for a "White version" and a "Black version." In the White version, they spoke English: "Oh, Mother, don't do that!" In the Black version, it was "Dig, Ma! That ain't hip!" I'll never forget that line. That's why reading a script for a Norman Lear show was such a treat, because all the characters just spoke like people.

All in the Family introduced profound topics with humor, and in this scene, with a taboo word. I still hate the word. I remember when Richard Pryor used to use it, but then as he got older and wiser, he stopped, realizing the harm in making it acceptable. But it was great how this episode used it [as George predicts Jenny's father, Louis, bickering with his wife, Helen, will use the "N-word"]. It's a startling moment—not so much for us actors, who had seen the script and been hearing the word in rehearsals all week, and were prepared. But it was shocking to the audience, who laughed and responded just as we wanted them to. That's not something that had been done before on TV, nor could it be done today.

"GLORIA SINGS THE BLUES"

GLORIA ADMITS THAT SHE DOESN'T THINK SHE LOVES MIKE ANYMORE TO EDITH, WHO IN TURN
PUTS HER DAUGHTER AT EASE BY REVEALING SHE ONCE BRIEFLY FELT THE SAME WAY ABOUT ARCHIE.

WRITTEN BY: **Michael Ross** and **Bernie West** ● DIRECTED BY: **John Rich**

ORIGINAL AIR DATE: **March 2, 1974**

NORMAN LEAR: It's interesting that despite the important storyline of Gloria feeling depressed and wondering whether she loves her husband, this episode is really known for the "sock and a shoe" routine. I remember as clearly as anything today how one day while making this episode, I walked into a rehearsal, and Rob and Carroll had come up with "sock and a shoe." We, the writers, had not in any way even approached it. It came strictly from the actors, working with the director. And to be given that, to be a writer on the show and be gifted with those kinds of performances, was amazing. The scene was a killer in terms of laughs, and it was a gift of the performers. To this day, I remember it so well, because there's so little in life that calls for that much laughter. I could not be more confident of anything than the fact that that laughter added time to my life.

So, which one should you do—a sock and a sock or a sock and a shoe? It doesn't matter; you've just got to laugh on your way to the answer.

SALLY STRUTHERS: I had so many wonderful scenes with Jean. Edith always had advice for Gloria. Most of the time, like in this episode, we were in the kitchen. And Edith would tell Gloria these wonderful stories—they were always odd, and yet they made sense.

ROB REINER: Over nearly fifty years, when people have come up to me and recalled a moment in the show, they've always talked about when Archie and I got into the argument in this episode—about how you put your socks and shoes on—more than any other scene we've ever done. That argument hadn't been in the script; it came out of an improvisation that Carroll and I did. It's one of those real things that people do in their lives that nobody ever comments about. We started riffing on it—is it a sock and a sock and a shoe and a shoe? Or a sock and a shoe and a sock and a shoe?—and it made its way into the script.

All four of us improvised a lot on the show. The way we put the show together, after our table read on Monday,

ARCHIE: Did you know that he puts on a sock and a shoe and
a sock and a shoe, instead of a sock and a sock and a shoe and a shoe?

GLORIA: What?

ARCHIE: What's the sense in asking you? You wear pantyhose.

we would have a run-through on Wednesday, in a rehearsal hall. And after the run-through, the writers, the actors, and the director would all be sitting around giving each other notes. I might say, "Carroll, why don't you take that line, let me say this, and then you'll say this?" We would all be pitching, "Wait a minute, what about this?" It was like a great jazz combo of people who could riff with each other. From the initial script, we'd take it onto the rehearsal floor, and often-

times some things would stay and others would change. Well, I remember one time, the great playwright Herb Gardner came to a rehearsal. In the theater, the author's words are sacrosanct, and you can't change anything without the playwright's approval. Herb looked at us and couldn't get over what we were doing. He said, "This is like creative communism!" We were like a machine, with everybody contributing. Norman set the tone and allowed it to happen that way.

I ALWAYS SAY THAT TV CAN BE DIVIDED into two eras, "BN" and "AN"—Before Norman and After Norman. That's how monumental he has been to the entire industry.

There are two parts to the genius of *All in the Family*. One is the political and social commentary, which of course was responsible for societal changes in America; it got Nixon's attention. It was part of the national discourse. I don't think there's been a show before or since that's had such an impact on the country. But here's the other part of the genius: No one would care about all that very important societal/political stuff in the show if the Bunkers were not relatable as a family. The key word in the show is "family." And this was one of the great family sitcoms. In fact, they could do a sidesplitting episode without mentioning a social issue at all—that's how well-drawn the characters were, how great the performances and writing and directing were. What did Archie and Mike arguing about putting on a sock and a shoe, or both socks, have to do with anything in society, other than fundamental differences between a young guy and an old guy?

When I went to CBS to pitch *Everybody Loves Raymond* and sat at their conference room table, I was surrounded by photos of all their greatest hits. When the president of CBS asked, "So what is this show? What will it be like?" I pointed to a picture of *All in the Family* on their wall and said, "Well, I'd like it to be like that." I said it as a joke, as if you could be like the greatest sitcom of all time. But it was something to aspire to, such greatness.

—*EVERYBODY LOVES RAYMOND* CREATOR PHIL ROSENTHAL

Season 5, Episode 7
"GLORIA'S SHOCK"

GLORIA AND THE BUNKERS ARE SURPRISED WHEN MIKE ANNOUNCES THEY WILL NOT HAVE CHILDREN.

WRITTEN BY: **Dixie Brown Grossman** • DIRECTED BY: **H. Wesley Kenney**

GUEST STARS: **Betty Garrett** as **Irene Lorenzo**

ORIGINAL AIR DATE: **October 26, 1974**

NORMAN LEAR: Throughout the series, Mike and Gloria had a lot of discussions about having children; they had lost a baby in the first season, and we were starting to think about them having a baby, as we would later plan for season 6. So this was another point in their discussion and decision.

The speech about the environment and ozone layer came from my own and possibly a few of the other writers' recognition of climate change early on. We made a few phone calls to get professional advice about what to say—it's not that we had the right language; it came from the counsel of other people we knew.

SALLY STRUTHERS: We were performance-ready every week by the time the two audiences came. We knew our lines forward and backward. But the night of this episode, Rob Reiner's mouth wouldn't work right. As Mike was getting very heated, telling Gloria about her hairspray and the disappearing ozone layer,

his line ends with "And God knows what it could do to the plants and crops!" Except he couldn't say "plants and crops." He'd get to the end of that sentence and say, "God knows what it could do to the cramps and plops!" He kept getting it wrong, the same way, take after take. Every time I would fall on the bed laughing, the audience would laugh, and Rob would get more frustrated. It became hilarious.

DIXIE BROWN GROSSMAN: I was in my early forties when I got my foot in the door with TV writing. I think Norman Lear was looking for women writers, because he sensed that there was a lack of that voice in television. One story idea I came up with for Don Nicholl, Bernie West, and Mickey Ross was from watching *60 Minutes*, which had a story about the growing number of young people who didn't want children. I thought that Mike and Gloria could announce something like that.

They liked the idea, and Bernie said, "No, let's have just Mike not wanting children, and it's him against the other three members of the family." In the two script drafts I wrote, Mike cited overpopulation, which was an issue being discussed a lot at the time. The whole show took place in the living room and kitchen. It was only later that the show's writing staff added a scene with just Mike and Gloria arguing in the bedroom; I have to confess that I did not write one word of the discussion about the dangers to the ozone layer from aerosols. But I do remember when the news came out about harmful CFCs in aerosols, and I'm glad the episode was so enlightening about that.

March 6, 1975

Mr Norman Lear
c/o all in the family
C B S Television City
Hollywood, California
U. S. A.

C-

Dear Mr Lear,

Your program has approached a number
of topical subjects with candor and integrity
concerning women, such as breast cancer, the
right to a childless marriage and others!

It seems to me in this year of 1975, International
women's year, you could take one small step
further for womankind and drop all the 'ding bats'
from Archie Bunker's lines. As vulnerable, loving
and sensitive as Edith is, it is inconceivable
that any woman would accept this offensive,
degrading appellation as a token of affection.

Who knows, it might even help your writers
develop some changes in a series and character
now wearing thin and repetitious,

Yours sincerely,

There was one line of mine that got such a big laugh that the clip was used in some of the later celebrations of the show. After Archie says how it's a big decision to bring a kid into the world, Mike replies, "Come on, Arch. The only reason a lot of people have kids is because they forgot to go to the drugstore." The way it's scripted, it then just says "(Looks at Archie, looks at Edith.)" And then Archie says to Edith, "Can't you keep your mouth shut?" And she says "I didn't say nothing."

I didn't know quite what the actors would do in that moment of looks between Mike's and Archie's lines. Sometimes you anticipate an actor will deliver a line a certain way, and then they don't. But Jean made the moment work so brilliantly, with a guilty look on her face as she could barely look over at Archie. And so at first, after Mike said his line and then looked over at Edith and Archie, the audience just sort of gasped. Birth control? You just didn't talk about stuff like that on television then! But when they saw Edith's reaction, they caught on, and there was this crescendo of laughter.

"ARCHIE AND THE MIRACLE"

A NEAR-DEATH EXPERIENCE CONVINCES ARCHIE THAT HE OWES
HIS LIFE TO GOD, WHICH LEADS TO AN ARGUMENT WITH ATHEIST MIKE.

WRITTEN BY: **Lloyd Turner** and **Gordon Mitchell** • DIRECTED BY: **H. Wesley Kenney**

GUEST STARS: **Betty Garrett** as **Irene Lorenzo** • **James Cromwell** as **Stretch Cunningham**

ORIGINAL AIR DATE: **November 23, 1974**

NORMAN LEAR: I never thought of Archie as a very religious person, in terms of churchgoing religion, but I also never thought about him as not believing in God, or not being frightened of God's wrath. So that middle ground is what this episode addresses. I also don't think of Mike as "anti-God"; he's just anti-what people make of God—the way people who do believe use God, as if to say that if you don't believe, you're not worthy.

ROB REINER: *All in the Family* wasn't just about liberal and conservative. It was also about somebody who believed in God and somebody who didn't, and we had those great religious arguments on the show. And of course it was clear that even though Archie was arguing for the existence of God, he was never really going to end up consistently going to church.

In her oral history for The Interviews, **BETTY GARRETT** *remembered:* Norman was always careful that whatever Archie said, which was just outrageous sometimes, there was always a rebuttal, which made a point that Archie was stupid to say whatever he had said. And one of my purposes, I think, in the script, was to be the person who cut him down and really set him straight. And also, to be a friend to Edith. So of the scripts I was involved with, in one I became foreman of his department, and that just enraged him, that a woman would be his boss. In another one I beat him at pool. Incidentally, I've never been able to play pool. Rob Reiner showed me how to just take the positions, and I think he made the shots in the close-up camera.

ARCHIE: They don't make guys like him no more.

STRETCH: No, not since my father died.

JAMES CROMWELL: When I came back to California after a year and a half hitchhiking around the world, I thought I was going to be a probations officer. But then a friend introduced me to Jane Murray, the *All in the Family* casting director. I met with her, and thought it didn't go well. And then a few months later, in July 1974, my agent called and said, "Get over to CBS right now."

I had never seen *All in the Family*. But I went to read again for Jane, and then the director, Wes Kenney, and then went up to meet Norman Lear. Within an hour or two, I went from never having done anything on film or television to a role on the biggest comedy on TV. And I later found out why: Carroll O'Connor had been refusing to appear in the last few episodes, and the producers had decided they would have to move on without him. So they wrote a script for the first episode I appeared in—season 5's "Archie Is Missing"—in which I had gone with Archie to Buffalo and had lost him there. I stayed a day or so afterward and called the cops and then came and announced to the family that Archie

wasn't there. That was the second show Carroll missed—and in the third one, we were going to hear that Archie was dead. Well, we were rehearsing that third show when Carroll realized the error of his ways and decided to return.

I had needed to adopt some mannerisms—and what I adopted without thinking about it was Art Carney's Ed Norton character from *The Honeymooners*; it was an homage to someone whose work I really admired.

WHEN I STARTED WRITING COMEDY with Mary Kay Place, there were very few women. We were lucky enough to have three great mentors in Larry Gelbart, Jim Brooks, and Norman Lear. I had always dreamed of being an op-ed writer, but from Larry I learned the power of getting your opinion on television. From Jim, who produced *The Mary Tyler Moore Show*, I got to experience the whole women's-lib thing. And then from Norman, I learned that you can be as bold as you want to be on television, and say the most shocking things, and you won't die. Your life won't be over, and the police won't come for you. And having grown up in a small town, where everyone is amiable and you never say anything too controversial, that was big news.

Today we have more than five hundred shows on the air, but when *All in the Family* aired, that was what you talked about at the water cooler the morning after the show. Norman had the nation by the tail. He had our national feelings organized like a town hall or public event. People fought and argued, and it caused a lot of conversations in families. *All in the Family* definitely changed the world—and changed the programming that evolved from it for multiple generations afterward.

There's a reason why Norman's work is reflected in the Smithsonian. Other people from Hollywood have taken their money and done some good things with it, but nobody has done it better or more nobly than Norman. He put his earnings right back into America, through his founding of People for the American Way and other work. He has done astounding things in the name of progress. People in Washington like to look down on Hollywood, and I have never understood that. Because the smartest people in Hollywood, like Norman, are changing hearts and minds. Washington is changing laws, which people can or cannot obey. But if you don't change their hearts and their minds, you don't really change much.

—*DESIGNING WOMEN* CREATOR LINDA BLOODWORTH-THOMASON

"ALL IN THE FAMILY"

A TANDEM *Production*

May 28, 1975

Thank you for your recent letter regarding
our series "ALL IN THE FAMILY." It means
a great deal to all of us when we hear from
our viewers even when the attitudes are
critical.

I must remind you that the character of
Archie Bunker speaks from a platform of
bigotry and prejudice, all of which stems
from ignorance. In all of our shows, whenever Archie does spout something that is
prejudiced, he is always answered by either
Mike, Edith or Gloria. I don't know the
segment you are referring to but I'm sure
that he was answered. This is one of the
prerequistes in the writing of the scripts.
In other words, this is the basic format of
the show.

We totally agree with you that there is a
need to spread love and brotherhood. We do
not produce message shows. We strive for
good entertainment and hope that we are telling
it as it is as far as subjects people are talking
and caring about. Incidentally, I would like to
quote to you Norman Lear, the executive producer
of our shows "We have lived for 2,000 years with
the Judeo-Christian ethic and we haven't beenable

"ALL IN THE FAMILY"
A TANDEM *Production*

-2-

to rid ourselves of bigotry yet. Why should
anyone expect a half-hour situation comedy show
to do what our own basic morality has failed
so far to - eliminate people's prejudices?"

Thank you again for your letter and we do hope
you continue to watch the show.

Sincerely,

Bina Bernard
Audience Response

Season 6, Episode 1
"THE VERY MOVING DAY"

GLORIA ANNOUNCES HER PREGNANCY THE DAY SHE AND MIKE MOVE NEXT DOOR TO THE BUNKERS.

WRITTEN BY: **Hal Kanter** • DIRECTED BY: **Paul Bogart**

GUEST STAR: **Betty Garrett** as **Irene Lorenzo**

ORIGINAL AIR DATE: **September 8, 1975**

NORMAN LEAR: The idea for Mike and Gloria to have a baby was great for us for story ideas—and equally great was the idea of Archie having a grandchild. And then the question became whether it would be a boy or a girl. And you'll be interested to know that the network wanted it to be a girl. We had a lot of silly conflicts with Program Practices—but this was possibly the silliest. Within days, toy companies came to us and to CBS for the rights to Archie and Edith's grandchild, and there hadn't really been much merchandising in general on a boy baby.

MIKE: When I move outta here tomorrow,
I'm gonna feel like a guy who just served a five-year sentence!

ARCHIE: Aw jeez, some tough sentence. Free room and board
and sleeping with the warden's daughter!

But their underlying reason was even stranger: They were sure that at some point, we would have Archie diapering the baby, and they didn't want to see a little doohickey. They were for some reason sure that I would put a camera right on it. And in no way would I put the camera deliberately on a child! Two months later, we were about to go into rehearsal with a script that called for Archie to be left alone with the baby, and a young man from Program Practices came to see me. He requested that if Archie diapered the baby, he would have the baby on his belly. As the father of three girls, I did wonder aloud if that was the way male babies were diapered. Then I caught a look from one of the writers overhearing this who had a son.

In the end, Archie did diaper the baby, who of course was a boy, and it was as dear as it was funny. And we didn't have the camera on his doohickey.

SALLY STRUTHERS: I had no idea they had come up with the idea for Gloria to be pregnant; I tended to learn things only by sitting around the table in rehearsal hall on Monday mornings and reading the script out loud. In many episodes I often had only three lines: "I'll help you set the table, Mom," "Michael, where are you going?" and "Oh, Daddy, stop it!" But every once in a while, there was something to sink my teeth into, like this pregnancy storyline, and that was thrilling.

In the last three seasons I was on *All in the Family*, Mike and Gloria moved to the house next door and had a baby. We were considered more for story ideas, and it became my favorite time on the show. By this point we were working with the best director, Paul Bogart, a wonderful man. I felt appreciated, and got to do some of my best work. And being pregnant on the show was hilarious. Costume designer Rita Riggs kept making me bigger and bigger stomach applications for under my costumes, and I just loved the look of it.

"ARCHIE THE HERO"

ARCHIE IS LAUDED AS A HERO AFTER PERFORMING MOUTH-TO-MOUTH ON BEVERLY LASALLE,
ONLY TO GET A SURPRISE WHEN HE DISCOVERS THAT BEVERLY IS A MALE DRAG ARTIST.

WRITTEN BY: **Lou Derman** and **Bill Davenport** ● DIRECTED BY: **Paul Bogart**

GUEST STARS: **Lori Shannon** as **Beverly LaSalle** ● **Sandy Kenyon** as **Jim Kitchener**
Bob Hastings as **Tommy Kelcy** ● **Billy Halop** as **Bert Munson**

ORIGINAL AIR DATE: **September 29, 1975**

NORMAN LEAR: The idea came first, for Archie to give mouth-to-mouth resuscitation to a cross-dressing person, who in the episode was a man dressing in drag as a performer. It's just a great, natural idea for an episode—although it was wonderful in every direction, because when we were casting, I remembered seeing Lori Shannon's musical act at the famous club Finocchio's in San Francisco, where I thought he was terrific.

I still think of Edith meeting Beverly at the front door, and how it didn't matter to Edith what exactly she was. Edith was all about love—this is just another human being, end of story. And I'm proud of the audience anticipation, seeing Archie come downstairs to be thanked by this person who was not a woman in his view. The look on Carroll's face when Archie learned he had given the "kiss of life" to someone who was in his eyes a guy—my God, was that funny.

BEVERLY: I'm afraid you don't understand, Mrs. Bunker. I'm a transvestite.

EDITH: Well, you sure fooled me. I mean, you ain't got no accent at all.

JACKIE BEAT, *Drag queen and writer*: I was about twelve years old when Beverly LaSalle first appeared on *All in the Family*. Before then, drag on TV was just Barney Fife in a dress on *The Andy Griffith Show*, or maybe someone in a sketch on *The Carol Burnett Show*. But it was never a full-fledged, fleshed-out character like Beverly.

At that age, just seeing Beverly means you are immediately struck with the thought, "Wait—this is a possibility?" I was young, so Beverly seemed so much older than me, and I thought, "That person is in New York." But still, if nothing else, just the fact that she existed put in my head that this is an option for what some people can do.

In Beverly's second episode, "Beverly Rides Again," Archie tries to fool his friend Pinky by setting him up with Beverly. Archie treats Beverly like an object, a prop, not a real person—"Come out with us, and embarrass my straight friend!"—but the show and the writers did not, and Beverly is allowed to keep her dignity, and even get a moment of revenge at the end. In that episode, I couldn't believe some of the things the show got away with. When Pinky hugs Beverly's shoulders and says, "I always like the girls with a little meat on their bones," I couldn't believe Archie's reply made it past the censors: "Rummage around there, you'll find a lot more." Archie might as well be telling him, "She's got a dick!"

Today it's a *RuPaul's Drag Race* world, but back then Lori Shannon was a real trailblazer. It was so smart for the show to hire an actual drag performer, rather than just put a male actor in a wig, because the character became so much more well-rounded. By using a real, working drag queen, it really came across. There's always a fine line, whenever you're dealing with someone from a specific community—even more so back then. Beverly really did ride that line pretty well, because on the outside, she's *not* just like you and me for most people. But ultimately, whether it's a racial thing or an LGBT thing, *All in the Family* showed that we don't have to be all the same—but the final message of the show, and these episodes in particular, was always the fact that deep down we actually are.

DON'T REMEMBER THE FIRST TIME I WATCHED *All in the Family*, but I do remember the first time the show had an effect on me. I was nine years old, and I was watching the show with my grandfather. The episode was "Archie the Hero." It's the one where Archie realizes the woman he gave CPR to is, in fact, a man. I will never forget sitting next to my grandfather, feeling my stomach drop as I watched Archie react in total disgust to the idea of his mouth being on the mouth of another man. I'm not sure I was cognizant of being gay, but I *did* know it would be a problem if I said what I was thinking: What's so bad about a man kissing another man?

Norman's shows are ubiquitous; therefore they had an untold impact on me as a person. *Maude* was my comfort food, the show that made me realize I wanted to write sitcoms when I grew up. And I truly believe *All in the Family* mirrored to this country the import of having moral character. But I don't think the show could be on network TV today, because Archie's voice would be, legally speaking, too terrifying for the conglomerates that own the television industry.

—*WILL & GRACE* CO-CREATOR MAX MUTCHNICK

(HE STARTS TO SIP BEER, BUT HIS HAND FREEZES IN
MID-AIR AS BEVERLY LASALLE ENTERS...DRESSED AS
SEEN EARLIER)

                    BEVERLY

          Oh there you are, Mr. Bunker.

                    ARCHIE

          Ah holy cow.

                    BEVERLY

          I'm sorry for interrupting,

          but I forgot something.

                    ARCHIE

(NERVOUSLY)

          Oh, you didn't forget nothin...You paid me

          my fare and everything.

                    KITCHENER

          Oh! You wouldn't be the one whose life

          he saved!

                    BEVERLY

          Yes I would.

                    KITCHENER

          I'm Jim Kitchener from the Long Island Press.

          I'd like to get a shot of the two of you

          together.

                    ARCHIE

          Hold it! Hold it! Before you do that, me

          and the lady got something to talk about in

          private.

(ARCHIE TAKES BEVERLY BY THE ARM, LEADS HIM TO A
TABLE)

KITCHENER

(TO MUNSON)

    I'll be right back.

(EXITS TO MEN'S ROOM)

                        ARCHIE

    What're you doin here? How'd you find me?

                        BEVERLY

    I called your house. Your son-in-law said

    I'd be sure to find you here.

                        ARCHIE

    I'll kill him later.

                        BEVERLY

    I'm opening at the Pink Tiger tonight...and...

                        ARCHIE

    Ssshhh!

                        BEVERLY

(TAKES TWO TICKETS OUT OF PURSE)

    I want you and your wife to be my guests at

    the show.

                        ARCHIE

    Yeah, yeah -- thanks a lot, but...Look willya

    do me a favor? Please...don't take your

    hair off in here. Not even for laughs. Them

    guys ain't liberal thinkers like you and me.

    They don't understand queers. You know what

    I mean?

                        BEVERLY

(LOOKS AT ARCH FOR A SECOND, THEN)

    Yes, I think I do.

"THE LITTLE ATHEIST"

ARCHIE AND MIKE ARGUE OVER BABY JOEY'S RELIGIOUS UPBRINGING DURING THANKSGIVING.

WRITTEN BY: **Lou Derman** • DIRECTED BY: **Paul Bogart**

GUEST STAR: **Betty Garrett** as **Irene Lorenzo**

ORIGINAL AIR DATE: **November 24, 1975**

NORMAN LEAR: In this episode, Archie and Mike are arguing about religion, and whether or not Joey should be brought up to believe in God. After arguing back and forth, Mike blows Archie a raspberry, and Archie believes that Mike's basically blowing a raspberry at God.

The network said, "You can't put that in the script." Usually, if the network objected to this kind of thing, which they did occasionally, I'd just say, "Let's wait until you see it on its feet. If you still have a problem, we can talk about it." This time, however, they were adamant. I suggested inviting clergymen from different religious factions to attend the pre-taping run-through. If they deemed it sacrilegious, well, I'd be willing to abide by their decision. Dick Kirschner from Program Practices rejected that idea, saying, "We don't program for clergymen." He said that of course the raspberry was not directed at God, but other people would not understand. By "other people" I knew he meant middle-of-the-country, so-called unsophisticated viewers.

"There is going to be a knee-jerk reaction," he said, "and we don't want that."

I could only reply, "So you're not programming for the clergy, but you're programming for the knee-jerkers."

ARCHIE: You know what that meathead just done?
He gave the Bronx cheer to the Lord, so help me!
And he's gonna bring up our grandson to do the same thing!

EDITH: Oh, Archie!

We shot the show we wanted to shoot, and later we got word that it had been accepted by the network anyway. All those hours spent discussing this, when we could have been doing something creative.

GARY SHIMOKAWA, *Associate Director*: CBS gave the show a hard time about any swearing. They allowed Norman to utilize swearing, but only two or three times per episode—any more than that and we're going to cut it out of the show.

They were particularly sensitive to use of the word "God." But in one episode I love—the first one of a two-parter that started season 4, "We're Having a Heat Wave"—I believe it's the first episode of network television to allow use of the word "goddamn." But the way it happens, it's like the writers had Archie immediately apologizing for it on the show. He explains that "God" is the most popular word in the Bible. And "the second word, 'damn,' that's a perfectly good word. You hear it all the time, like they dammed the river to keep it from flooding.

And you read in the Bible that some guy was damned for cheating or stealing or having insex in the family. And who damned him? Who else? God! God damned him, Edith. Beautiful words right out of the Holy Book!"

SALLY STRUTHERS: There had been one episode where I had had to walk down the stairs in a bikini, and I really didn't want to do it. But I did, and I was miserable. And after that, my mail was littered with letters from guys in prison. And because Mike was an atheist—not Rob Reiner, but the character, Mike—people would send him Bibles in the mail. They were worried for his soul. He would write them back, saying "I'm a nice Jewish guy who went through a bar mitzvah. I believe in God, but thank you." And then there were people who would read the credits and quickly write down names, and write letters to "the lovely Miss Carroll O'Connor." So the prisoners were attracted to me, and the Christians were worried about Rob. And people thought Carroll O'Connor was a woman.

DEAR ALL IN
the FAMILY
I WOUNLD
LiKE A
PiCTURE
OF JOEYS
ON YOG
Show

PLease

OdeDME
ONC PLease

#0617

SHAPIRO

You've got a son... a healthy son --
with a complete inventory.

SFX: BABY CRIES

GLORIA

Look at him, Michael, he's getting
pinker and pinker.

MIKE

Is that a terrific boy? Isn't
Joey terrific?

GLORIA

Joey -- are you sure?

MIKE

Of course. Wouldn't I know my
own son? I love you, honey...

(HE KISSES HER)

It wasn't too bad was it?

GLORIA

No, it wasn't.

MIKE

How do you feel about a second one?

GLORIA

(JOKING)

Not now, Michael, I have a headache.

(THEY KISS)

SFX: BABY CRIES

(THEY BREAK KISS, LOOK OFF TOWARDS
BABY AND SMILE)

CUT TO:

"JOEY'S BAPTISM"

AFTER ARGUING WITH MIKE ABOUT RELIGION, ARCHIE TAKES JOEY TO CHURCH AND BAPTIZES HIM ON HIS OWN.

WRITTEN BY: **Milt Josefsberg, Mel Tolkin,** and **Larry Rhine** ● DIRECTED BY: **Paul Bogart**

GUEST STARS: **Clyde Kusatsu** as **Reverend Chong**

ORIGINAL AIR DATE: **February 23, 1976**

NORMAN LEAR: At this point in the series, the audience had a big emotional investment in Archie Bunker. And so the scene Archie has with his baby grandson in this episode is so meaningful for the sake of the character of Archie, and Carroll O'Connor made it wonderful. Watching Archie talk so lovingly to Joey at the baptismal font, I was awash in Archie's feelings, the need to do something for his grandson, and the joy in the fulfillment of the moment. And I think that's the way it came off for the audience, too.

SALLY STRUTHERS: In the scene where Archie baptizes Joey, even though he's really doing something against his daughter's wishes, there is such love in the way he speaks to his baby grandson that you love him for it. It was when Archie was tender that Carroll just broke your heart. It was wonderful that Carroll could play those moments, that the writers could write those moments, and that the audience could partake of that brilliance. And their hearts were already so accepting of Archie that when he did do something so tender and real, they were genuinely moved.

PHIL DORAN: My writing partner, Doug Arango, and I were the same age as Rob Reiner and Sally Struthers, so we were hired to write stories for them. Having Gloria and Mike have a baby seemed like the next logical thing to do to give us a big block of stories to tell for season 6. We weren't breaking ground by doing that—but we did do it better and funnier. At the time of this episode, I remember talking with the other writers about how my wife and I had just had a baby. I

grew up in a Jewish family, and went to Hebrew school and got bar mitzvahed. My parents wanted us to have a ritual circumcision for my son, and I said, "No way— we'll just have it done in the hospital and that's that." And from that incident, we came up with a story about Archie insisting on having Joey christened.

I learned so much just being around Norman Lear. I've since run a lot of writers' rooms on shows, and as it was on *All in the Family*, I like to stay open to contributions from everyone who can make the show better. The way Norman said it has always stayed with me: "Listen to the smallest voice."

CLYDE KUSATSU: I considered myself still starting out as an actor at the time I was on *All in the Family*. I had been a theater major at Northwestern University from 1966 to 1970, and I had a professor corner me one time when I was a freshman and say, "Why do you want to be an actor? There's only *The King and I* and *The Teahouse of the August Moon*. How can you possibly think of making a living?"

That had been crushing. Now I was playing Reverend Chong, and what was unique about the role was that the *All in the Family* writers didn't make any kind of excuses or back story for why Edith's Episcopal minister is Chinese-American. He's just there, part of the American scene. I looked at it as a wonderful opportunity, because each time I appeared, the country saw a person who looked like me, who spoke clearly, without an accent, who was just another American.

By this point, Carroll had become such an icon as Archie Bunker, and I had heard that some other

ARCHIE: Throwin' rocks is, what do you call,
an age-old religious custom, there, for bringin' people around.
All your ancient people, there, threw rocks, until
they got axes and spears, and later on guns to do God's work.

guest stars had been nervous. The pressure was really immense, because they taped only two shows, the 5:30 and the 8 p.m.—and there were usually no "pickups," or reshoots of scenes if you messed up. It was like doing a twenty-five-minute play, where you really had to hit your marks. You had to be ready, almost at the very beginning, at the table read.

The *All in the Family* writers were some of the greats of American TV comedy, going all the way back

to Sid Caesar's *Your Show of Shows* and other classics. And they had set up that first scene where Archie meets the reverend so beautifully. All it took was for Carroll to walk into the reverend's office, take one look at me, and the audience would erupt. They knew the setup, what Archie was thinking, and what was about to happen. The running bit in the scene—and it continued in future episodes in which the reverend returned—was similar to the running joke about the name of the other

> EDITH: Maybe God don't care if you get sprinkled in church or not.
> Maybe the rain is God's way of baptizing the whole world.

reverend, Felcher: Archie would never get my name right, first calling me "Chang," and when I corrected him with "Chong," he would just say "Whatever." The

rhythm of it was like an old-time comedy routine. And by the end of the scene, I got to turn it around on him, calling him "Mr. Binker," and when he said "Bunker," I just said "Whatever." I knew the key to making my whole appearance work would be saying that killer line—"Whatever"—just the right way. So the pressure was on in my mind to say it at the same level Carroll had, to really make it work.

That evening, after the first show, we were all seated at tables during the dinner break, when I saw Norman across the room. He spotted me and started making his way over to me, wearing that porkpie hat, and everybody was watching. He came up to me, looked at me, and said "You're funny!" To hear something like that from Norman Lear—I felt like I'd just been knighted, or gotten a blessing from the Pope.

I WAS TWENTY-THREE YEARS OLD when *All in the Family* first aired, and it was obvious to me that it was groundbreaking. I was only a couple years out of college, but living in New York and finding my way as a writer. I thought I would be a playwright or maybe a journalist. But *All in the Family* really hit home, and it was so different from the dumbed-down comedies of the past that I set my sights on television.

Archie Bunker was a bigot—but somehow America tuned in faithfully anyway, because in the hands of Carroll O'Connor he was that guy everybody knew but tolerated, and in the hands of Norman Lear the show walked a tightrope every week in tone, deftly balancing the comedy with the social satire and the bold political statements. It was at once a family comedy and a comment on America. It goes down in history as one of the all-time greats.

Norman was nearing fifty when he had his first major hit TV show in *All in the Family*. Pretty inspiring. And now, in his late nineties, he's still kicking ass and making a statement. I think that today, the broadcast networks have become fearful of any content that might stir the pot and offend advertisers. But I give audiences more credit. And so do premium cable and streaming services. Could there have been a Tony Soprano without Archie Bunker? Could there have been a Murphy Brown? I think not.

—*MURPHY BROWN* CREATOR DIANE ENGLISH

ARCHIE (CONT'D)

CROSSES HIS FINGERS)

be saved as young as possible. 'Cause
they're growin' up in a wicked world
which you know is like a regular Sodom
and Glockamorrah. You folly me?

CHONG

At a respectable distance. Mr.
Bunker, somehow I have the feeling
the child's parents are against his
being baptized, and in that case...

ARCHIE

Wait a minute! Now, wait a minute!
Just suppose I slip you a couple
of bucks for the poor box, which
don't have to wind up there.   And
your boss Reverend Fletcher.

CHONG

Felcher.

ARCHIE

Whatever, he don't have to know nothing
about it. What do you say, Chang?

CHONG

Chong.

ARCHIE

Whatever.

CHONG

I say no, Mr. Binker.

ARCHIE

Bunker.

CHONG

Whatever.

DISSOLVE TO:

0622

OUR BLK SHIRT
HIS JACKET + PANTS.

ALL OF *ALL IN THE FAMILY*
Seasons 4–6

Season 4
1973-74

Episode 1
"We're Having a Heat Wave"
WRITER: **Don Nicholl**
DIRECTORS: **John Rich, Bob LaHendro**
AIR DATE: **September 15, 1973**

★

Episode 2
"We're Still Having a Heat Wave"
WRITERS: **Michael Ross, Bernie West**
DIRECTORS: **John Rich, Bob LaHendro**
AIR DATE: **September 22, 1973**

★

Episode 3
"Edith Finds an Old Man"
WRITERS: **Susan Harris, Michael Ross, Bernie West**
DIRECTORS: **John Rich, Bob LaHendro**
AIR DATE: **September 29, 1973**

★

Episode 4
"Archie and the Kiss"
WRITER: **John Rappaport**
DIRECTORS: **John Rich, Bob LaHendro**
AIR DATE: **October 6, 1973**

★

Episode 5
"Archie the Gambler"
WRITERS: **Steve Zacharias, Michael Leeson, Michael Ross, Bernie West**
DIRECTORS: **John Rich, Bob LaHendro**
AIR DATE: **October 13, 1973**

★

Episode 6
"Henry's Farewell"
WRITER: **Don Nicholl**
DIRECTORS: **John Rich, Bob LaHendro**
AIR DATE: **October 20, 1973**

★

Episode 7
"Archie and the Computer"
WRITERS: **Lloyd Turner, Gordon Mitchell, Don Nicholl**
DIRECTORS: **John Rich, Bob LaHendro**
AIR DATE: **October 27, 1973**

★

Episode 8
"The Games Bunkers Play"
WRITERS: **Susan Perkis Haven, Dan Klein, Michael Ross, Bernie West**
DIRECTORS: **John Rich, Bob LaHendro**
AIR DATE: **November 3, 1973**

★

Episode 9
"Edith's Conversion"
WRITER: **Ray Taylor**
DIRECTORS: **John Rich, Bob LaHendro**
AIR DATE: **November 10, 1973**

★

Episode 10
"Archie in the Cellar"
WRITER: **Don Nicholl**
DIRECTORS: **John Rich, Bob LaHendro**
AIR DATE: **November 17, 1973**

★

Episode 11
"Black is the Color of My True Love's Wig"
WRITER: **Michael Morris**
DIRECTORS: **John Rich, Bob LaHendro**
AIR DATE: **November 24, 1973**

★

Episode 12
"Second Honeymoon"
WRITERS: **Michael Ross, Bernie West, Warren S. Murray**
DIRECTORS: **John Rich, Bob LaHendro**
AIR DATE: **December 1, 1973**

★

Episode 13
"The Taxi Caper"
WRITER: **Dennis Klein**
DIRECTORS: **John Rich, Bob LaHendro**
AIR DATE: **December 8, 1973**

★

Episode 14
"Archie is Cursed"
WRITERS: **John Rappaport, Michael Ross, Bernie West**
DIRECTORS: **John Rich and Bob LaHendro**
AIR DATE: **December 15, 1973**

★

Episode 15
"Edith's Christmas Story"
WRITERS: **Don Nicholl, Austin and Irma Kalish**
DIRECTOR: **John Rich**
AIR DATE: **December 22, 1973**

★

Episode 16
"Mike and Gloria Mix it Up"
WRITERS: **Michael Ross, Bernie West**
DIRECTOR: **John Rich**
AIR DATE: **January 5, 1974**

★

Episode 17
"Archie Feels Left Out"
WRITERS: **Paul Lichtman, Howard Storm, Don Nicholl**
DIRECTORS: **John Rich, Bob LaHendro**
AIR DATE: **January 12, 1974**

★

Episode 18
"Et Tu, Archie"
WRITERS: **Mickey Rose, Lila Garrett**
DIRECTORS: **John Rich, Bob LaHendro**
AIR DATE: **January 26, 1974**

★

Episode 19

"Gloria's Boyfriend"

WRITERS: **Bud Wiser, Don Nicholl**
DIRECTOR: **John Rich**
AIR DATE: **February 2, 1974**

★

Episode 20

"Lionel's Engagement"

WRITERS: **Michael Ross, Bernie West**
DIRECTOR: **John Rich**
AIR DATE: **February 9, 1974**

★

Episode 21

"Archie Eats and Runs"

WRITERS: **Paul Wayne, George Burditt**
DIRECTOR: **John Rich**
AIR DATE: **February 16, 1974**

★

Episode 22

"Gloria Sings the Blues"

WRITERS: **Michael Ross, Bernie West**
DIRECTOR: **John Rich**
AIR DATE: **March 2, 1974**

★

Episode 23

"Pay the Twenty Dollars"

WRITERS: **Robert L. Goodwin, Woody Kling**
DIRECTOR: **John Rich**
AIR DATE: **March 9, 1974**

★

Episode 24

"Mike's Graduation"

WRITER: **Don Nicholl**
DIRECTOR: **John Rich**
AIR DATE: **March 16, 1974**

Season 5
1974–75

Episode 1

"The Bunkers and Inflation: Part 1"

WRITERS: **Don Nicholl, Michael Ross, Bernie West**
DIRECTOR: **H. Wesley Kenney**
AIR DATE: **September 14, 1974**

★

Episode 2

"The Bunkers and Inflation: Part 2"

WRITERS: **Don Nicholl, Michael Ross, Bernie West**
DIRECTOR: **H. Wesley Kenney**
AIR DATE: **September 21, 1974**

★

Episode 3

"The Bunkers and Inflation: Part 3"

WRITERS: **Don Nicholl, Michael Ross, Bernie West**
DIRECTOR: **H. Wesley Kenney**
AIR DATE: **September 28, 1974**

★

Episode 4

"The Bunkers and Inflation: Part 4"

WRITERS: **Don Nicholl, Michael Ross, Bernie West**
DIRECTOR: **H. Wesley Kenney**
AIR DATE: **October 5, 1974**

★

Episode 5

"Lionel the Live-In"

WRITERS: **Jeffery Mackowsky, Woody Kling**
DIRECTOR: **H. Wesley Kenney**
AIR DATE: **October 12, 1974**

★

Episode 6

"Archie's Helping Hand"

WRITERS: **Norman and Harriet Belkin**
DIRECTOR: **H. Wesley Kenney**
AIR DATE: **October 19, 1974**

★

Episode 7

"Gloria's Shock"

WRITER: **Dixie Brown Grossman**
DIRECTOR: **H. Wesley Kenney**
AIR DATE: **October 26, 1974**

★

Episode 8

"Where's Archie?"

WRITERS: **Barry Harman, Harve Brosten**
DIRECTOR: **H. Wesley Kenney**
AIR DATE: **November 2, 1974**

★

Episode 9

"Archie is Missing"

WRITERS: **Lloyd Turner, Gordon Mitchell**
DIRECTOR: **H. Wesley Kenney**
AIR DATE: **November 9, 1974**

★

Episode 10

"The Longest Kiss"

WRITERS: **Dawn M. Stephens, Lou Derman, Bill Davenport**
DIRECTOR: **H. Wesley Kenney**
AIR DATE: **November 16, 1974**

★

Episode 11

"Archie and the Miracle"

WRITERS: **Lloyd Turner, Gordon Mitchell**
DIRECTOR: **H. Wesley Kenney**
AIR DATE: **November 23, 1974**

★

Episode 12

"George and Archie Make a Deal"

WRITER: **David P. Harmon**
DIRECTOR: **H. Wesley Kenney**
AIR DATE: **November 30, 1974**

★

Episode 13

"Archie's Contract"

WRITER: **Ron Friedman**
DIRECTOR: **H. Wesley Kenney**
AIR DATE: **December 7, 1974**

Episode 14

"Mike's Friend"

WRITERS: **Roger Shulman, John Baskin**
DIRECTOR: **H. Wesley Kenney**
AIR DATE: **December 14, 1974**

★

Episode 15

"Prisoner in the House"

WRITERS: **Lou Derman, Bill Davenport, Bud Wiser**
DIRECTOR: **H. Wesley Kenney**
AIR DATE: **January 4, 1975**

★

Episode 16

"The Jeffersons Move Up"

WRITERS: **Don Nicholl, Michael Ross, Bernie West**
DIRECTOR: **H. Wesley Kenney**
AIR DATE: **January 11, 1975**

★

Episode 17

"All's Fair"

WRITERS: **Lloyd Turner, Gordon Mitchell**
DIRECTOR: **H. Wesley Kenney**
AIR DATE: **January 18, 1975**

★

Episode 18

"Amelia's Divorce"

WRITERS: **Lou Derman, Bill Davenport**
DIRECTOR: **H. Wesley Kenney**
AIR DATE: **January 25, 1975**

★

Episode 19

"Everybody Does It"

WRITERS: **Lou Derman, Bill Davenport, Susan Ware**
DIRECTOR: **H. Wesley Kenney**
AIR DATE: **February 8, 1975**

★

Episode 20

"Archie and the Quiz"

WRITER: **Michael Morris**
DIRECTOR: **H. Wesley Kenney**
AIR DATE: **February 15, 1975**

★

Episode 21

"Edith's Friend"

WRITERS: **Barry Harman, Harve Brosten**
DIRECTOR: **H. Wesley Kenney**
AIR DATE: **February 22, 1975**

★

Episode 22

"No Smoking"

WRITERS: **Lou Derman, Bill Davenport**
DIRECTOR: **H. Wesley Kenney**
AIR DATE: **March 1, 1975**

★

Episode 23

"Mike Makes His Move"

WRITERS: **Robert Arnott, Lou Derman, Bill Davenport**
DIRECTOR: **H. Wesley Kenney**
AIR DATE: **March 8, 1975**

Season 6
1975–76

Episode 1
"The Very Moving Day"
WRITER: **Hal Kanter**
DIRECTOR: **Paul Bogart**
AIR DATE: **September 8, 1975**

★

Episode 2
"Alone at Last"
WRITER: **Hal Kanter**
DIRECTOR: **Paul Bogart**
AIR DATE: **September 15, 1975**

★

Episode 3
"Archie the Donor"
WRITER: **Bill Davenport and Larry Rhine**
DIRECTOR: **Paul Bogart**
AIR DATE: **September 22, 1975**

★

Episode 4
"Archie the Hero"
WRITERS: **Lou Derman, Bill Davenport**
DIRECTOR: **Paul Bogart**
AIR DATE: **September 29, 1975**

★

Episode 5
"Mike's Pains"
WRITERS: **Lou Derman, Milt Josefsberg**
DIRECTOR: **Paul Bogart**
AIR DATE: **October 6, 1975**

★

Episode 6
"Chain Letter"
WRITERS: **Milt Josefsberg, Lou Derman**
DIRECTOR: **Paul Bogart**
AIR DATE: **October 20, 1975**

★

Episode 7
"Mike Faces Life"
WRITERS: **Mel Tolkin, Larry Rhine**
DIRECTOR: **Paul Bogart**
AIR DATE: **October 27, 1975**

★

Episode 8
"Edith Breaks Out"
WRITERS: **Lou Derman, Bill Davenport**
DIRECTOR: **Paul Bogart**
AIR DATE: **November 3, 1975**

★

Episode 9
"Grandpa Blues"
WRITERS: **John Rappaport, Mel Tolkin, Larry Rhine**
DIRECTOR: **Paul Bogart**
AIR DATE: **November 10, 1975**

★

Episode 10
"Gloria Suspects Mike"
WRITERS: **Lou Derman, Milt Josefsberg**
DIRECTOR: **Paul Bogart**
AIR DATE: **November 17, 1975**

★

Episode 11
"The Little Atheist"
WRITER: **Lou Derman**
DIRECTOR: **Paul Bogart**
AIR DATE: **November 24, 1975**

★

Episode 12
"Archie's Civil Rights"
WRITERS: **Larry Rhine, Mel Tolkin**
DIRECTOR: **Paul Bogart**
AIR DATE: **December 1, 1975**

★

Episode 13
"Gloria Is Nervous"
WRITERS: **Milt Josefsberg, Ben Starr**
DIRECTOR: **Paul Bogart**
AIR DATE: **December 8, 1975**

★

Episode 14
"Birth of the Baby: Part 1"
WRITERS: **Lou Derman, Bill Davenport, Larry Rhine, Mel Tolkin**
DIRECTOR: **Paul Bogart**
AIR DATE: **December 15, 1975**

★

Episode 15
"Birth of the Baby: Part 2"
WRITERS: **Milt Josefsberg, Ben Starr**
DIRECTOR: **Paul Bogart**
AIR DATE: **December 22, 1975**

★

Episode 16
"New Year's Wedding"
WRITERS: **Lou Derman, Bill Davenport, Milt Josefsberg, Ben Starr**
DIRECTOR: **Paul Bogart**
AIR DATE: **January 5, 1976**

★

Episode 17
"Archie the Babysitter"
WRITERS: **Lou Derman, Bill Davenport**
DIRECTOR: **Paul Bogart**
AIR DATE: **January 12, 1976**

★

Episode 18
"Archie Finds a Friend"
WRITERS: **Mel Tolkin, Larry Rhine**
DIRECTOR: **Paul Bogart**
AIR DATE: **January 26, 1976**

★

Episode 19
"Mike's Move"
WRITERS: **Milt Josefsberg, Ben Starr**
DIRECTOR: **Paul Bogart**
AIR DATE: **February 2, 1976**

★

Episode 20
"Archie's Weighty Problem"
WRITERS: **Larry Rhine, Mel Tolkin**
DIRECTOR: **Paul Bogart**
AIR DATE: **February 9, 1976**

★

Episode 21
"Love By Appointment"
WRITERS: **Lou Derman, Bill Davenport**
DIRECTOR: **Paul Bogart**
AIR DATE: **February 16, 1976**

★

Episode 22
"Joey's Baptism"
WRITERS: **Milt Josefsberg, Mel Tolkin, Larry Rhine**
DIRECTOR: **Paul Bogart**
AIR DATE: **February 23, 1976**

★

Episode 23
"Mike and Gloria's House Guests"
WRITERS: **Larry Rhine, Mel Tolkin, Milt Josefsberg**
DIRECTOR: **Paul Bogart**
AIR DATE: **March 1, 1976**

★

Episode 24
"Edith's Night Out"
WRITERS: **Douglas Arango, Phil Doran, Lou Derman**
DIRECTOR: **Paul Bogart**
AIR DATE: **March 8, 1976**

EMMYS
1974

**Best Supporting Actor
in a Comedy Series**
ROB REINER

I'm Henry Fonda. Tonight, we're going to take a look at
the best of ALL IN THE FAMILY, one of the most acclaimed and
also one of the most controversial shows ever seen on television,
starting with the character of Archie Bunker right down to the
kind of themes the show has dealt with. Menapause, homosexuality,
rape, mental retardation, cancer- sounds like a real fun show,
doesn't it? And yet, we all know it is. Now, I'm not going to
comment on the contribution ALL IN THE FAMILY's made on the American
scene. We all know there have been pro's and con's- except to say
that I wouldn't be here if I weren't one of its biggest fans.
(APPLAUSE)
We're in Studio 41, CBS Television City in Hollywood. You're
watching Norman Lear, the creator of ALL IN THE FAMILY talking to
the studio audience about tonight's show. (NORMAN:) Anyway, as I
mentioned earlier, tonight, because this is the 100th airing of
ALL IN THE FAMILY, we will be presenting one hour of what we hope
you all will feel is the best of ALL IN THE FAMILY. (APPLAUSE)
Ladies and gentlemen, I'd like you now to meet the cast of ALL
IN THE FAMILY, four magnificent players- the primary players in
our Company who have provided more laughter and therefore, in our
opinions, have added more to our lives... I'm talking about the
people, the writers, producers, actors, technicians, who work with
them; and has laughed with them and have laughed with them for
these five years. We all feel has added time to our lives through
that laughter.

#0609　　　　　ACT I

REG PANTS
NAVY LEGION SHIRT
WINTER COAT
NAVY N.Y. HAT
RIBBON BAR
SHARP SHOOTER MEDAL

0612　　　　　ACT I

NO socks   slippers
pjs w/ green piping

06006　　　　　ACT II

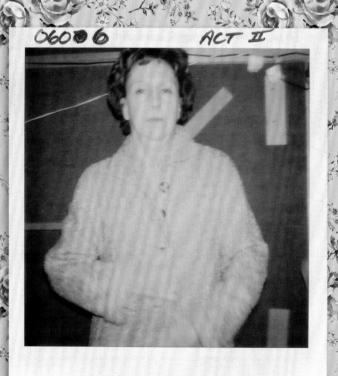

#06127

TOP
COAT, SCARF GOOD HAT HANDBAG
Beige shoes.

THE COSTUMES

In her oral history for The Interviews, costume designer **RITA RIGGS** *remembered:* After the first batch of *All in the Family* episodes had aired, Norman asked me if I would come in and work with the production designer, Don Roberts, and see if we could give the show a "look." So Don and I gave a kind of nostalgic, sepia, "family album" look to that show. The set was always in that sepia. That was the concept—to open everybody's family album and recognize some of those characters. Archie was the American working man out of the '30s who believed he was the class equal of everyone in our country, which I think is the basis of our democracy.

Archie had seven "white" shirts. Because of the requirements of television, particularly in those days, they were tan shirts from Brooks Brothers made of Oxford cloth so they would take in the light. In those days, white read so badly on camera that almost everything was dyed a cocoa brown. The beauty of those shirts is that they came that way from Brooks Brothers. But Archie wouldn't have been caught dead in a Brooks Brothers shirt. So we re-cut the cuffs and collars so they simply looked like every man's white shirt. Edith

Bunker ironed those every day.

Archie had one pair of pants for those seven years, because Carroll became superstitious about those pants. We kept those pants mended and functioning, and let them out a little bit as age and success took their toll.

Archie's hat was like a beacon of the American gentleman. Carroll loved that hat, and so did I. It was kind of a tan fedora with a black grosgrain ribbon trim. An everyman's hat. That hat became part of that persona, and there was only one when we started. I have never forgotten coming back from the 5:30 show for the 8 o'clock show—and the hat was gone! Some fan in the audience probably now has the original Archie Bunker hat. We made it through the 8 o'clock show with something improvised from my loft. But I then had three of those hats made, and sometimes five, so that at all times, we were protected.

Archie's coat was the only one we had, a Mackinaw that probably came out of CBS Wardrobe. Because there was no duplicate, after Archie's hat was stolen, we used to hire one person to sit from 5:30 to 8 p.m. and guard all those special things.

0607

Thanksgiving outfit w/ apron
8 months

0614 ACT I

It was hard to find fashionable little skirts and tops for Gloria that would still be in the show's sepia color palette. So we made a lot of her little flippy skirts and cute little smocked tops. When Gloria was pregnant, we just made her clothes and made wonderful little tummies that grew and grew and grew.

Sally was short so that to get her into camera range, with Carroll and Jean and particularly Rob, she wore the tallest platforms you have ever seen, with those little, cute short skirts. Thank God at that time, platforms were fashionable!

Gloria always wore young things even as time went by. But I think we made a progression with Mike. He was really despicable-looking in the beginning, with those awful tie-dyed shirts. I think we tried to add to his stature. I loved chambray shirts, and that was very much a statement politically in the '70s. All the protesters and students and the working class wore chambrays and jeans.

LIZA STEWART, *Costumer:* On Norman's shows where the characters were wealthier, like *Maude* and *The Jeffersons*, we might shop at Ohrbach's, or the May Company, or Bullock's. But the Bunkers were lower-middle-class, and a lot of the clothes that Rita originally bought for them were from the Salvation Army. They had that older look to them—they were already "broken down," so she didn't have to spend the money to break them down and age them. Rita would send me to the Salvation Army in Pasadena, and I would buy clothes by the brown-bag-ful, things that we would clean and repair or refit or cut.

The last thing you'd ever want to do is hold up the camera and the entire company of hundreds of people. So if you bought an outfit, you bought three. Was a character going to get hit in the face with a pie? Was someone going to get caught in the rain and get wet? Would we need to match an actor's outfit with a stunt person's? We had to pre-plan everything and have backups.

By Thursday afternoon, the cast would have a dress rehearsal in front of all the producers and writers. There would be no makeup involved, but everyone wanted to see the clothes. The CBS censors would be there, too. And everyone would confer: yea or nay? If they didn't like an outfit, you had less than twenty-four hours to come up with something new. The wardrobe all had to be ready for the first show on Friday at 5:30.

#0608

GREEN CORDS BELT
BOOTS
BLUE YELLOW STRIPE SHIRT
CORD JACKET

0605   BOTH ACTS

JEANS W/ BELT
GREY HOOD SWEAT SHIRT

0605   ACT I

NAVY DICKY.   ENTERS W/
NAVY STOCKINGS   LIGHT BLUE
RED SHOES — Thero   RAINCOAT
Red plaid dress   LARGE HANDBAG
TORTOUSE HAIR COMBS

0612   ACT I

8th month pad,
1- blue rain coat
2- Mike army jacket

WIG FROM FIRST YEAR
of STRAWBERRY curls

Tiny SEED
PEARLS
GRADuated

FRESH
FLOWERS in Hand

my old
~ FINGERTIP VEEL

FLASHBACK
to GLORIA AND MEATHEAD
The WEDDING

"GRANDMOTHER'S
DRESS REWORKED
FIT WAIST
AND Petticoats AND FLOUNCES
For SALLY STRUTHERS

Rita Riggs

VINTAGE
Thrift STORE
"The PALACE"
'SEPIA IVORY

EDITH

Oh, you don't like it.

ARCHIE

Listen, I've got a big surprise for
the two of youse, if you're expectin'
me to say somethin' against women
wearin' pants, that's a long time
ago... before you women came a long
way baby.

EDITH

Then you do like it?

ARCHIE

No, but if you want to wear pants to
show off your independence, plus your
keester, go ahead it don't offend me
as long as you throw an apron over it
and make me dinner. Now let me get
to my chair.

Season 6, Episode 24

"EDITH'S NIGHT OUT"

In Episode 24 of Season 6, "Edith's Night
Out," Edith receives a pantsuit as a thank-you
gift from Mike and Gloria. Unfortunately,
Archie hates it. Many women wrote in to the
show thanking them for "helping pants for
women come out of the closet."

EDITH Bunker

Civil Rights Script

no pleats.?? Gunnel—
should we cut a slim
skirt with only one pleat
in Back?

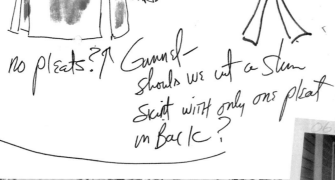

ACT II Court Room

carrying bag&coat
brown shoes and hat

Season 6, Episode 12

———

**"ARCHIE'S CIVIL
RIGHTS"**

0618

GREY BROWN sweater   ben hat
NAVY Knit tie   Shirt
miss match jacket-pants
heavy over coat.
His own shoes

0603

NAVY PANTS, NAVY TURTLE NECK
SNEEKERS BLUE, NAVY BANDANA
KERCHIEF, MELON OVER BLOUSE

0602   ACT II

green tie
stripe (pink) shirt

0601   FAMILY   ACT II

brown knit stripe pants
en shirt + belt
leather jacket w/ 9 button

0611

PINK muslin smock · BROWN PANTS
JEANS · APRICOT TOP
chiffon TOP
BUTTERFLY HAIR

Season 6, Episode 10

"GLORIA SUSPECTS MIKE"

BERNADETTE PETERS: *All in the Family* was a huge hit—the kind of show no one missed watching, everyone talking about each episode after it aired. So I was thrilled and honored to be asked to be on the show. As a young actress, I was warmly welcomed and made to feel part of the show's "special family." I was cast alongside Rob Reiner, a wonderful actor. It was fun to play the role of a femme fatale, someone very much in charge (and not much like me). I felt very comfortable taking Rob's lead, while Sally was adorable and so kind. I went on to work with Norman again on another series, *All's Fair*, with the brilliant actor Richard Crenna. What special memories I have from being part of making history!

0620

dirty apron
brown pants
grey-red stripe shirt

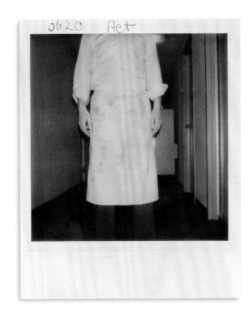

0620 Act

BILLY CRYSTAL: It was October of 1975, and I was a young standup comic living in New York. I came to L.A., and my managers set up a night for me at the Comedy Store. Jim Brooks and Carl Reiner, among others, were there and when I was done a charming man in a funny hat introduced himself to me.

"Hello, I'm Norman Lear."

Can you imagine? Two weeks later, I was home on Long Island and my phone rang and a woman asked if it was me and could I hold on for Norman Lear? Oh my God...

"Hi, Billy, we met at The Comedy Store"—as if I wouldn't remember—and he explained they had a part that he'd thought of me for. Could I come out to L.A. to be on *All in the Family*?

I had done a few talk shows at the time—Dinah Shore, Mike Douglas, Merv Griffin—but to be on the number-one show and, to me, the best show on television was incredible.

Honestly, the script wasn't great when I first got it, and Norman told me it needed work. But that was their process (the first time I heard that word). The premise was I was Mike's best friend, and my fiancée and I were to be married. However, Rob and Sally couldn't attend because they didn't have anyone to take care of their newborn, so we got married in their house.

My scenes were only with Rob and Sally as Carroll and Jean weren't in the episode but I did get to sit in Archie's chair. Rob and I hit it off immediately, and

we created a backstory of how they were best friends. My name was "Al the Nut Boy"...and we used the "nut boy" tag over and over again: "You're a nut boy...Tell me again...You're a nut boy...I LOVE THIS MAN!"

Rehearsals were great fun, and Norman from the beginning told me, "Don't be shy, jump in." Paul Bogart was the director, and he was charming, smart, and funny. Rob was a revelation to me. Looking back it was already evident that he'd become the great director he is. Rob was very strong in working on the script with the writing staff, suggesting cuts and moments, and he would always say to me, "What do you think"? Remember, I was so new in my career and without many credits, yet they included me as a seasoned pro.

Taping night at CBS was so exciting. The audience seemed to love the relationship between us, from the time the front door opened and I entered, jumping into Rob's arms as he screamed, "YOU'RE A NUT BOY! I LOVE THIS MAN!" The show was scheduled to air the week after Rob and Sally's baby was born, so the ratings were huge as people thought they'd see the baby—but they got the nut boy instead.

I love that I was on *All in the Family* because to me it was the greatest comedy half hour ever, because Norman Lear himself wanted me to play this guy and because not only did I get to play Rob's best friend, but it went so well that we decided to just keep it going for these forty-seven years.

Once in a while, a long while, someone will see me and call me "Nut Boy"...but very rarely. If they do, it's usually someone in my family...or Rob.

Seasons 7 & 8

THE HUMAN EXPERIENCE

10 Episodes that Shook Things Up

As a sitcom progresses, if often gets harder and harder for the writers to come up with new situations the characters haven't encountered before. And that was true on *All in the Family*. The writers loved the characters, and wanted to deliver great material to these actors they respected so deeply. We knew that we wanted to stop the show at the end of the eighth season, because we felt we had shown all 360 degrees of all of the characters. We proceeded through that year as if we were going to end, but at some point, Carroll decided he wanted to go on. He and Jean agreed to return for a ninth season; I continued with my plans to leave the show, as did Rob and Sally. Meanwhile, in the eighth, even though we had thought we had said it all, we ended up being able to mine the characters for wonderful stories, including the beautiful moment in the season finale where Archie and Mike hug goodbye.

—NORMAN LEAR

Season 7, Episodes 1, 2, and 3
"Archie's Brief Encounter"

Season 8, Episodes 4 and 5
"Edith's 50th Birthday"

Season 7, Episodes 6 and 7
"Archie's Operation"

Season 8, Episodes 10 and 11
"Archie and the KKK"

Season 7, Episode 15
"The Draft Dodger"

Season 8, Episodes 13 and 14
"Edith's Crisis of Faith"

Season 7, Episode 21
"Mike the Pacifist"

Season 8, Episode 19
"Two's a Crowd"

Season 8, Episode 3
"Cousin Liz"

Season 8, Episode 24
"The Stivics Go West"

Season 7, Episodes 1, 2, and 3
"ARCHIE'S BRIEF ENCOUNTER"

AFTER A FLIRTATION WITH A WAITRESS LEADS TO A KISS, ARCHIE MUST FACE AND RECONCILE WITH EDITH, WHO DISTRACTS HERSELF FROM HER PAIN BY WORKING ROUND-THE-CLOCK AT THE SUNSHINE HOME.

WRITTEN BY: **Mel Tolkin** and **Larry Rhine** ● DIRECTED BY: **Paul Bogart**

GUEST STARS: **Janis Paige** as **Denise** ● **Scott Brady** as **Joe Foley** ● **Teddy Wilson** as **Whitney Monroe**
André Pavon as **Carlos** ● **Jason Wingreen** as **Harry Snowden** ● **Harry Davis** as **Sol Kleeger**
Maxine Elliott Hicks as **Mrs. Bradley** ● **Bella Chronis** as **Sylvia Freedman**

ORIGINAL AIR DATE: **September 22** and **September 29, 1976**

NORMAN LEAR: I first saw Janis Paige on Broadway in *The Pajama Game* and thought she was fantastic. So I kept her in mind for *All in the Family*, although it was much later. I don't remember exactly where the idea for Archie to flirt with an affair came from—other than the need twenty-six times a year to come up with stories for episodes. But of course it was from thinking: What could happen in human nature? What goes on all the time? It's not a very complicated idea to land on.

However, what made the idea work was the amazing performances from these actors. Every time I think of Carroll and Jean, and here Janis, I realize how much the talent of those actors motivated the depth to which the show's writers reached for stories. Because this was a reach for the actors, having Archie do something a little far afield from the usual. But we were working with people who we knew were going to deliver brilliantly on these difficult subjects. The third episode in this story arc only works so well because of Jean Stapleton. She showed her character finding a strength in herself, and that's how she forgave Archie. We knew Edith had that strength, but for her to realize she had it—that was really quite a moment.

In the first episode, when Archie is telling Denise about his history, he talks about having been stationed in Foggia, Italy, in World War II, as was I. I had to think about doing that, whether I should use any part of my own background for the character. And I realized that there was a lot of my father in Archie, so why not a little of me? Not in his personality, but in where he had been. This was a lovely opportunity to do that.

JANIS PAIGE: I had been up for a different part in an earlier episode a month or so before this one, but then Norman called and said he had something much better for me coming up: Denise, the waitress, who found Archie funny when nobody else did, and laughed at all his jokes.

And then of course, we had that kiss—at which point the audience absolutely erupted. Most of them were angry, because Edith was so loved, and rightly so. She was so loyal, and would never do anything like Archie was doing in kissing Denise. She just wasn't vulnerable to any of that stuff. She was a very principled human being—and so was Archie, but he got tempted. And I was the instigator. They blamed me for everything. I was the villain. I know that when the episode aired, the reaction was powerful from all over the country and all over the world.

On that tape night, during the break between the two audience shows, Norman came rushing into the makeup room where we were all getting fixed up again and said, "I cannot tell you the reaction that kiss has had! I am not going to cut away from it. If this goes over by ten or eleven minutes, I'm going to turn it into a three-parter." They did end up turning it into a three-parter, and I still get fan mail about it.

We don't come close in this business very often to feeling like we've achieved perfection, but working with brilliant writers and brilliant actors like Carroll O'Connor—and in a later episode where Denise returns and meets Edith at Archie's restaurant (Season 9, Episode 9, "Return of the Waitress"), when I got to have a scene with Jean Stapleton—well, Norman got the best of everybody, and so I was given the best. To work with these actors, you had to be good, because they gave so much of themselves back to you. They were the most generous actors I've ever worked with.

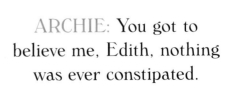

ARCHIE: You got to believe me, Edith, nothing was ever constipated.

"ARCHIE'S OPERATION"

ARCHIE IS DISMAYED TO LEARN THAT HIS UPCOMING OPERATION MAY BE PERFORMED BY
A BLACK FEMALE DOCTOR, AND EVEN MORE SO WHEN HE LEARNS THAT SHE WILL
ALSO BE HIS BLOOD DONOR. TO MAKE MATTERS WORSE, THE SIZE OF THE HOSPITAL BILL
ADDS TO ARCHIE'S WORRIES ABOUT HIS CONTINUED UNEMPLOYMENT.

PART 1 STORY BY: **Calvin Kelly** and **Jim Tisdale** • TELEPLAY BY: **Milt Josefsberg** and **Mort Lachman**
PART 2 WRITTEN BY: **Larry Rhine** and **Mel Tolkin** • DIRECTED BY: **Paul Bogart**

GUEST STARS: **Liz Torres** as **Teresa Betancourt** • **Vinnette Carroll** as **Dr. Wynell Thatcher**
Milton Selzer as **Dr. Seymour Shapiro** • **Danny Dayton** as **Hank Pivnik** • **Frances Fong** as **Nurse**

ORIGINAL AIR DATE: **October 20** and **October 27, 1976**

NORMAN LEAR: After doing a show a week for seven years, we were thinking about what else could happen to Archie, Edith, Mike, or Gloria—and it wasn't that unusual that a man of Archie's age should require some medical help. So why not surgery? It was a way for us to find Archie in the setting of a hospital, and see what he's like post-surgery.

Similarly, introducing the character of Teresa Betancourt was another way to test the Archie character. In the seventh season, you try to shake things up and make them a little different. I thought the world of Liz, too; after having seen her onstage, I was eager to work with her. It's a similar story with Vinnette Carroll. She had done so much on Broadway, starting as a performer and then conceiving and directing such shows as *Don't Bother Me, I Can't Cope* and *Your Arms Too Short to Box with God*. This happened often with me—I would see a performance that knocked me out, and then imagine a scene on the show that I was doing with that actor, with that performance in a role on my show. That's how she came to be cast as Dr. Thatcher. She had a really strong presence and made a good foil for Archie. It was similar to how I had felt about Bea Arthur: She was someone who could fire back.

LIZ TORRES: At this point in my career, I was the pitch-in person on *The Tonight Show*. If somebody didn't show up, they could always count on me. One night when I did the show, Carroll O'Connor was also a guest. After the show, I was told that Carroll wanted to meet me, and I said, "Me?" I had my backup dancers and a crew of, like, twenty-five people with me, and everyone got so excited, because Carroll was on the number-one show. They told me, "Liz, you've got to go meet him!" So I went upstairs and sat on the couch with him, and had a lovely conversation.

Carroll asked me about my background in New York. I said I had gone to NYU, and before that, to Charles Evans Hughes High School. He stopped me there—"Charles Evans Hughes High School? I taught at Charles Evans Hughes High School!" I couldn't believe the connection. What were the chances?

Apparently at that time, the *All in the Family* producers were already thinking about Archie adopting a little girl. But Carroll decided he wanted me, because I was funny. Carroll convinced Norman to use me on one show. I couldn't wait to do it. They told me I was going to be a tough nurse. Her name was Teresa Betancourt—which is a French last name, but Carroll told me he had taught with a Hispanic woman named Betancourt.

I asked them, is she Puerto Rican? I had just finished doing *The Ritz*, replacing Rita Moreno on Broadway, and I was full of vim and vigor and Puerto Rican–ness. I said what if I do a Puerto Rican accent, and Archie will really have a tough time? And it worked like gangbusters. Teresa was a good foil for "Mr. Bonkers," as she called him.

I was supposed to do only one show, but the audience just ate it up. And so a few episodes later they wrote "Teresa Moves In," where the Bunkers are going through a hard time with Archie unemployed and with

bills pending from his operation, and I move in as a boarder into Mike and Gloria's old room. Once they got me in the house, though, that kind of changed things. I was living there and couldn't be as tough as I was. I certainly would have fallen in love with Edith, as I did in real life with Jean Stapleton, who was like an angel, a ray of sunshine walking into the room. So I think Teresa became a little too nice.

I'm very proud of the shows I did—and I loved sitting in Archie's chair! I learned more about acting from Carroll O'Connor—he was a born teacher. Carroll was really magical—and it was a magical show. Everyone has an Archie in their family, and everyone can relate to him.

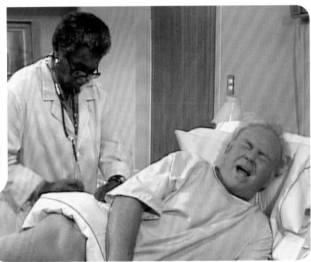

TERESA: Did you want a ward,
a semi-private room, or a private room?

ARCHIE: Any room at all as long as there ain't
a guy in it with hoses up his nose.

"THE DRAFT DODGER"

THE BUNKERS SHARE CHRISTMAS DINNER WITH ARCHIE'S FRIEND PINKY PETERSON,
WHOSE SON DIED IN THE VIETNAM WAR, AND MIKE'S FRIEND DAVID BREWSTER, A DRAFT DODGER.

WRITTEN BY: **Jay Moriarty** and **Mike Milligan** ● DIRECTED BY: **Paul Bogart**

GUEST STARS: **Liz Torres** as **Teresa Betancourt** ● **Eugene Roche** as **Pinky Peterson**
Renny Temple as **David Brewster**

ORIGINAL AIR DATE: **December 25, 1976**

NORMAN LEAR: The idea for this episode came from the writers Jay Moriarty and Mike Milligan, who at the time were working on *The Jeffersons*.

It was a perfect episode to write as our Christmas show. I remember thinking how serious Christmas is, if one thought about it that way. Because you have a whole family with such an enormous investment in an occasion, and any little thing that could disappoint a member of the family was magnified because of the timing. It made for a wonderful opportunity to tell good stories that got to the heart of a family dynamic.

I served in World War II, although I have to say that it's hard at this time of life to remember it exactly as it was—it always so surprises me that I was there. With my background, I loved the discussion in the episode. There was a mixed reaction to it when we heard from viewers, just as Archie has a very different view on the ideology of the draft dodger than does David and, it turns out, Pinky. There were some negative letters—there always were—but by and large the response was lovely, and I do think the episode was much appreciated.

I love the way the episode ends, with Archie stunned and utterly inarticulate, only able to say that he has to take time later to sort things out in his mind. He had taken something for granted about "draft dodging," and then learned that people he cared about thought that it was actually an honor to be called a draft dodger. That was such an intricate, difficult, won-

derful, exciting moment. And it still was forty-three years later, when we re-created it for *Live In Front of a Studio Audience*.

LIZ TORRES: During the big Christmas dinner scene, I had my back to the cameras. And when Carroll started his big speech, I began crying. I held my shoulders down and sat absolutely still, hoping it couldn't be seen. In the middle of the speech, Carroll looked at me—and I was so embarrassed. I knew that I shouldn't be crying, but it was such a moving moment for me. That night, I was so spent, I felt like I crawled out of that set. People talk about how Carroll was "an actor's actor," and there was the proof. He had done a lot of theater, and it showed.

GLORIA

It's Christmas Eve, ~~let's not~~ NOW DON'T GO makeN

a ~~whole~~ big crisis out of this.

*A
JUST A MINUTE, SIS.*

MIKE

(JUMPS UP)

~~Look,~~ Arch, what David did took a

lot of guts!

ARCHIE

What do you mean a lot of guts?

DAVID

My own father didn't understand,

why should he?

MIKE

~~Arch,~~ When the hell are you going

to admit the war was wrong?

ARCHIE

(CROSSES BETWEEN PINKY AND
DAVID)

I ain't talkin' about the war. I

don't wanna talk about that rotten

damn war no more. I'm talkin'

about somethin' else. And what he

done was wrong! Sayin' he won't go.

What do you think? The whole people

of this country can say whether or

not they wanna go to war.

(MORE)

ARCHIE (CONT'D)

You couldn't get a decent war off
the ground that way. All the young
people would say no, sure they would,
'cause they don't wanna get killed!
And that's why we leave it to the
Congress! 'Cause them old crocks
ain't gonna get killed and they're
gonna do the right thing. And get
behind the President and vote yes!

PINKY

Arch, if my opinion is of any
importance here...

ARCHIE

Certainly your opinion is important!
(CROSSES TO HIS CHAIR)
Gold Star father, your opinion is
more important than anybody else's
in this room. And I wanna hear that
opinion. And I want these young
people here to hear that opinion.
Now you tell 'em, Pinky, you tell
'em.

PINKY

I understand how you feel, Arch.
My kid hated the war, too, but he
did what he thought he had to do.

(MORE)

                    PINKY (CONT'D)

And David here did what he thought

he had to do. But David is alive

to share Christmas dinner with us,

and if Steve were here, he'd want

to sit down with him. And that's

what I want to do.

(TO DAVID)

Merry Christmas, David.

                    DAVID

Merry Christmas, sir. _____   GLORIA
                                        DADDY...
               ARCHIE

No, no, no.

(ARCHIE WALKS AWAY, EDITH
FOLLOWS)

                    EDITH

Archie, please sit down and eat. ___   A
                                          NO, NO, NO...
But, Archie, it's Christmas.

               ARCHIE

I can't. I gotta work this ~~thing~~

out, Edith. I can't think about

that.

                    EDITH

But, Archie, you asked Pinky what
                       TO
~~he would do~~, and you ~~saw~~ *SEE* what he's

doin' and you oughta do the same.

Come on.

                    (MORE)

(SHE LEADS HIM BACK TO TABLE)

                    EDITH (CONT'D)

There's a drumstick for you.

                    ARCHIE

Oh, Edith, I ain't thinkin' about

eatin'.

                    MIKE

I'll take it, MA.

                    ARCHIE

Leave it on the plate. Leave it

on the plate. ~~But,~~ WELL, I don't wanna

stop none of yoose from eatin'

Edith's nice Christmas dinner here,

so... youse might as well eat it.

But, I'll tell ya one thing. When

~~the~~ dinner's over I still gotta

work this ~~thing~~ out, so you better

remind me to do that, Edith.

                    EDITH

I will.

                    ARCHIE

Everybody eat, eat.

SLOW DISSOLVE TO:

MEMORANDUM

DATE: November 24, 1976

RE: ALL IN THE FAMILY "The Draft Dodger"

As last discussed following the taping of this episode on November 19, 1976, we wish to reinterate the fact that Archie's "...that God damned war!" (underlined only) is considered unacceptable for broadcast and again request that it not be present in the episode as delivered to CBS for broadcast. We would ask that his alternate line "..that rotten war" be used instead.

Your cooperation is appreciated.

JAY MORIARTY: I came up with the idea of a draft dodger, a friend of Mike's, showing up at Christmastime, having snuck back across the border to visit his mom in the hospital. It was six or seven pages, with arguments like "What if Jesus were drafted? Would he go fight in Vietnam, and kill?" My agent sent it to Norman's company, and a month or so later told me they passed on it. Later, when my writing partner Mike Milligan and I were working on *The Jeffersons*, we realized we had a perfect Christmas show for *All in the Family*, so we made an appointment for me to pitch it directly to Norman. By 1976, the war was over, but it was always in the news, particularly because part of presidential candidate Jimmy Carter's platform was offering amnesty to kids who went to Canada. Hearing the pitch, Norman immediately said, "Let's do it." And when we exited his office, he turned to his assistant and said to her, "Jay just gave us a reason for doing next season." To hear that from my idol was amazing.

At another meeting that fall, Norman suggested that at the same time Meathead's draft-dodger friend is there, Archie's friend, a Gold Star father who lost his son in Vietnam, will also be at Christmas dinner. At first I thought, "Wow, is that a little too coincidental?" And then I realized, "Damn, why didn't we think of that? That's great drama!" I remember when both *All in the Family* and *The Jeffersons* were sharing a stage

at the Metromedia complex on Sunset Boulevard, the production company was booming, and they were physically expanding the studio space. One day I saw a sign in the mud where they were digging that read "Dig Deeper—Norman Lear." That's what Norman was always saying to the writers. He always encouraged us to go farther and find the emotion of the story.

On the night of the taping, I sat in the audience next to Carroll's wife, Nancy O'Connor, and tears were running down her face. As the dinner turned into an argument about the war, the whole audience was frozen. Everyone could feel the passion in the arguments, the same ones people had been having at home. The generation gap was all across the country, and so many young people would complain, "My dad's just like Archie Bunker."

That night, the whole performance became so much more than it had been on paper, and more even than it was in rehearsal. Carroll got so carried away in his performance that he ad-libbed a word, saying "I don't wanna talk about that goddamn war no more!" The producers loved it and wanted to keep it in. The fight went all the way to the head of CBS, William Paley, in New York. The producers argued to be able to use the word, saying, "If you can't damn war, then what can you damn?" But CBS insisted that the most frequent complaint letters they got were for using the name of God. This was a rare example where Norman

THE JEFFERSONS

5752 west sunset boulevard los angeles, california 90028 (213) 462-7111

November 22, 1976

Dear Norman,

We are still reeling from the stunning performances we saw at 5:30 and 8:00 Friday by the <u>All In The Family</u> cast. We want to thank you for making "The Draft Dodger" possible; and we want you to know that we are very proud to have been involved in the development of the script.

While we're at it, we also want to thank you for all the fantastic experiences we've had working for you and <u>The Jeffersons</u> during the past two seasons. The fact that you and Tandem/TAT are making television and social history is not lost on us; and we are thrilled to know that we are a part of the whole process.

With much affection and respect,

Jay Moriarty & Mike Milligan

norman lear

December 6, 1976

Dear Jay and Mike,

Thank <u>you</u>. If it hadn't been for you guys, I couldn't have received the note from you about the ALL IN THE FAMILY <u>you</u> made possible.

I love you, too.

NL:jj

> ARCHIE: I ain't talkin' about that war! I don't want to talk about that goddamn war no more! I'm talkin' about somethin' else! And what he done was wrong! Sayin' he won't go! Whaddya think, that all people of this country can say whether or not they wanna go to war? You couldn't get a decent war off the ground that way!

must have backed down. We ended up recording Carroll saying the words *rotten damn* at a later taping, and we "flew in a wild line," meaning we overdubbed the scene with those words for the version to be aired. Now it says "I ain't talking about that rotten damn war!" It doesn't quite match Carroll's lips, but you wouldn't notice it unless you're really looking for it.

At the time, I thought for sure ninety-plus percent of viewers were going to agree with Meathead on this one. But actually, it was 50/50. We got one review in the *Chicago Tribune* saying, "I just watched the most rotten show I have ever seen." Like now, the country was incredibly divided and polarized. And the brilliance of Norman Lear is, he turned that into comedy.

MIKE MILLIGAN: I was one of the few writers of my age within the company who had also been in the military, entering in 1966 and getting out in early 1970. To be clear, I spent my entire enlistment protecting an area that is still safe to this day: Chicopee Falls, Massachusetts.

I remember coming home from basic training and wearing my heavy blue uniform around the house in August, I was so proud of that damn thing. It wasn't until halfway through the miasma that was the war that it became clear what was really going on there. There was a sea change in American culture, politically and philosophically, and for me as well.

By the point we were writing this episode, I felt like I had a little skin in the game. I knew a couple of people who did go to Canada. Society in general thought that was so horrible, but I didn't feel that way. So this was a subject that was personal to me, maybe more than to others.

When you write a script as a freelance writer for a show, it gets rewritten by that show's writing staff. On *All in the Family*, most of the writers were experienced comedy pros who had written for great shows

going back to the 1950s—and as such, most of them were from the World War II generation and had served themselves. But it was also a liberal-minded group, so it's not like they all agreed with Archie. They did such a lovely job with this script, and massaged it nicely in their edits. I particularly like how the rest of the characters react to Archie. He had his beliefs in the U.S. of A., and the others were very nurturing to him. Nobody told him he was being an ass. There was no wisecrack about him from Meathead. The characters let him go, giving him room to vent, and I thought that was huge.

I'm not aware of what reaction the episode got when it aired. In 1976, in many people's minds, veterans were still "baby killers" for the actions the U.S. took in Vietnam. Veterans' groups weren't very vocal in those days, because of the shit they were going to take; thankfully at some point our attitudes switched from "baby killer" to, now, "Thank you for your service." I'm sure there were a lot of veterans who didn't like the episode, because maybe they thought it was questioning their decision. We didn't mean to suggest that anyone who was in the military should have gone to Canada instead. That wasn't the message of the show at all. It was a message about democracy and freedom.

"MIKE THE PACIFIST"

MIKE FEELS GUILTY FOR RESORTING TO VIOLENCE AFTER DEFENDING
A SUBWAY PASSENGER FROM HER ABUSIVE HUSBAND.

WRITTEN BY: **Phil Doran** and **Douglas Arango** ● DIRECTED BY: **Paul Bogart**

GUEST STARS: **Nita Talbot** as **Marcia** ● **Wynn Irwin** as **Howard** ● **Sudie Bond** as **Old Woman**
Richard Lawson as **Angry Black Man** ● **William Lanteau** as **Doctor** ● **William Pierson** as **Wino**
Al Mancini as **Pickpocket** ● **Jerrold Ziman** as **Lawyer** ● **Vanda Barra** as **Clarise**
Eddie Goldberg as **Old Man** ● **Gerry Black** as **Conductor**

ORIGINAL AIR DATE: **February 12, 1977**

NORMAN LEAR: We wanted to do a story that tackled the question of violence: What happens when a man who would never consider himself violent, and could never imagine himself participating in an act of violence, suddenly is in a situation that in an instant demands that of him? How would he react to that?

After Mike punches the guy to separate the fighting couple and save the wife, he has a reaction of disbelief that he could have committed a violent act. It's a powerful moment for him, and shows that it's not just Archie who can be a hypocrite or not live up to his ideals. We hoped to be nonpartisan that way—and although I think we were a bit partisan, I'm very proud of that. We hoped to show 360 degrees of human beings, who need to think more seriously about who they are and how they perform, how they react to life's struggles.

MIKE: You've moved us through three cars already.

ARCHIE: There was a gang war in the first car.

MIKE: What gang? It was three kids fighting over a strap to hold on to.

ARCHIE: I'll bet if you went back now the little one would be hanging from that strap.

SALLY STRUTHERS: This entire episode took place on a subway car, the set for which they built on a platform that they could move to jiggle us, without us having to jiggle ourselves, which I thought was brilliant. The big issue in the episode was whether and how Mike should get involved in preventing a violent attack on the subway. Mike starts out saying, "I don't want to get involved"—but at some point in life you have to get involved.

I also got to jump on someone's back in the episode, which I remember because I fell on the floor during one of the tapings and hurt my arm. Because the show's editor would always edit things together from each of the two tapings, we were taught to be incredibly exact in our movements, so that it wouldn't make editing difficult. In eating scenes, we paid so much attention to that during rehearsal, because they wanted us to lift a fork and take a bite of food at the same place in the script every time, no matter what. If you reach for a glass, remember where you put it down. We were rehearsed like automatons. And that moment with me getting hurt, shooting that subway scene, and then carrying my injured arm around, was not part of the rehearsal. So there was a moment where we stopped taping. I had been excited for my husband-to-be, Bill, to be sitting in the studio audience for that show, because it was such a good episode. And when we stopped, Bill, who was a doctor, came running out of the audience to take a look at my arm.

ORMAN'S SHOWS were on in repeats when I got home from school. I'd watch *All in the Family*, and I loved that there was a character named Gloria. Norman always embraced the conversation in his work, and that's what Mike Royce and I tried to capture in our reimagining of his *One Day at a Time*—those great, raw, honest, hard, and hilarious conversations.

All in the Family encouraged discourse. Everyone was themselves, and through conversation they would find their way toward each other—maybe not all the way to each other, but toward one another, certainly. Norman wants the world to be better, and cares about people. He wants his art to reflect the world, and to encourage us to be our best selves. His fingerprints are all over his work that way. There is certainly nothing like *All in the Family* on TV today, and that's a shame.

—*ONE DAY AT A TIME* (2017–20) CO-CREATOR GLORIA CALDERÓN KELLETT

Season 8, Episode 3

"COUSIN LIZ"

EDITH DISCOVERS THE TRUE NATURE OF HER COUSIN LIZ'S RELATIONSHIP WITH
HER LONGTIME "ROOMMATE" VERONICA, AS THEY GATHER TO MOURN LIZ'S DEATH
AND DECIDE OWNERSHIP OF AN ANTIQUE SILVER TEA SET.

STORY BY: **Barry Harman** and **Harve Brosten** ● TELEPLAY BY: **Bob Weiskopf** and **Bob Schiller**
DIRECTED BY: **Paul Bogart**

★ EMMY AWARD: Outstanding Writing in a Comedy Series ★

GUEST STAR: **K Callan** as **Veronica Cartwright**

ORIGINAL AIR DATE: **October 9, 1977**

NORMAN LEAR: I love in this episode that when Edith learns that her cousin and her "roommate" were really lovers, were really a married couple, she accepts it compassionately and without reservation. I guess that could surprise some people, because Edith isn't really very worldly. But you don't have to be worldly to love. And that's who Edith was; she was all about love. There was actually a book written about Edith: *Edith the Good*, by a Los Angeles pastor, Spencer Marsh, who examines the character as someone who truly listens to God. I loved reading that.

I have heard people say that at this time there weren't too many gay characters on TV, and even wonder if we had concerns about doing an episode like this. Well, I didn't think we needed to be afraid of doing anything that was human. This was all part of the human experience—and if that had not been shown on television before, that was of no concern to us. We presented the character of Veronica not really as "different," but simply the way I and the other writers experienced gay people in our everyday lives. In our experience, every day there were gay people whom I never knew were gay until they let me know. And that's the way the character was played by K Callan, whom I adore.

K CALLAN: On the first day of rehearsal for *All in the Family*, Carroll came over to me and said, "I learn my lines right away, but that's just the way I work. So you just do whatever you need to do." And I saw what his process was. He already knew his lines, so he could from then on become Archie, with his mind going in that direction. He would sit in the Archie chair all day long, and would come up with improvisatory thoughts. He'd add this and that, and in fact, he added a great moment to this episode. When Archie finally says that Veronica can keep the silver tea set, she hugs him, and he says, "Well, there, didn't you get something out of that?" Carroll would come up with these wonderful lines that were so funny and worked for the moment.

The night we shot the episode—during the break between the early taping and the later one, when the actors would have supper and get notes about the performance—I heard the producers walking down the halls, saying, "It didn't go well—it was just awful!" And I thought, "What's wrong with them? I thought it went just fine!" But then in the second taping, Carroll just lit the place up. It was a whole different show, and I really understood the power of charisma and what he brought to the show.

VERONICA: We loved each other in a different way.

EDITH: Well, what way?

VERONICA: Well, this was more like a marriage.

EDITH: A marriage? Oh well, it couldn't be.
You and cousin Liz was both g—Ohh. You mean…You and cousin Liz…

VERONICA: Yes.

EDITH: Ohhhh.

I was told that the episode was conceived in response to the campaign by Anita Bryant, who was a singer and orange juice spokesperson, to fire school-teachers for being gay. That's why my character, Veronica, was a teacher. I've been told that when the episode was finished, CBS said they weren't going to air it. And I heard Norman's response was, "Well, you won't be airing anything else from me."

I know this episode is still shown at gay and lesbian events, and afterward people will come up to talk to me about it. And I have heard often from fans. Once, many years ago, I was on a cruise, and a young man came up to me and said, "Thank you so much. It changed my life. I was a teenager who knew I was gay, but my parents thought being gay was sinful and awful. We watched that episode together, and afterward, my father said something like, 'Well, I guess they're just people like everybody else.'"

Once we had the internet, when I would get an email with something like that, I would forward it to the episode's writers, Bob Schiller and Bob Weiskopf. I was so glad to be able to pass the reaction on to the writers, because as the actor, you're just the face of it. The writers don't often get the applause for what they've done, but they should know fans appreciate the power of their words.

"EDITH'S 50TH BIRTHDAY"

EDITH NARROWLY ESCAPES A HOME-INVADING RAPIST, AND MUST FIND THE STRENGTH TO FILE A POLICE REPORT.

WRITTEN BY: **Bob Weiskopf** and **Bob Schiller** • DIRECTED BY: **Paul Bogart**

★ EMMY AWARD: Outstanding Directing in a Comedy Series ★

GUEST STARS: **David Coleman Dukes** as **Lambert** • **Jane Connell** as **Sybil Gooley**
John Brandon and **Ray Colella** as **Cops**

ORIGINAL AIR DATE: **October 16, 1977**

NORMAN LEAR: When I was first pitched this story idea, it was by the writers of *One Day at a Time*. And I remember thinking that yes, it would be an interesting, groundbreaking story for Bonnie Franklin's character, Ann Romano—but it would be more interesting if this terrible situation were to happen to a middle-aged woman instead. And so we moved the idea over to *All in the Family* and reworked it for Edith. Rape has nothing to do with youth or appearance; it has to do with power. And showing that any woman, including a mother figure like Edith, would be in danger at the hands of a predator like this character would really make a statement.

I remember Jean being uncomfortable about doing this episode—but, as a great actress, wanting to do it. Her head said, "I want to do it," but her body, her emotions, were truly tested. And as a result, my God, what a great performance!

Toward the end of the first episode, there's the famous moment where Edith gets away from her attacker by taking her burning birthday cake from the oven and throwing it in his face, and then kicking him in the nuts. That got such a huge explosion of relief and applause from the live audience, who had been watching this menacing situation happen before their eyes. When she kicked him and pushed him out the door, we had close to three hundred people reacting with utter joy and excitement, rising from their seats as one. It

was glorious, and I remember our subsequent decision not to use the full audio, because the cheers just went on too long. So Edith ran out of there, and *bam*—we cut the sound.

When we were writing, we reached out to a woman named Gail Abarbanel, who was and is a social worker at the Santa Monica Rape Treatment Center. She gave us invaluable advice, and her guidance led to us making this storyline a two-part episode, because it would be hard for Edith to go through such a trauma and then come out of it all within twenty-something minutes. So we had the second episode concentrate on the impacts of the assault on Edith and her family, and how she reclaims her life. As a result of all the press the episode received, and Gail received, the Santa Monica Rape Treatment Center was able to grow. For years I have stayed involved with their work and their fundraisers. I've always felt great about that, because I admire so much what Gail has done over the years.

ROB REINER: This was as dark and dramatic as we'd ever gotten. Nobody ever thought we could do a dark and dramatic episode like this and get laughs—and yet, one of the funniest scenes of any show we did is in the second episode here, where Archie and Mike go back to the house to try to find the attacker. We have a bat, and we are trying to squeeze through the door at the same time, which is a little bit of physical, old-fashioned slap-

NORMAN: I'll tell you what I remember. I was combining a story that
Hal Kantor wanted to do. The basic idea of which I've always loved --
that there's somebody phoning that's threatening and the answer to
why does she pick up the phone is she's expecting a very important
call from Archie out of town. Everytime she goes to that phone
it's the threat again. This was an obscene call but I saw it getting
to the point where the obscene call would be threatening. Now,
they wrote on "One Day At A Time" a second act in which a guy is
in the house and they spent hours with two different groups
representing anti-rape techniques. So they got a portrait of a
guy that's real and a way of handling him that's real. And they
wrote a second act that I thought would play wonderfully with
Bonnie. Dramatic, only a little funny. With Edith, I thought, it
could be very funny and extrememly dramatic. There's a guy in the
house. He's announced intention. He's going to have her. Archie's
away, she's got all night, he's got plenty of time and she talks
him out of it. I do remember, 'you musn't be frightened', and she
has just read something about this. Or for some reason she...
it's fresh in her mind what she's supposed to do.

MORT: As I remember it, we said what she would instinctively do,
that she found it, not out of instruction, but out of Edith, that
what she tried to do was the right thing to do. It wasn't that
she was trained or learned anything...

NORMAN: If some expert said to her, "God, that's right out of the
book." But she didn't get it out of the book.

NL: On the "Rape" story, it occurred to me that if we get
something else happening, and we really have her meeting an
interesting guy and we're ahead - I mean, the camera's ahead
of Edith and everybody else - if we do that, you've got the
strongest two-parter if at the end of the second part he
successfully alone with Edith in the home. Archie is away
for a few hours, whatever. And other things are in the story
to carry over. In other words, you're going to watch Arche
wherever he is. And the guy is closing in on her as she's talking
her way out of it, as Archie's on his way back or whatever's
happening to him, and Mike and Gloria. It would be the greatest
irony in the world if the three of them for some reason were
right next door.

MJ: That's a good idea.

6

BW: I think the less she knows about this guy, the better.

WM: So Archie would leave at the end of the first act?

ML: You mean the second act.

MJ: It would seem that we have some nonsequitor there. We have two scenes that have no relation with each other. The scene where she's at the market and then the scene where Archie has the fight with her and leaves.

BW: Archie's going to have the fight first.

NL: It may not be a fight. Maybe a whole other invention.

MJ: I'd like to bring something up. I think at the start, where she's in the market, there should be something said between her and another woman about doing something. She says "No, I can't. Tonight is the night Archie is going bowling." Or Archie's going to be away. 'Cause why would a rapist come to the house when the husband can be in or out at any minute?

LR: Milt, that could be where we find out he's the rapist. When he overhears it at the market that Archie is going out bowling, or whatever, and she's going to stay home and work on something for the Sunshine Home herself. And when he does his take on that, the audience knows without saying "I am the rapist."

BS: How old is he?

NL: She could turn fifty, I would think. He's turned 51.

LR: That was about three years ago when he was 50. So she's 50.

WM: I kind of like what Milt say. They don't have to have an argument, but Archie goes bowling and he could...

MJ: What I don't like about the argument is that we have so many of them. If for once - all right he doesn't have to worry for two weeks - he has gone over to Mike and Glorias to play a birthday party for Edith's 50th birthday. The first time he's ever done

7

MJ: (CONT'D.)
something for her.

NL: That's all right. Or Gloria and Michael are planning a surprise there and he's there helping. Who should come.

MJ: Fine. In other words this lends us such a pleasant thing going on rather than...

NL: We can have some fun with that. As a matter of fact they are all over there and they keep calling her and she keeps saying "I will. I will. I'll be right there." And the rapist is making her answer the phone. And she's making excuses, "The only reason I can't come over..." and the guy is looking at her, whatever. There are fifteen people in the dark, waiting to yell "surprise!" That's wonderful.

"ALL IN THE FAMILY"

"Edith's 50th Birthday"

BUNKER HOUSE - SATURDAY MORNING

1.   Archie, Mike and Gloria set up Edith's 50th birthday. Archie has planned a surprise party at the Stivic's house at three that afternoon. Friends of Edith and people from the Sunshine Home invited so party is in afternoon. Edith, in kitchen, calls Archie so he tells Gloria and Mike he'll be over in a few minutes to help with the decorations, etc. Gloria compliments Archie -- one of the nicest things he's ever done -- Mike says the only nice thing. They EXIT.

* * *

2.   Archie and Edith in kitchen. Edith is finishing a birthday cake. Archie wants to know whose birthday -- Edith says "Mine." Archie pretends he forgot all about it. "How old are you going to be, Exith?" "I won't tell," she says. "Then I will," he says. "Okay," says Edith, but tell the truth and lie by a few years. Candles, jokes, etc. Edith asks Archie to take her out to dinner -- they'll come home for birthday cake and coffee. Archie likes the cake and coffee idea at home, along with the rest of the meal. Edith is a superb cook. Edith reluctantly agrees to cook her own dinner. INTO LIVING ROOM: She'll just go next door to invite Gloria and Mike. Archie quickly says he'll do it. He'll yell out window. Opens window, it falls with a thud. Archie tells Edith

to get it fixed, somebody's liable to get killed. But don't get it fixed on Saturday, it'll cost a fortune. He has to go next door anyway to sit for Joey -- Mike and Gloria are leaving to go somewhere for the day and he promised.

Edith offers to sit -- "Why spoil your Saturday, Archie?" Archie says "Why spoil your 50th birthday?" He'll sit -- Edith can come over at three this afternoon and relieve him if she wants. By three P.M., Archie says he'll be ready for a nap. They agree -- Edith will go next door at three.

Edith has to go marketing for her birthday dinner. Archie says get a case of beer - it's on sale - shows coupon. He leaves to go next door and Edith starts to get ready to leave for supermarket.

3.   SCENE AT CHECK-OUT COUNTER AT MARKET

Edith and man discussing the beer. Talk with checker, about Edith's birthday. She leaves. We, the audience, find the man is the suspected rapist after he leaves.

NL: I have no way of expressing how much I think a great show is inherent in this. It's such an incredible irony that everyone who loves her is gathered next door, and wouldn't come near her, which can be emphasized, because they wouldn't interrupt the surprise at all. They wouldn't think of coming near her because they wouldn't think of interrupting a surprise. And she is trapped with a rapist. I mean, Jesus, what a sensational conceit. It is marvelous. I missed something that we talked about which I didn't know I missed until we're talking here just now which I think would help it tremendously...is to use Gloria's kitchen. 'Cause I know we can't have the two livingrooms. But use Gloria's kitchen so we have the excitement of the party to cut to. Maybe it's set up so Edith is expected through the back door. They told Edith to come in the back door because they're going to surprise her in the livingroom. So they want her to come in the back door, so they would have a similar set up in that house that the Bunker's have. I don't remember ever seeing if we've ever seen Gloria's kitchen but maybe we haven't.

ML: Oh, yes. Frequently.

NL: We have. I just can't remember. And so when she walks in the livingroom they have it fixed or whatever. They yell surprise when she comes in that way. So we use the kitchen and Archie yelling out, "Shaddup, she's coming any second!" I mean it's fun, there's laughs to cut to

stick in the middle of this very tense and dramatic episode. But that's what was good about *All in the Family*. We tried things that had never been done on TV before, and found ways to make them funny without undercutting the seriousness of the subject.

GAIL ABARBANEL: I had been a social worker at Santa Monica Hospital since 1974, working with many different types of patients. One day, I was asked to see a woman in our ER who had been walking on the beach on a Sunday afternoon and was raped by a stranger. She ended up in our ER a few days later—not as a rape victim, but because she had made a suicide attempt. I was very moved by her experience, and decided to

see every rape victim who came to our hospital ER. Many came at night so I put myself on call to be there at the moment they reached out for help. And that was the beginning of what became the Rape Treatment Center, now an international model for victim care.

At that time, there were very few rape crisis centers in the country or in the world. Rape was a hidden crime and very misunderstood. Few victims came forward and those who did were often blamed and disbelieved. There was so little awareness. Most of our knowledge was about stranger rape; no one had yet even coined the term *acquaintance rape*. One day, out of the blue, I received a call from Norman Lear. He told me they were thinking about doing an episode of *All in the Family*, and asked me to come meet with him and the writers. I was a little hesitant because I had never consulted on a television show before. That's when Norman presented an incredible opportunity. He said, "If you could talk to 40 million people about rape, what would you want to say?" I accepted the invitation.

The collaboration was an amazing experience for me and a gift to the work of the Rape Treatment Center. Norman and his writers were so open. They really wanted to understand the impacts of rape on victims and common responses to this kind of trauma. I suggested that they focus on both the victim and her family, and how important it is for victims to have support from their significant others. And so the writers portrayed Archie's reactions and his attempts to be supportive. It became one of the poignant times in the series when Archie was, in his own way, very tender with Edith.

I met with the writers several times, and there was a lot of interchange and discussion. They were all committed to getting it right. We talked a lot about the initial reactions many victims have—shock and disbelief, and fears about personal safety. Many victims say, "I thought he was going to kill me." The writers addressed this with Edith's fear that the attacker might hurt Archie when he came home to pick up the punch bowl. Many victims try to resume normal activities to block thoughts and feelings about the trauma. Edith kept doing the laundry. A big issue for victims is their decision about reporting the crime. They struggle with fears of retaliation if they do report and feelings of social responsibility to help prevent it from happening to someone else. Edith struggled with this dilemma too.

I remember feeling like they were covering a lot of territory. I was pushing for them to do more than a short half hour, because this was one of the first times this issue would be dealt with on national television. It was a great opportunity to educate the public and do it in a sensitive way. Edith was such a beloved character, and I saw the power of embedding the issue in a comedy show: When you make people laugh, it can deepen their capacity to feel empathy and compassion, and in the 1970s, most television shows wouldn't have dared to have a beloved main character get raped. By portraying this happening to Edith Bunker, *All in the Family* brought the issue of rape into people's living rooms in a way that they could see and emotionally feel some of the realities of being raped.

Their decision to have Edith be a victim was a way to address stereotypes about who gets raped and how and where these crimes occur. It was not a "stranger in a dark alley." Edith was attacked in her own home. Depicting the support she received would give other victims the courage to come forward and seek help. In fact, during the production of the show, a number of women in Norman's company came forward and told him that they had been victims and had never told anyone or sought help, and he was profoundly moved.

Norman truly changed the nation's consciousness about rape. And he enlightened Hollywood. After *All in the Family*, other shows began to tackle the issue. Norman continued to work with the Rape Treatment Center. He joined our board, spoke at many of our events, and helped us raise money. His partnership changed

my life and helped bring justice and compassionate care to so many victims. The Rape Treatment Center now sees about one thousand new victims a year—adults and children. We have a special facility for child victims called Stuart House. Even today, people of all ages remember this show, and mention it to me. It changed my life, and the life of so many others.

2.

in the middle of what I hope will be stark drama in the second act. I mean I think Archie's coming in is glowing. I know it's tougher to find it without Archie coming in but it's glowing what can be absolutely great. The two of them alone, and we must find a way in which Edith's saves herself. Not the inadvertent appearance of another human being. Now there's a million reasons for doing the show. But one of the original reasons was, a woman can save herself if she does the right thing. Now Edith either inadvertently does the right thing and learns it was the right thing or she simply does it without making the comment...succeeds in getting rid of him. I don't know why the first act is loaded with opportunities to be funny. And it isn't 'cause the situation is so good. Marvelous...I don't think it's fully realized here, but it's easy to realize. And the second act potential... Jesus...here is America's most loveable leading television lady, a most adored woman in that kind of peril. For me, in dramatic terms anyway, totally worked out the reason why everybody is immediately next door, and wouldn't come near her. And can't wait for her to get there and she's in that kind of peril?

                    EDITH
(RAISES UP)

        Wouldn't you like a cup of coffee,

        instead?

                    LAMBERT

        I don't drink coffee.

                    EDITH

        I got Sanka.

                    LAMBERT
(PUSHES HER BACK DOWN)

        Lady, you're stalling. It ain't

        gonna do you any good. This is

        gonna happen. So just relax, okay?

                    EDITH

        Listen, I gotta get outta here. I

        gotta get ready for my birthday

        party...

                    LAMBERT

        Happy birthday!
(TOSSES SHIRT AWAY)

                    EDITH

        Oh, oh, thank you.

                    EDITH

        There's somethin' burnin'

        in the kitchen.

                    LAMBERT

        What is it?

EDITH

It's in the kitchen.

LAMBERT

All right. All right. C'mon.

C'mon. C'mon.

EDITH

There's somethin' burnin' in the

kitchen.

(EDITH RUNS TO KITCHEN.
LAMBERT IS FOLLOWING. THEY
EXIT)

INT. BUNKER KITCHEN

(SMOKE IS COMING OUT OF THE
OVEN. EDITH CROSSES TO STOVE,
LAMBERT FOLLOWING. SHE GRABS
POT HOLDERS, TAKES CAKE OUT.
HE TURNS OFF THE OVEN)

EDITH (CONT'D)

Ahhh! There's a fire! Fire! My

birthday cake! My birthday cake

is burnin'.

LAMBERT

Lady, get rid of it! Get rid of it!

(EDITH TURNS, LOOKS AROUND,
TURNS BACK TO LAMBERT AND
SHOVES CAKE IN HIS FACE, RUNS
TOWARD KITCHEN DOOR. HE
CATCHES HER, HOLDING HER, SHE
BREAKS HIS GRASP, SHOVES HIM
OUT THE DOOR)

(INTO: NARRATION - PART II)

"ARCHIE AND THE KKK"

ARCHIE UNKNOWINGLY JOINS A NEW LOCAL CHAPTER OF THE KU KLUX KLAN AND MUST DISSUADE THE VIGILANTE GROUP FROM CARRYING OUT THEIR PLANS TO ATTACK MIKE FOR WRITING A NEWSPAPER EDITORIAL.

WRITTEN BY: **Bob Weiskopf, Bob Schiller,** and **Mort Lachman** • DIRECTED BY: **Paul Bogart**

GUEST STARS: **Dennis Patrick** as **Gordie Lloyd** • **Roger Bowen** as **Mitch Turner** • **Jason Wingreen** as **Harry Snowden** • **Danny Dayton** as **Hank Pivnik** • **Owen Bush** as **Charley** • **Victor De Rose** as **KKK Applicant**

ORIGINAL AIR DATE: **November 27** and **December 4, 1977**

NORMAN LEAR: Even with all the fear Archie has for different groups, and the way he talks about them, there was a line he would not cross. He would not sink to violence, and I'm filled with pride when I remember that we showed that. Archie goes to great lengths to protect Mike, the son-in-law he's been calling Meathead all these years, going so far as to reveal to these KKK members that he had received blood from a Black woman. "I'm Black and I'm proud!" Carroll's performance here was so wonderful.

ARCHIE

Well, that there titular authority,

that's up to his mother, ain't it?

MITCH

What I mean is, well, how about you

joinin' all of us in a little reprimand?

ARCHIE

Well, yeah, I ain't drivin' tonight.

Anything you got, with water 'cause

ginger ale gives me dispoopsia.

MITCH

No, no. I'm talking about a warning

to him to either change his views or

keep them to himself.

ARCHIE

I been tryin' to do that for seven

years.

(TO MITCH)

I'm a little thirsty. When are you

gonna serve the repriand?

MITCH

Then you will join us in teaching

him a lesson he'll never forget?

ARCHIE

If I can help you teach that meathead

son-in-law of mine to become a God-

fearin', patriotic American, you got

Archie Bunker as a member for life.

FADE OUT.

END OF ACT II

Season 8, Episodes 13 and 14
"EDITH'S CRISIS OF FAITH"

BEVERLY LASALLE IS MURDERED IN A BRUTAL HATE CRIME, CAUSING EDITH TO LOSE HER FAITH IN GOD AT CHRISTMASTIME.

STORY BY: **Erik Tarloff** • TELEPLAY BY: **Bob Weiskopf** and **Bob Schiller** • DIRECTED BY: **Paul Bogart**

GUEST STARS: **Lori Shannon** as **Beverly LaSalle** • **Allan Melvin** as **Barney Hefner** • **Ron Vernan** as **Doctor**

ORIGINAL AIR DATES: **December 18** and **December 25, 1977**

NORMAN LEAR: Brainstorming for these episodes, it took weeks of thinking to find a reason why we thought Edith could lose her faith in God. And then we realized, "Well, if she had a friend who was killed for being gay, or being a transvestite…if God could see that happen to a Beverly LaSalle, could that force her to lose her faith in God?"

We realized we couldn't lose her faith and regain it in the same episode. It just wasn't possible; time had to go by and it was too much. So we knew this would take place in two parts. Weeks and weeks went by again as we discussed it. The death of Beverly LaSalle would cause her to lose her faith—and then for part two, what on earth could get her to regain it? Finally, somebody in the room asked, "When Edith loses her faith in

God, what happens to Archie?" And oh, what a revelation that was! That whatever strength Archie had as a human being, so much of it rested on how strong his wife was. And her strength rested in her faith.

The night it was taped, this episode had the audience near tears. I thought it was the best show we'd ever made. When the cast and I flew to Washington in September 1978 for the installation of Archie's and Edith's chairs into the Smithsonian Institution, President Carter invited us all to the White House. There in the Oval Office we listened to our president talk about episodes he and Rosalynn had seen and remembered, especially "the one where Edith lost and regained her faith."

ERIK TARLOFF: When I had my first meeting to pitch stories to *All in the Family*, the head writer, Mort Lachman, was interested when I suggested, "What if Edith needs to see a shrink?" He said, "That's terrific. Why does she need to see a shrink?" I didn't know yet. He told me to come back another day with the answer, so I did. One possible reason was that Edith had never had an orgasm, and when she discovers they exist, she wants one. Another possible reason was that she loses her faith. They liked both of those, and ended up doing them as separate episodes.

The orgasm story became the episode "The Joys of Sex" in season 7. *All in the Family* was known as a show where the writing staff would rewrite every script extensively—and in fact, I've heard Norman say that the

RECEIVED

FEB 7 1978

January 4, 1978

Mr. Norman Lear
T.A.T. Productions
Sunset Blvd.
Los Angeles, Calif.

Dear Norman Lear:

It is a rare occasion that prompts me to write to the producer of a TV show --- as a matter of fact, I think this is my first time. However, I felt compelled to write you and let you know of my feelings about a recent "All in the Family" episode.

The second installment about the female impersonator, Beverly, was so very touching and moving. Both my husband and I --- without any words or conversation between us --- sat and cried our eyes out at the very sensitive sequence between Edith and Mike in the kitchen. I think you have done an extraordinary job of enlightening the public about the true feelings many sons-in-law have about their mothers-in-law and portraying the deep affection that can exist in such a relationship. My husband and my mother shared this special closeness during the course of her lifetime.

Thank you, thank you, thank you for your wonderful programs. I enjoy your programs so very much and so does my husband. We wish you continued success and many, many years of fruitful endeavors.

mrk/ts

Con Edith's
Crisis of Faith
Program Dept.

Just saw your show "All In The Family" and am completely fed-up. How **DARE** you put on a show like this Christmas week?

Beverly was the best part of the show.

How could you "kill off" such a beautiful character, this week? your timing stinks; and so does your writing!

You just lost a family fan.

Merry X-Mas

The two-part program on the death of "Beverly" has done more for compassion; love of mankind and Christianity than all of this Anita Bryants could ever do.

Thank you for the show and God Bless you.

Don't Cancel

Dear Mr. Lear,

Just another letter from a fan pleading with you to try to continue "All In the Family." Even without Mike and Gloria, couldn't Archie & Edith perhaps move to a retirement village & have occasional visits from the kids. A new setting for the Bunkers would provide hysterical situations.

We love them. They're a part of our lives. Please try.

Thank you!

EDITH BUNKER: Why don't you sit down?

BEVERLY: In this dress? Are you kidding? [imitating Mae West]
One false move and you'll have wall-to-wall foam rubber.

highest praise he's ever paid a script is, "It will make a good rewrite." That can be frustrating for a writer who thinks his script was actually pretty good, but it was just part of the way that operation worked. With "The Joys of Sex," I noticed at the table read that very little in the script had changed during the development process. If they left your work alone, that was a real tribute to your writing. But then, at the table read, Carroll O'Connor said, "Oh, no—when Archie sleeps with Edith, she has an orgasm!" It was really interesting that politically, he was able on the show to be the opposite of who he really was, but when it came to sex, he was suddenly protective about his character. So the writers had to change and rewrite everything.

"Edith Loses Her Faith" was rewritten quite extensively, particularly part one. In the outline I'd initially worked out with Mort, and then in my initial draft, the victim of the murder was not Beverly LaSalle but a young minister friend of Mike's. Archie gives him a hard time: "How can you be friends with an atheist?" Then the minister goes out to get ice cream and

is killed. In the second episode, the key questions we had to answer to make it work were "Why does anyone care about Edith losing her faith? Why is this an issue for everyone else in the story?" Even for Mike, an atheist, and certainly for Archie, Edith's faith was their bedrock. The whole family rested on it, whether they believed it or not; it provided an underpinning for the family's cohesion.

I wasn't there for the episode's rehearsals, so I didn't hear firsthand what the actors felt about the emotion of the script. I did attend the taping and remember the audience's loud gasp when it was announced that Beverly had died. And I remember Mort telling me when I first pitched the idea that because Jean was very religious, and her faith was so important to her, he thought she'd really like a storyline like this for Edith. It would give her a chance to be more than just a "dingbat" and explore the Edith character more as an actress, while still being true to the character. Jean was always looking to bring depth to Edith, as she did more and more through the years.

IT'S HARD TO UNRAVEL Norman Lear's impact on my sense of humor because those shows were part of my life from so early. Basically, he was everything. His reality was my reality. Norman's writing was sharp, honest and unafraid. The idea that people in families can love each other, even when they have different ways of understanding the world, was paramount to *All in the Family*, and that was really the central theme of *Transparent*. *Transparent* asked the question "Will you still love me if…" and I think *All in the Family* was asking that with every episode.

In retrospect, we're realizing that *All in the Family* was one of the first shows to feature openly queer characters who weren't offensive stereotypes. Edith had a trans friend, Beverly. Beverly was murdered in a gay-bashing incident on the show, and Edith's pain and distress at her friend's death showed that, yes, trans people are human and loved. These messages about queer and trans people were nowhere else on television back then. I'm sure watching the show gave me the desire to stick up for those of us who are seen as Other, to celebrate all the people society tries to crush.

—*TRANSPARENT* CREATOR JOEY SOLOWAY

Season 8, Episode 19

"TWO'S A CROWD"

A DRUNKEN ARCHIE UNKNOWINGLY GIVES MIKE INSIGHT INTO THE WAY
ARCHIE GREW UP AFTER THEY GET LOCKED IN THE STOREROOM OF ARCHIE'S PLACE.

WRITTEN BY: **Phil Sharp** • DIRECTED BY: **Paul Bogart**

ORIGINAL AIR DATE: **February 12, 1978**

NORMAN LEAR: The scenes between Mike and Archie in this episode say more about how Archie became Archie than any other scene or episode we made in nine years of the series. We wanted to examine what would happen if the very foundations of Archie's beliefs were tested. We didn't get to thinking about it until that eighth year, but it's an obvious factor in Archie's or anybody else's beliefs, the relationship he had with his father—and indeed I spent years coming to terms with the relationship I had with mine.

The scene with Archie and Mike in the storeroom, and Archie, a little drunk, opening up about his childhood, is as strong a scene as we could ever have managed to come up with to deal with such an important topic. Archie talks about how his father spanked him, and I can still see so clearly the moments when he talks about his father's strong hand. He loved his father, and he was defending him, and in fact all fathers. And yet, Archie's expression shows that, as he relives those memories, a terrible seed of doubt has been placed in him. It's a heart-wrenching moment, ending in a beautiful father-son moment between Archie and Mike, as

Mike takes the old store awning and covers the sleeping father-in-law he now understands maybe a little better.

ROB REINER: This is one of the best episodes we ever did. These two characters have been at each other's throats for years, but here, you find out that Archie really loves Mike, and Mike loves him. After so many seasons, you've made an investment in these characters, and now you get to find out some real feelings they had for each other.

We also get to find out where Archie got some of the beliefs he has, from his own upbringing. In a normal situation, I don't think Archie would ever reveal that to Mike. But here they are, stuck in the storeroom after so long a time, and they're drinking, and adverse situations like that bring those things out in people. This episode provided a great way to show new things about these two characters, even after eight seasons. The setup was just right for deeper feelings to come out, and it worked so well because the loving feelings Carroll and I had for each other as people could be infused into the show.

MIKE: I don't believe it. We're trapped in here. We're trapped in here!

ARCHIE: Aw, stop your yellin', there. You're only trapped in here with me.
Look who the hell I'm trapped in here with.

                    MIKE

Did you ever think that possibly

your father just might be wrong?

                    ARCHIE

Wrong, my old man? Don't be stupid.

My old man, let me tell you about

him. He was never wrong about

nothin'.

                    MIKE

Yes, he was, Arch.

                    ARCHIE

Huh? ~~Don't tell me my father was~~ *Your father who made you —*

wrong. Let me tell you somethin'.

Your father, the breadwinner *of the house* ∧ there,

the man who goes out and busts his

butt to keep a roof over your head

and clothes on your back. You call

your father wrong? Your father,

your father's ∧*that's* the man who comes home

bringin' you candy. Your father's

the first guy to throw a baseball to

you, and take you for walks in the

park, holdin' you by the hand. My

father held me by the hand. Oh, hey,

my father had a hand on him, I'll

tell you, *Buddy*.

                    (MORE)

ARCHIE (CONT'D)

(HOLDS UP HIS HAND)

    He busted that hand once and he busted

it on me! To teach me to do good.

My father, he shoved me in a closet

for seven hours to teach me to do

good. 'Cause he loved me, he loved

me. Don't be lookin' at me! Let

me tell you somethin', you're

supposed to love your father 'cause

your father loves you.

(A BEAT)

    Now how can any man that loves you,

tell you anything that's wrong!

What's the use in talkin' to you.

(A BEAT, HE RISES, CROSSES
AND LIES DOWN ON A TABLECLOTH
THAT IS ON THE FLOOR. HE
FALLS ASLEEP. AFTER A FEW
BEATS, MIKE RISES, CROSSES TO
ARCHIE, CAREFULLY COVERS HIM
WITH AWNING, LIES DOWN HIMSELF,
GETS UNDER COVER)

             MIKE

Good night, Shoebootie.

(AFTER A BEAT MIKE TURNS, SPOON
FASHION TO ARCHIE. PUTS HIS
ARM AROUND ARCHIE, PATS HIS
STOMACH. ARCHIE MUTTERS ABOUT
ALICE FAYE AS HE TURNS, FACING
MIKE. THEY GET INTO EMBRACE
WHICH NOW LEAVES THEM CHEEK TO
CHEEK)

"THE STIVICS GO WEST"

MIKE AND GLORIA LEAVE ARCHIE AND EDITH TO ADJUST TO LIFE WITHOUT THEM
AS THEY START THEIR NEW LIVES IN CALIFORNIA.

WRITTEN BY: **Bob Weiskopf** and **Bob Schiller** ● DIRECTED BY: **Paul Bogart**

GUEST STARS: **Clyde Kusatsu** as **Reverend Chong**

ORIGINAL AIR DATE: **March 19, 1978**

NORMAN LEAR: At the end of the eighth season, we all were feeling that the show needed to come to a close. Sally and Rob each wished to move on. They adored what we'd done together, as did I, as did Carroll and Jean— but it was time. Carroll eventually changed his mind, and convinced Jean to join him for a ninth season. And so everybody was involved in making the decision how to allow Mike and Gloria to move on.

We didn't want them killed in a car crash or anything, so this was the best idea that we had, that they would be moving. California was consistent with the writing we'd established that Mike wanted to do, so California would be the place.

I had known Sally Struthers least well in the beginning, of the four principals. I originally envisioned

her character as like a Kewpie doll, but with an inner strength that would grow over the seasons. By this episode, Gloria has become the head of the family, and in charge. Sally was perfect as Gloria.

The farewell scene was a tearjerker. After the goodbyes, Gloria and Joey are waiting in the cab and Edith rushes back into the house in tears. Then Mike and Archie are alone on the front porch. We'd seen them disagreeing about everything for eight years, but there was love between these two men. Mike understood how much Archie loved his daughter and his wife, and how hard it had been to support a family with the education he'd had. And Archie, who perhaps couldn't really understand everything about Mike, knew that he loved and would take care of his daughter and grandson. They have a moment where they hug, when the two men are alone. That emotional moment of parting, I can still see that as clearly as if I saw it yesterday.

CLYDE KUSATSU: After first appearing in "Joey's Baptism" [see page 128], I was very humbled and grateful that I got asked back for this episode, especially because it was when Rob and Sally were leaving the show. That night the audiences for both tapings were filled with families, friends, and industry greats. And I never saw Rob so nervous. It was almost like going back to high school or college and being nervous about who's out there. I saw that these actors who had done this show so beautifully could get butterflies, and that calmed me down as well. Later on, I would find out that Rob's dad, Carl Reiner, had been in the audience, because when he was casting the film *Oh, God!*, he recognized me in the casting office as he walked by. And so I ended up being cast in the film and doing a nice little scene that Carl directed.

ROB REINER: We had all decided that this was going to be the end of the series—all of us, not just Carroll and Jean and Sally and me, but also the writers and Norman. So we wrote this to be the last show, and Carroll was the one who pushed for it harder than anybody else. He didn't want to do the show anymore. And then at some point he said, "Wait a minute—maybe I'll do more." And he went on to do a ninth season of *All in the Family*, and then four seasons of *Archie Bunker's Place*.

But everything was originally tailored for this to be the last episode. That's why Archie and Mike had such a beautiful moment of goodbye. And it was totally real—there was no acting in that moment. There on the screen, that was the real feeling I had for Carroll and his feeling for me. It transcended the characters.

SALLY STRUTHERS: The actors on *All in the Family* were signed up only through the eighth season, and there's no way some of us would have entertained renewing. I wanted to do other things, and Rob had big plans—he had already bought the rights to the book *The Princess Bride*, and was kicking at the gate to get out and let his creative juices flow.

I remember shooting this episode, knowing it was the last for me, and having that goodbye hug on the porch with Edith and Archie, which was heartbreaking. When I was very young my father hadn't been around much because he was a doctor and a workaholic; then, when I was six or seven, he left my mother and my sister and me. Carroll had become like a real father to me, off-screen as well as on-screen. He and his wife, Nancy, took me under their wing, and even introduced me to my husband. And so hugging Carroll goodbye within the scene was especially difficult, to know that I wouldn't be working every day with him for several months of the year. And I worshiped—I don't want to put that in the past tense—I worship Jean. She was our company angel, our litmus test of taste, who didn't say or think negative things, and gave to us all from her brain and from her heart. And so as I said goodbye as Gloria, leaving the Bunker house, I didn't feel any regret, but I certainly felt great sorrow for what I would be missing.

ARCHIE: You just take very good care of Gloria and Joseph.

MIKE: Those are two things you never have to worry about, Arch.

                    EDITH

          Goodbye, Joey.

(KISSES HIM)

                    GLORIA

          Say goodbye to Grandpa.

                    ARCHIE

          So long, Joe, so long, Joe.

                    ~~EDITH~~

          ~~Put on your coat.~~

                    ARCHIE

          So long, Joe.

                    EDITH

          I love you, Mike.

(GLORIA AND JOEY EXIT)

                    MIKE

          I love you, Ma.

(EDITH AND MIKE EMBRACE)

(MIKE TURNS TO ARCHIE, THEY
STARE AT EACH OTHER)

                    ARCHIE

          Hey, the taxi meter's runnin' ~~out~~ *on*

          there ~~on you.~~ *you know.* It's gonna be at

          least a fifteen dollar ride out

          there. You don't want to ~~hear two~~ *add to it,*

          ~~you know, there is no use in doin' that~~

          ~~of you, you know you shouldn't do~~

          ~~all that.~~ Chargin' up... *they charge*

(THEY EXIT) *you enough for them...*

EXT. BUNKER PORCH

                    EDITH

        Gloria, Gloria... goodbye.

                    GLORIA

        Goodbye, Ma.

                    EDITH

        Goodbye, Michael.

(KISSES GLORIA AND JOEY AGAIN.
RUNS BACK INTO THE HOUSE.
GLORIA EXITS PORCH)

                    MIKE

        Arch...

                    ARCHIE

(TAKES MIKE'S HAND)

        Hey listen, have a good trip there,

        huh. Have a good trip.

                    MIKE

        Yeah. I know you always thought

        I hated you, but I love you.

(HE HUGS ARCHIE, THROUGH WHICH:)

                    ARCHIE

        Hey, yeah, you be sure and send

        postcards every now and then, will

        you because your mother-in-law,

        she's gonna, she's gonna wanna know

        that you're all right, you know.

(ARCHIE GIVES IN TO THE HUG.
MIKE BREAKS HUG)

ALL OF *ALL IN THE FAMILY*
Seasons 7 and 8

Season 7
1976–77

Episode 1
"Archie's Brief Encounter: Part 1"

Episode 2
"Archie's Brief Encounter: Part 2"
WRITERS: **Mel Tolkin, Larry Rhine**
DIRECTOR: **Paul Bogart**
AIR DATE: **September 22, 1976**
★

Episode 3
"Archie's Brief Encounter: Part 3"
WRITERS: **Larry Rhine, Mel Tolkin**
DIRECTOR: **Paul Bogart**
AIR DATE: **September 29, 1976**
★

Episode 4
"The Unemployment Story: Part 1"
WRITERS: **Ben Starr, Chuck Stewart**
DIRECTOR: **Paul Bogart**
AIR DATE: **October 6, 1976**
★

Episode 5
"The Unemployment Story: Part 2"
WRITERS: **Chuck Stewart, Ben Starr**
DIRECTOR: **Paul Bogart**
AIR DATE: **October 13, 1976**
★

Episode 6
"Archie's Operation: Part 1"
WRITERS: **Calvin Kelly, Jim Tisdale, Milt Josefsberg, Mort Lachman**
DIRECTOR: **Paul Bogart**
AIR DATE: **October 20, 1976**
★

Episode 7
"Archie's Operation: Part 2"
WRITERS: **Larry Rhine and Mel Tolkin**
DIRECTOR: **Paul Bogart**
AIR DATE: **October 27, 1976**
★

Episode 8
"Beverly Rides Again"
WRITERS: **Phil Doran, Douglas Arango**
DIRECTOR: **Paul Bogart**
AIR DATE: **November 6, 1976**
★

Episode 9
"Teresa Moves In"
WRITER: **Michael Loman**
DIRECTOR: **Paul Bogart**
AIR DATE: **November 13, 1976**
★

Episode 10
"Mike and Gloria's Will"
WRITERS: **Bill Richmond, Gene Perrett**
DIRECTOR: **Paul Bogart**
AIR DATE: **November 20, 1976**
★

Episode 11
"Mr. Edith Bunker"
WRITERS: **Mel Tolkin, Larry Rhine**
DIRECTOR: **Paul Bogart**
AIR DATE: **November 27, 1976**
★

Episode 12
"Archie's Secret Passion"
WRITERS: **Michael Loman**
DIRECTOR: **Paul Bogart**
AIR DATE: **December 4, 1976**
★

Episode 13
"The Baby Contest"
WRITERS: **Marion Zola, Ed Haas, Larry Rhine, Mel Tolkin**
DIRECTOR: **Paul Bogart**
AIR DATE: **December 11, 1976**
★

Episode 14
"Gloria's False Alarm"
WRITERS: **Phil Doran, Douglas Arango**
DIRECTOR: **Paul Bogart**
AIR DATE: **December 18, 1976**
★

Episode 15
"The Draft Dodger"
WRITERS: **Jay Moriarty, Mike Milligan**
DIRECTOR: **Paul Bogart**
AIR DATE: **December 25, 1976**
★

Episode 16
"The Boarder Patrol"
WRITERS: **Mel Tolkin, Larry Rhine**
DIRECTOR: **Paul Bogart**
AIR DATE: **January 8, 1977**
★

Episode 17
"Archie's Chair"
WRITERS: **Phil Doran, Douglas Arango**
DIRECTOR: **Paul Bogart**
AIR DATE: **January 15, 1977**
★

Episode 18
"Mike Goes Skiing"
WRITERS: **Ben Starr, Chuck Stewart**
DIRECTOR: **Paul Bogart**
AIR DATE: **January 22, 1977**
★

Episode 19
"Stretch Cunningham, Goodbye"
WRITERS: **Phil Doran, Douglas Arango, Milt Josefsberg**
DIRECTOR: **Paul Bogart**
AIR DATE: **January 29, 1977**
★

Episode 20
"The Joys of Sex"
WRITERS: **Erik Tarloff**
DIRECTOR: **Paul Bogart**
AIR DATE: **February 5, 1977**
★

Episode 21
"Mike the Pacifist"
WRITERS: **Phil Doran, Douglas Arango**
DIRECTOR: **Paul Bogart**
AIR DATE: **February 12, 1977**
★

Episode 22
"Fire"
WRITERS: **Michael Loman, Larry Rhine, Mel Tolkin**
DIRECTOR: **Paul Bogart**
AIR DATE: **February 19, 1977**
★

Episode 23
"Mike and Gloria Split"
WRITERS: **Mort Lachman, Milt Josefsberg, Mel Tolkin, Larry Rhine**
DIRECTOR: **Paul Bogart**
AIR DATE: **February 26, 1977**
★

Episode 24
"Archie the Liberal"
WRITERS: **Ben Starr, Chuck Stewart**
DIRECTOR: **Paul Bogart**
AIR DATE: **March 5, 1977**
★

Episode 25
"Archie's Dog Day Afternoon"
WRITERS: **Mort Lachman, Milt Josefsberg, Chuck Stewart, Ben Starr**
DIRECTOR: **Paul Bogart**
AIR DATE: **March 12, 1977**

Season 8
1977–78

Episode 1 & 2
"Archie Gets the Business"
WRITERS: **Larry Rhine, Mel Tolkin**
DIRECTOR: **Paul Bogart**
AIR DATE: **October 2, 1977**
★

Episode 3
"Cousin Liz"
WRITERS: **Barry Harman, Harve Brosten, Bob Weiskopf, Bob Schiller**
DIRECTOR: **Paul Bogart**
AIR DATE: **October 9, 1977**

★

Episode 4 & 5
"Edith's 50th Birthday"
WRITERS: **Bob Weiskopf, Bob Schiller**
DIRECTOR: **Paul Bogart**
AIR DATE: **October 16, 1977**

★

Episode 6
"Unequal Partners"
WRITERS: **Chuck Stewart, Ben Starr**
DIRECTOR: **Paul Bogart**
AIR DATE: **October 23, 1977**

★

Episode 7
"Archie's Grand Opening"
WRITERS: **Mel Tolkin, Larry Rhine**
DIRECTOR: **Paul Bogart**
AIR DATE: **October 30, 1977**

★

Episode 8
"Archie's Bitter Pill: Part 1"
WRITERS: **Mel Tolkin, Larry Rhine, William C. Rader, M.D.**
DIRECTOR: **Paul Bogart**
AIR DATE: **November 6, 1977**

★

Episode 9
"Archie's Bitter Pill: Part 2"
WRITERS: **Larry Rhine, Mel Tolkin**
DIRECTOR: **Paul Bogart**
AIR DATE: **November 13, 1977**

★

Episode 10
"Archie and the KKK: Part 1"
WRITERS: **Bob Weiskopf, Bob Schiller, Mort Lachman, Milt Josefsberg**
DIRECTOR: **Paul Bogart**
AIR DATE: **November 27, 1977**

★

Episode 11
"Archie and the KKK: Part 2"
WRITERS: **Bob Weiskopf, Bob Schiller**
DIRECTOR: **Paul Bogart**
AIR DATE: **December 4, 1977**

★

Episode 12
"Mike and Gloria Meet"
WRITERS: **Bob Weiskopf, Bob Schiller**
DIRECTOR: **Paul Bogart**
AIR DATE: **December 11, 1977**

★

Episode 13
"Edith's Crisis of Faith: Part 1"
WRITERS: **Erik Tarloff, Bob Weiskopf, Bob Schiller**
DIRECTOR: **Paul Bogart**
AIR DATE: **December 18, 1977**

★

Episode 14
"Edith's Crisis of Faith: Part 2"
WRITERS: **Mel Tolkin, Larry Rhine, Erik Tarloff**
DIRECTOR: **Paul Bogart**
AIR DATE: **December 25, 1977**

★

Episode 15
"The Commercial"
WRITERS: **Ben Starr, Ron Bloomberg**
DIRECTOR: **Paul Bogart**
AIR DATE: **January 8, 1978**

★

Episode 16
"Super Bowl Sunday"
WRITERS: **Bob Weiskopf, Bob Schiller**
DIRECTOR: **Paul Bogart**
AIR DATE: **January 15, 1978**

★

Episode 17
"Aunt Iola's Visit"
WRITERS: **Michael Loman, Albert E. Lewin**
DIRECTOR: **Paul Bogart**
AIR DATE: **January 22, 1978**

★

Episode 18
"Love Comes to the Butcher"
WRITER: **Phil Sharp**
DIRECTOR: **Paul Bogart**
AIR DATE: **February 5, 1978**

★

Episode 19
"Two's a Crowd"
WRITER: **Phil Sharp**
DIRECTOR: **Paul Bogart**
AIR DATE: **February 12, 1978**

★

Episode 20
"Stale Mates"
WRITERS: **Bob Weiskopf, Bob Schiller**
DIRECTOR: **Paul Bogart**
AIR DATE: **February 19, 1978**

★

Episode 21
"Archie's Brother"
WRITERS: **Larry Rhine, Mel Tolkin**
DIRECTOR: **Paul Bogart**
AIR DATE: **February 26, 1978**

★

Episode 22
"Mike's New Job"
WRITERS: **Mel Tolkin, Larry Rhine**
DIRECTOR: **Paul Bogart**
AIR DATE: **March 5, 1978**

★

Episode 23
"The Dinner Guest"
WRITERS: **Bob Weiskopf, Bob Schiller, Larry Rhine, Mel Tolkin**
DIRECTOR: **Paul Bogart**
AIR DATE: **March 12, 1978**

★

Episode 24
"The Stivics Go West"
WRITERS: **Bob Weiskopf, Bob Schiller**
DIRECTOR: **Paul Bogart**
AIR DATE: **March 19, 1978**

The Emmys
1977

Outstanding Lead Actor in a Comedy Series
CARROLL O'CONNOR

The Emmys
1978

Outstanding Comedy Series
MORT LACHMAN, EX. PROD., MILT JOSEFSBERG, PROD.

★

Outstanding Lead Actor in a Comedy Series
CARROLL O'CONNOR

★

Outstanding Lead Actress in a Comedy Series
JEAN STAPLETON

★

Outstanding Continuing Performance by a Supporting Actor in a Comedy Series
ROB REINER

★

Outstanding Writing in a Comedy Series
BOB WEISKOPF, TELEPLAY; BOB SCHILLER, TELEPLAY; BARRY HARMAN, STORY; HARVE BROSTEN, STORY – "COUSIN LIZ"

★

Outstanding Directing in a Comedy Series
PAUL BOGART – "EDITH'S 50TH BIRTHDAY"

★

THE SET

MICHAEL BRITTAIN, *Assistant to Art Director Don Roberts*: *All in the Family* was TV's first thirty-minute comedy shot on videotape, as opposed to film. And that meant everything about designing and decorating sets had to be changed.

The art director for the first ABC pilot's set was Edward S. Stephenson. For the second pilot, the art director was Henry C. Lickel. Then, beginning with the third pilot, the art director was Don Roberts, who was just starting out in the business but who went on to be incredibly accomplished in television. The things Don added to the set's design were based on his childhood home in Wilmington, California.

NORMAN LEAR: I was in a car going out to JFK Airport, and we drove down a few city blocks in Queens. Later, I pointed to a house in my mind's eye and said, "That's the kind of house Archie would live in." I had the crew go find a house in Queens. And that's what we laid out in L.A., months later, with the living room, kitchen, and staircase.

PETER CLEMENS, *Assistant Art Director*: The way it worked in Norman's company, the same stage would be used for multiple productions. Today, a multi-camera sitcom set will stay standing from the beginning of the season through the end. But we used the same stage, stage 11 at Metromedia Studios in Hollywood, for both *All in the Family* and *The Jeffersons*. That meant that twice each week, we would have to strike one show, and then, overnight, put up the sets for the other.

When the set arrived on the stage each week to be reassembled, the walls had to be joined, the seams at the corners covered up. And we'd do that with masking tape and touch-up paint that would be kind of fudged as an extension of the wallpaper. One time I think we actually repapered part of the set, such as on the stairway—but then we had to coat it with a tea-colored wash to make it look older.

JAMES COMISAR, *Founder and President of The Comisar Collection, which preserves television memorabilia*: Every stitch of wallpaper on those walls was probably a close-out or discontinued even by the time the show had started. They just went to the bargain bin for the wallpaper, just as they did for the furniture. Since the Comisar Collection has acquired the set, we've had painters come in to hand paint some of the flowers that are missing on the wallpaper, because there's no way to replace it.

The prints that hung on the walls were the lowest-grade artwork you could ever possibly purchase. No artist names, no identifying markings, but just stuff from the '60s you could get at a dime store. I'm sure that, like the chairs, the artwork must also have been acquired from thrift outlets. The problem is, go try to find another to match if you needed to.

There was an inset of faux stained glass in the cabinet door. Real glass might create reflections, so the stained-glass effect is just paint on a piece of plexiglass.

Much of the wood on the set is real wood, but it was painted with a faux woodgrain by the art department, to add a theatrical touch that looks a little bit more distinct for camera. Back then,

cameras were primitive. So they also would just paint pieces of masking tape and stick them over any dings in the wood. They didn't have to sweat the details as much back then. Anything from the brown family would look good enough on camera.

Most of Edith's bric-a-brac in the living and dining rooms has to do with animals. There was a golden elephant sitting by the front door, on the table by the couch. On the buffet, center stage, there were ceramic plates featuring blue jays and other birds, and a camel played very prominently on the counter near the dining room.

PETER CLEMENS: The entire floor of the Bunker living room and dining room set was covered with a light-colored indoor/outdoor carpeting that was then painted with vinyl latex paint. The living room "rug" was created with a big stencil design, and the "wood floor" of the dining room was actually just a design painted on the same carpet. It was done in order to keep the floor even, so that the camera could roll anywhere onto the set.

But the paint had to be refreshed because of the constant traffic. So we'd have to bring in painters and bring out the stencils again.

One of my final jobs in the TV business, before I left to work for Universal Studios, was to pack up Archie's chair and send it to the Smithsonian, after having it reconditioned. After so many years of use, the chair had been falling apart. It had been kind of spuriously repaired several times, but was always a tumble-down wreck of a chair. The cushions got flatter over time, and the antimacassars would get dirty and would have to be replaced—and then they finally dispensed with the antimacassars altogether. Before sending the chair to the Smithsonian, we sent it to an upholsterer in Beverly Hills, Oscar Bazan, who reconditioned it, and glued it all back together again.

MICHAEL BRITTAIN: After the end of *Archie Bunker's Place*, the set went to Western Studio Service for storage. But after a while standing upright in storage, the walls were a mess.

JAMES COMISAR: I was walking through a massive warehouse, working on another project, when I saw a bit of a set wall sticking out. They store set walls sort of like dominoes, side by side by side, standing up; and when they do, gravity begins to take its toll. I saw a few inches of wallpaper, and my brain said, "That's the Bunker home!" I met with Norman Lear, and asked him for the set. He was going to have to think about it—but when he heard that Johnny Carson had just given me his set a few weeks before, he said yes right on the spot. "If it's good enough for Johnny, it's good enough for me."

MICHAEL BRITTAIN: I identified everything from *All in the Family* in that warehouse, and put it on trucks to send it to James Comisar. In those days, they used Masonite for the walls—and even as they were driving the *All in the Family* set to be restored, pieces of the walls were flying off onto the highway. The walls were disintegrating.

JAMES COMISAR: Since 1993, 168 structural pieces and furnishings from the *All in the Family* set have been maintained and conserved in climate-, light- and humidity-controlled storage at the Comisar Collection archive. They're part of television's tangible history—and a part of the story of our lives.

Season 9

AND THAT'S A WRAP

4 Episodes that Closed the Arc

I was not as involved in season nine. Carroll became showrunner, and in doing so, made some big changes: the show returned to the CBS Television City lot, and was now filmed without a live audience. That's a very different experience for actors as their comedic timing would be totally different without an audience to respond to. But I think Carroll, having taken on active, behind-the-scenes roles while still playing Archie, was thinking about the direction and the production. I also have to say that there was only one man who could ever realize Archie Bunker as he was realized, and that was Carroll O'Connor. I'll never be anything but deeply indebted to that man.

—NORMAN LEAR

Season 9, Episode 1
"Little Miss Bunker"

———

Season 9, Episodes 12 and 13
"California, Here We Are"

———

Season 9, Episode 20
"Stephanie's Conversion"

———

Season 9, Episode 1
"LITTLE MISS BUNKER"

EDITH'S NE'ER-DO-WELL COUSIN FLOYD LEAVES HIS DAUGHTER, STEPHANIE, WITH ARCHIE AND EDITH.

WRITTEN BY: **Mel Tolkin** and **Larry Rhine** • DIRECTED BY: **Paul Bogart**

GUEST STARS: **Danielle Brisebois** as **Stephanie Mills** • **Marty Brill** as **Floyd Mills**
Jason Wingreen as **Harry Snowden** • **Bhetty Waldron** as **Woman** • **Santos Morales** as **Ticket Agent**
Bern Bennett as **Sports Broadcaster** (voice)

ORIGINAL AIR DATE: **September 24, 1978**

NORMAN LEAR: At the start of season 9, the only person who wanted to continue in the show and their role was Carroll. And so with Mike and Gloria gone, we had to find a new entity, to introduce a new something, that would bring out a brand-new side of the character of Archie Bunker, something for him to have to deal with. We decided on the problems of being a father to a small girl at his age. So we introduced the character of Stephanie for that purpose. Later on, at the end of season 9, Jean wanted to move on, too. Her husband was back east, and she wanted to go back, too. Just talking about that time, I'm experiencing it myself all over again....That's the sadness that I talk about, that the show is over.

DANIELLE BRISEBOIS: Norman Lear had seen me in *Annie* on Broadway, right about the time when I was getting too big for the role I was in, Molly. The producers wanted me to wait six months, and then possibly play the role of Annie.

My mother used to joke with people backstage at *Annie*, asking, "Did Hollywood call today?" She told them, "One day, I'm going to call you from Hollywood." So we went to L.A. for two weeks to try to make something happen. Charles Strouse, who wrote the music for *Annie*, had also co-written the theme song to *All in the Family*. So we were able to get in to meet with Norman Lear that way.

I spent some time talking with Norman in his office, and afterward, as we were shaking hands to say goodbye, my mother asked, "Danielle, did you sing to Norman?" I said I hadn't, so Norman brought us into this little room and said he'd be right there. My mother had brought along a tape I used to use when I was six and did a nightclub act in New York, with the song "City Lights." It's a belt song, a way to show off your voice. And so when Norman came back into the room, I sang it. And suddenly, there was applause outside the door. Norman had gathered everyone outside the door to listen.

Norman said to me, "You've just done so much for me. Now what can I do for you?" And I replied, very cheekily, "You can give me a job!" I already loved *All in the Family*, as well as *Maude* and *The Jeffersons*. And I came from Brooklyn, where everybody knows an Archie Bunker in their family.

The characters of Mike and Gloria had just left, so my meeting was perfect timing, because they were trying to figure out what to do with the show. And Carroll seemed really taken with the idea, when we met, of having a kid on the show.

So they wrote a part for me—my mom called back to New York to tell the people at *Annie* that we'd be staying in L.A. And she started that phone call with, "I'm calling from Hollywood...."

_____

FLOYD: Gee, Arch,
I hate to ask for help.

ARCHIE: Good, 'cause I hate to
give it. Especially if it's money.

FLOYD: Oh no, this ain't
about money.

ARCHIE: Then you got a chance.

FLOYD: I need you to watch
Stephanie for a few weeks.

ARCHIE: You had a better
chance at money.

_____

RECEIVED

NOV 0 3 1979

Janeen M. Fischer

Oct. 19, 1979

Dear Archie + Edith,

My granddaughter who
will be four next month,
loves Stephanie. Would it
be possible for you to send
her a picture of the three
of you? It will mean a
lot of happiness for her.

Thank you very much.

Sincerely,

"CALIFORNIA, HERE WE ARE"

THE BUNKERS ARRIVE IN CALIFORNIA FOR CHRISTMAS TO LEARN THAT THE STIVICS ARE PLANNING TO GET DIVORCED.

WRITTEN BY: **Milt Josefsberg, Phil Sharp, Bob Schiller,** *and* **Bob Weiskopf** ● DIRECTED BY: **Paul Bogart**

★ EMMY AWARD: **Outstanding Supporting Actress in a Comedy or Comedy-Variety or Music Series** ★

GUEST STARS: **Danielle Brisebois** as **Stephanie Mills** ● **Cory R. Miller** as **Joey Stivic**
Rob Reiner as **Mike Stivic** ● **Sally Struthers** as **Gloria Stivic**

ORIGINAL AIR DATE: **December 17, 1978**

NORMAN LEAR: Rob and Sally had just left *All in the Family* at the end of the previous season, but it wasn't hard to get them to come back on the show as guest stars for these two episodes; I called Rob at four o'clock on a Friday afternoon and Sally Saturday morning, and asked if they were free. They loved their roles and the continuity of the Bunkers' storyline, and I think they were happy with the notion of wrapping up those performances.

For some weeks as we had approached what we knew to be Rob and Sally's final episodes in season 8, it had been quite emotional. Now these episodes brought up new emotions, as we found out Mike and Gloria were headed for a divorce. I wasn't afraid that fans would be upset by the divorce; if I had been, I wouldn't have done it, so close to what would be the overall ending for *All in the Family*. But the divorce did feel like an ending within an ending.

DANIELLE BRISEBOIS: After Rob Reiner and Sally Struthers had left *All in the Family* at the end of the previous season, there was definitely excitement in the air to have them back for this episode. I was really excited not just to work with them, whom I'd watched on the show, but I was also excited to get to meet Joey! I remember the episode where Joey was born, and that it was such a big deal—they even made a doll of his character. So I was excited to get to do this episode

with the Joey character. I'm going to get to meet and play with Joey? It was the equivalent of getting to meet Tabitha from *Bewitched!* So the whole week was fun for me—and I remember there were definitely a lot of emotions flying around the set that week.

SALLY STRUTHERS: Mike and Gloria had left the show and moved to California—but wouldn't you know, the next year on *All in the Family*, they wrote this episode where Edith, Archie, and Stephanie go out to California to visit them. And I, Sally Struthers, was pregnant when they shot that episode.

They didn't want to mention that I was pregnant, because it would be too awkward with the storyline that Mike and Gloria were splitting up. So costume designer Rita Riggs had to costume me in a way that hopefully didn't show it yet. I obviously was heavier than the last time viewers saw me, so they wrote a line when I was in the bathroom, crying to Edith about how my marriage wasn't working, and then all of a sudden, I let out a great lament: "And I'm fat!"

The funniest part about doing this episode is what happened afterward. Rita had made me the most beautiful baby-blue and wine-colored jacket and skirt, and there were beautiful boots that matched. It was a glorious outfit, and I asked her at the end if I could have it because it fit me so well. A few weeks later, in December, my husband and I were headed to Lake

Tahoe before going to Oregon for Christmas. This was in the days when you dressed nicely to travel.

We got to Tahoe late at night, in the worst snowstorm they'd had in thirty years. From our rental car we could hardly see ten feet in front of us, and had to retrieve housekeys and a map to the place we would be staying from where the realtor had left them, behind a billboard. The snow was a foot high, and the streets were dark by the time we felt we were in the right neighborhood. Finally, there was a house with its lights on, where you could tell the people inside were watching TV.

I knocked on the door to ask about the address we were looking for. It was probably the most surreal moment of my life when a woman answered the door, and as I started to say, "Hi, my husband and I are looking for…" I saw her eyes get big. She turned to look at her TV, then back at me, with her mouth hanging open. When I looked around the corner into their living room at the TV, there I was, in this episode, wearing that very same outfit. The woman could hardly talk, but managed finally to say, "The house is right next door."

ALL IN THE FAMILY WAS MUST-SEE VIEWING in our house when I was growing up. I was fourteen when it came on the air. Even at that age I was blown away by it. I'd never seen a show that could be shocking and hilarious in the same moment. I could also relate to it because my parents were ardent liberals, while my grandfather was an old-school New Yorker who still pronounced "toilet" as "terlet."

While my writing style is nothing like his, I always took to heart Norman's insistence on honesty in the work. It was never enough just to be funny. There always needed to be an emotional investment to the stories we were telling. It's a lesson that has always served me well. Oh, and Norman Lear was the first person to point out that I was going bald. It was our very first meeting with him. Obviously, I was nervous. It was *Norman Lear*! He couldn't have been sweeter or more disarming. At one point the conversation turned to a photo on his desk of him in his youth. He still had hair then. He told us that he was just starting to lose his hair when the picture was taken.

"Like David." My jaw dropped. Up until then I truly had no idea.

—*THE POWERS THAT BE*, *FRIENDS*, AND *EPISODES* CO-CREATOR DAVID CRANE

"STEPHANIE'S CONVERSION"

ARCHIE RELUCTANTLY AGREES TO REGISTER AT THE LOCAL TEMPLE TO HONOR
STEPHANIE'S JEWISH HERITAGE AND CONTINUE HER RELIGIOUS EDUCATION.

WRITTEN BY: **Patt Shea** and **Harriett Weiss** • DIRECTED BY: **Paul Bogart**

GUEST STARS: **Danielle Brisebois** as **Stephanie Mills** • **Clyde Kusatsu** as **Reverend Chong**
Michael Mann as **Rabbi Jacobs**

ORIGINAL AIR DATE: **February 18, 1979**

NORMAN LEAR: By the ninth season we had done so much with these characters, and what we always wanted to continue doing was to stretch. And so we went through a lot of thinking: What kind of situation would get Archie to stretch? We came up with the idea of this little girl he was coming to love, and responsible for raising, having a different religious background. We considered, should we do a Catholic thing? A Jewish thing? A this or a that?

Now, as I think back at it, I love what we were doing there. Archie had used derogatory words for every group, including Jews, and here he is, putting a new Star of David necklace on Stephanie. It's such a loving moment, and a testament to how powerful Carroll was as an actor.

DANIELLE BRISEBOIS: Growing up in the Flatlands neighborhood in Brooklyn, we were the only non-Jewish family on an all-Jewish block, and all my friends were Jewish. My best friend was Orthodox, so I understood a lot of the traditions and beliefs. It wasn't a mystery to me when Stephanie turned out to be Jewish, and I worked hard to get it right. In fact, later, on *Archie Bunker's Place*, Stephanie had her bat mitzvah. The show brought in a female cantor to come to the set and work with me for a few weeks before the taping, to teach me Stephanie's Torah portion phonetically so I could be as respectful as possible to the religion.

I don't know what happened to the Star of David that Archie gives Stephanie in this episode—but I do still have the overalls I wore in the first show I did, "Little Miss Bunker," because they were actually mine. Some of the other clothes I had to wear on the show, I didn't like. There was a lot of rust and gold and brown. Nobody really had hip clothes on the show. But that was part of the statement about the Bunkers.

Carroll was a joy to work with. He loved to sing together on the show. And he knew his character so well. In the scene at the end of this episode, where we're on the front porch and Archie gives Stephanie the Star of David necklace, we improvised a lot of that. Carroll kind of went off script, and I had learned always to follow his lead. I know that scene meant a lot to viewers. Especially for Jewish viewers, I think it really gave them a connection. Many times, I would go somewhere—particularly when the show moved back to CBS' Television Studios, which is in the Fairfax District in Los Angeles—and people would ask where my star was. Or they would say, "Such a lovely Jewish girl." I would say, "I'm not actually Jewish, but I love it." And my mother would say to me, "Are you happy? You wanted to be Jewish, and you got your way."

PATT SHEA: CBS had promised Jean Stapleton that they'd bring some women writers onto *All in the Family*. Mort Lachman, the showrunner, told my partner, Harriett Weiss, and me at eleven o'clock one

ARCHIE: You know, you gotta love somebody to give 'em one of them.
I mean, you gotta love everything about them.

---

morning about Jean's goal to hire women writers. He asked us to write up an audition piece for him to give to her at one o'clock that afternoon. So we did, and Jean liked it.

Jean was a wonderful woman. I had worked on the show years earlier as an extra, before I became a writer. And Jean treated me the same way as an extra that she later would as a writer. She was the kindest and most gentle woman.

This was at a time when women were just break-ing into comedy. In fact, when we were working on *All in the Family* and *Archie Bunker's Place*, there were two old-time male writers on the show. One of them really thought women can't be comedy writers—they can be actresses, and they can be comedians, but they really can't be comedy writers. And his wife is the one who told us that's what he would say. But in that last year of *All in the Family*, Harriett and I wrote quite a few of the scripts. We really loved working on that show. It was so much fun.

1/3/79
4:50 P.M.

I'm Norman Lear.

ALL IN THE FAMILY has two sets of stars --
our cast -- and you, our audience.

So, how would you like to come to California
for a weekend at our expense -- to attend
ALL IN THE FAMILY's 200th Episode Anniversary
Celebration on February 19th?

To qualify, drop a note to ALL IN THE FAMILY.
Give us your address, phone number, and a paragraph
as to why you would like to be with us. We
will select 200 couples from all over the country.

See you in February.

200th Episode Celebration

The 200th Episode Celebration of *All in the Family* aired on Sunday, March 4, 1979. Directed by Walter C. Miller, it was hosted by Norman Lear and taped in front of a live audience on February 19, 1979 at the Mark Taper Forum of the Los Angeles Music Center.

One hundred couples from forty-eight states were selected in a random drawing to attend the show, followed by an after-show party with the cast members.

ALL OF *ALL IN THE FAMILY*
Season 9

Season 9
1978–79

Episode 1
"Little Miss Bunker"
WRITERS: **Mel Tolkin, Larry Rhine**
DIRECTOR: **Paul Bogart**
AIR DATE: **September 24, 1978**

★

Episode 2
"End in Sight"
WRITER: **Nate Monaster**
DIRECTOR: **Paul Bogart**
AIR DATE: **October 1, 1978**

★

Episode 3
"Reunion on Hauser Street"
WRITERS: **Milt Josefsberg, Phil Sharp**
DIRECTOR: **Paul Bogart**
AIR DATE: **October 8, 1978**

★

Episode 4
"What'll We Do With Stephanie?"
WRITERS: **Larry Rhine, Mel Tolkin**
DIRECTOR: **Paul Bogart**
AIR DATE: **October 15, 1978**

★

Episode 5
"Edith's Final Respects"
WRITERS: **Sam Greenbaum, Bob Schiller, Bob Weiskopf**
DIRECTOR: **Paul Bogart**
AIR DATE: **October 22, 1978**

★

Episode 6
"Weekend in the Country"
WRITERS: **Phil Sharp, Milt Josefsberg**
DIRECTOR: **Paul Bogart**
AIR DATE: **October 29, 1978**

★

Episode 7
"Archie's Other Wife"
WRITERS: **Bob Schiller, Bob Weiskopf**
DIRECTOR: **Paul Bogart**
AIR DATE: **November 5, 1978**

★

Episode 8
"Edith vs. the Bank"
WRITERS: **Mel Tolkin, Larry Rhine**
DIRECTOR: **Air Date: Paul Bogart**
AIR DATE: **November 19, 1978**

★

Episode 9
"Return of the Waitress"
WRITERS: **Milt Josefsberg, Phil Sharp**
DIRECTOR: **Paul Bogart**
AIR DATE: **November 26, 1978**

★

Episode 10
"Bogus Bills"
WRITERS: **Bob Schiller, Bob Weiskopf**
DIRECTOR: **Paul Bogart**
AIR DATE: **December 3, 1978**

★

Episode 11
"The Bunkers Go West"
WRITERS: **Mel Tolkin, Larry Rhine**
DIRECTOR: **Paul Bogart**
AIR DATE: **December 10, 1978**

★

Episodes 12 and 13
"California, Here We Are"
WRITERS: **Milt Josefsberg, Phil Sharp, Bob Schiller, Bob Weiskopf**
DIRECTOR: **Paul Bogart**
AIR DATE: **December 17, 1978**

★

Episode 14
"A Night at the PTA"
WRITERS: **Larry Rhine, Mel Tolkin**
DIRECTOR: **Paul Bogart**
AIR DATE: **January 7, 1979**

★

Episode 15
"A Girl Like Edith"
WRITERS: **Bob Schiller, Bob Weiskopf**
DIRECTOR: **Paul Bogart**
AIR DATE: **January 14, 1979**

★

Episode 16
"The Appendectomy"
WRITERS: **Phil Sharp, Milt Josefsberg**
DIRECTOR: **Paul Bogart**
AIR DATE: **January 21, 1979**

★

Episode 17
"Stephanie and the Crime Wave"
WRITERS: **Mel Tolkin, Larry Rhine**
DIRECTOR: **Paul Bogart**
AIR DATE: **January 28, 1979**

★

Episode 18
"Barney the Gold Digger"
WRITERS: **Winston Moss, Bob Schiller, Bob Weiskopf, Phil Sharp, Milt Josefsberg**
DIRECTOR: **Paul Bogart**
AIR DATE: **February 5, 1979**

★

Episode 19
"The Return of Archie's Brother"
WRITERS: **Tom Sawyer, Bob Schiller, Bob Weiskopf**
DIRECTOR: **Paul Bogart**
AIR DATE: **February 11, 1979**

★

Episode 20
"Stephanie's Conversion"
WRITERS: **Patt Shea, Harriett Weiss**
DIRECTOR: **Paul Bogart**
AIR DATE: **February 18, 1979**

★

Episode 21
"Edith Gets Fired"
WRITERS: **Mort Lachman, Harriett Weiss, Patt Shea**
DIRECTOR: **Paul Bogart**
AIR DATE: **February 25, 1979**

★

Episode 22
"The Family Next Door"
WRITERS: **Mel Tolkin, Larry Rhine**
DIRECTOR: **Paul Bogart**
AIR DATE: **March 11, 1979**

★

Episode 23
"The Return of Stephanie's Father"
WRITERS: **Larry Rhine, Mel Tolkin**
DIRECTOR: **Paul Bogart**
AIR DATE: **March 25, 1979**

★

Episode 24
"Too Good Edith"
WRITERS: **Harriett Weiss, Patt Shea**
DIRECTOR: **Paul Bogart**
AIR DATE: **April 8, 1979**

The Emmys
1979

Outstanding Supporting Actress in a Comedy or Comedy-Variety or Music Series
SALLY STRUTHERS –
"CALIFORNIA, HERE WE ARE"

★

Outstanding Lead Actor in a Comedy Series
CARROLL O'CONNOR

All in the Family's Legacy

THE LAUGHTER CONTINUES

5 Encores

No discussion about *All in the Family* could be complete without including its enduring and widespread effect on the television landscape, and how it has been permanently enshrined as a treasured piece of American culture. Of the countless shows that have been on television, *All in the Family* ranks as arguably the show whose spinoffs were not only critical and popular hits in their own right, but also continued *All in the Family*'s mission to reflect and remark on the American experience. The show's impact on American culture was codified when the United States Postal Service issued an *All in the Family* stamp and the Smithsonian Institution took possession of Archie and Edith's chairs. And in 2019, two television specials re-created—live—in front of a studio audience, episodes of the show for television audiences across the country.

The Stamp

The Spin-Offs

The Smithsonian

Live in Front of a Studio Audience:
'All in the Family' and 'The Jeffersons'

Live in Front of a Studio Audience:
'All in the Family' and 'Good Times'

As part of the United States Postal Service's "Celebrate the Century" series, *All in the Family* was immortalized on a stamp issued in November 1999.

THE SPIN-OFFS
1971–1994

MAUDE **(1972–78)**

GOOD TIMES **(1974–79)**

THE JEFFERSONS **(1975–84)**

CHECKING IN **(1981)**

ARCHIE BUNKER'S PLACE **(1979–83)**

GLORIA **(1982–83)**

---

704 HAUSER **(1994)**

NORMAN LEAR: From the moment I saw Bea Arthur in rehearsal as Cousin Maude in season 2, I knew the network would ask me to give Bea her own spinoff. Then, in the first season of *Maude*, we had James Evans, played by John Amos, come pick up his wife, Florida Evans, played by Esther Rolle. The very day that played in New York, I got the call from CBS that they could see a show set around them, which became *Good Times*.

So in just a few years, I had gone from having one show on the air to having four. I would be in my office, and representatives from each show's writing staff would come in, one after another, to pitch me the stories they were working on that week. I can't say that allowed me to stay involved with every story on every show, but I don't recall missing much of *All in the Family*. I stayed pretty close.

It was during this time that Bud and I realized that in order both to keep creating shows and retaining ownership and distribution, rather than being just CBS employees, we needed help. So, I replaced myself within our company, Tandem Productions, with a business guy I had great belief in, Alan Horn, who now runs Disney. I remember having lunch with him at the Beverly Hills Hotel, and telling him that I had asked all of my comedy friends, like Larry Gelbart, Mel Brooks, and Carl Reiner, if they would like to take my job. These were guys who were already doing one or two shows, and they all said they didn't see how they could do that and couldn't see how I was doing it. I remember telling them that if someone had come to me and asked me to take over four shows, I don't think I could have done it either.

But our company had a culture in which if the climate demanded another leg, I grew another leg. If it demanded another neck, I grew another neck. If I hadn't been planted in that soil, I never would have been able to come in and run four shows that were already on the air and doing well. These years in the early- to mid-'70s were a stressful time, but the expression I use to describe them is "joyful stress." There is stress in life from which one can simply get joy.

"Maude" #0406
Polling Party Scene

yoke?

MAUDE
1972–78

Edith's cousin Maude Findlay (Bea Arthur) lives with her fourth husband, Walter (Bill Macy), her daughter, Carol (Marcia Rodd in the *All in the Family* pilot and Adrienne Barbeau in the series), and Carol's son, Phillip (Brian Morrison and Kraig Metzinger). The Findlay's housekeeper, Mrs. Naugatuck (Hermione Baddeley), is hired to fill the void left by Florida Evans (Esther Rolle), who gets spun-off into her own series. Maude's politics often put her at odds with their conservative Republican neighbor Arthur (Conrad Bain) and his wife, Vivian (Rue McClanahan).

GOOD TIMES
1974–79

Maude's maid, Florida Evans (Esther Rolle), lives in the projects of Chicago with her husband James (John Amos) and their children, J.J. (Jimmie Walker), Thelma (Bern Nadette Stanis), and Michael (Ralph Carter), and their neighbor, Willona (Ja'net Dubois), who adopts Penny (Janet Jackson).

THE JEFFERSONS
1975–84

The Bunkers' next-door neighbors George (Sherman Helmsley), Louise (Isabel Sanford), and Lionel (Mike Evans and Damon Evans) move up to the East Side of Manhattan in the same apartment building as Tom and Helen Willis (Franklin Cover and Roxie Roker), their daughter Jenny (Berlinda Tolbert), and Harry Bentley (Paul Benedict), along with the building's money-hungry doorman, Ralph Hart (Ned Wertimer). While George battles with their maid, Florence (Marla Gibbs), Louise often contends with her mother-in-law, "Mother" Jefferson (Zara Cully).

CHECKING IN
1981

The Jefferson's maid, Florence, gets a job as executive housekeeper in a Manhattan hotel.

ARCHIE BUNKER'S PLACE
1979–83

After Edith's death, Archie concentrates on raising Stephanie (Danielle Brisebois) and tending to his bar, co-owned by Murray (Martin Balsam), as well as its employees including Veronica (Anne Meara), and regulars including Barney (Allan Melvin).

GLORIA
1982–83

Gloria (Sally Struthers), now divorced from Mike and raising Joey (Christian Jacobs) on her own, moves back to New York and works for veterinarians (Burgess Meredith and Jo de Winter).

704 HAUSER
1994

African-American Ernie (John Amos) and Rose (Lynnie Godfrey) Cumberbatch live in the Bunkers' old house with their son, conservative-leaning "Goodie" (T.E. Russell) and his white, Jewish girlfriend, Cherlyn Markowitz (Maura Tierney).

RECEIVED

APR 1 8 1980

NORMAN LEAR

april 4,1980

Dear Mr. President:

Who can deny that we are all living in very trying times. It seems that each day brings a new crisis, equally as unanswerable as yesterdays crisis. Now we are faced with another national calamity. Not as mind boggling as some but nevertheless an other chunk from the foundation.

Now Mr. President, I can fully appreciate the weighty problems that rest on your shoulders and you need one more like you need an other Iran. However, you are the voice of the people and we the people of America need to know where you stand on all issues, large or small.

PLEASE READ THE ENCLOSED NEWS RELEASE.

Now I ask you Sir," Are we, the public, going to allow Mr. Lear to kill Edith off without a fight-------are we going to stand passively by and permit our beloved Edith to die an ignominious death?" She is family. If we allow Mr. Lear and Archy to "kill her off" then how long will it be before Mickey does away with Minnie, the POP is taken out of the corn, Jack Armstrong refuses his Wheaties. I tell you, we don't have to many things to hang on to anymore. When they take a-way our dingbats we are really in deep trouble. There is no need to end her life this way. Why can't she go to college, be an American Ambassador, a congresswomen, president (After your next term is up), anything as long as she is not lost to us forever.

Please Mr. President, we need your support. Let us know that you care. Let Mr. Lear and Archie know publicly that we will per-sonally oppose any move to Kill our Edith.

The Hitlers of the world come and go but OUR EDITH LIVES ON.

Thanking you for your time and consideration, I remain,

ALL OF NORMAN'S SHOWS "WERE" TV. They *were* my first "other families" I really got to know. I don't think I could be overstating it to say they're how I developed my personal view of the importance of family in making it through tough times and laughing in the best times. They're also how and why I connected so much with storytelling as an art form. Finally, they provided comfort and joy to most of us regular folks living totally mundane American lives. They set the standard that TV could be not just mainstream entertainment, but at its best it could also be smart and important, both reflecting the culture and moving it forward.

I remember crying for the first time at a TV show when Edith died on *Archie Bunker's Place*, and Archie sat on the bed crying, holding Edith's slippers. I have often aspired to make TV shows that make people feel emotions in both directions. For me, a show that could make me laugh that deeply and cry that much and still entertain a whole family watching together—that is the best this medium can offer.

—TV AND FILM WRITER, EXECUTIVE PRODUCER AND DIRECTOR GREG BERLANTI

Thank you again for sharing your thoug[...]

Sincerely,

Norman Lear

Norman Lear

P.S. If you wish to remember Edith by way of a donation to the Edith Bunker Memorial Fund for the E.R.A., a check may be sent to:

June 27th, 1980

Dear Norman Lear :-

After reading your letter and you still decided to the death of Edith Bunker, I could not believe you could be so dead against Edith. There are so many ways you could find to preserve Edith, than pull the plug.

And at the end of your letter where you write you will create in her name a Memorial Fund of $500,000.°° for the E.R.A., I became extremely angry that you would donated one half million dollars to E.R.A.

It is not a charity :- Why not donate to several charities.

To me E.R.A. is for Homo's — Homosexuality + Lesbians 90% — 10% are innocent E.R.A. members

(see other side)

SMITHSONIAN INSTITUTION

THE NATIONAL MUSEUM OF HISTORY AND TECHNOLOGY

WASHINGTON, D.C. 20560

April 24, 1979

Mr. Norman Lear
Tandem/TAT Productions
5752 Sunset Boulevard
Los Angeles, California   90028

Dear Mr. Lear:

On behalf of the National Museum of History and Technology, I would like to thank you for your donation to this museum of the "Archie" and "Edith Bunker" chairs, furnishings, and corresponding set designs. Because it has united comedy with serious social concerns, "All in the Family" has been a landmark in the history of American entertainment. We are proud to have such pivotal props from the show's set in our collections; moreover, the Bunker exhibit has been one of the most popular attractions in the museum since the day of its opening. The gift has been entered into our permanent records in the name of Tandem/TAT Productions, through you.

Our staff and guests thoroughly enjoyed the cast's presentation party last September. Once again, thank you for your generous contribution to the Smithsonian Institution.

THE SMITHSONIAN

RYAN LINTELMAN, *Curator, Entertainment Collection*: The Smithsonian has been around since 1846 as a national museum collecting great works of art. Our Museum of American History was originally called the Museum of History and Technology, a Cold War–era project to show off the greatest American achievements in technology and the arts. It wasn't until around the Bicentennial in 1976 that we changed our focus and started integrating more social and cultural history. And as part of that, my predecessor, Carl Scheele, was the first curator who focused on entertainment. He was looking for things that expressed the idea that entertainment is not something separate from the historical developments of the nation. It's not just diversion, but actually helps people to understand the world around them. And what better show to talk about that than *All in the Family*?

DWIGHT BOWERS, *Former Curator, Entertainment Collection*: The entertainment collection at the National Museum of American History really began with *All in the Family*. Archie and Edith Bunker's chairs were the first large artifacts we collected. We had not truly embraced props from television, but this allowed us to do it. *All in the Family* was such a groundbreaking achievement in American culture, and the chairs were seen as an equivalent of the Nixon-Kennedy debate in popular culture, because they were the locus for Archie and Edith's dialogues about current affairs.

Date ___13 April 1979___   Accession Number ___1978.2146___

THE NATIONAL MUSEUM OF HISTORY AND TECHNOLOGY

SMITHSONIAN INSTITUTION

ACCESSION MEMORANDUM

Department of ___Cultural History___   Division of ___Community Life___

Norman Lear   for

Accession From (include address):   Tandem/TAT Productions
5752 Sunset Blvd.
Los Angeles, California   90028

Credit Line ___Norman Lear   for   Tandem/TAT Productions___

Recorded as ___Gift___   Number ___Deed of Gift # 2246___

(gift, bequest, transfer, exchange, purchase, found-in-the-collections, collected for or made at NMHT)   (Deed of Gift, Purchase Order, Transfer Order, etc.)

Catalog Number

Index Number	Object (include dimensions)	Catalogue Number
.01	CHAIR, wing, upholstered, used by "Archie Bunker" W 26" x D 31" x H 40"	
.02	CHAIR, lolling (Martha Washington), back and seat upholstered (velour thistle motif on white satin-weave ground), wooden arms and legs, used by "Edith Bunker" W 25" x D 26" x H 35"	
.03	TABLE, wood, with semi-circular top, three turned legs, and lower shelf W 24" x D 12" x H 24"	
.04	DOILY, lace, white	
.05	ASHTRAY, glass, amber-colored, squared form with pebbled outer surface W 6" x L 6" x H 1 1/2"	
.06	BEER CAN, "Best Quality Beer", empty Anheuser-Busch can, with yellow paper label H 4 3/4" x D 2 1/2"	
.07	BEER CAN, "Best Quality Beer", empty Anheuser-Busch can, with yellow paper label H 4 3/4" x D 2 1/2"	
.08	DESIGN, Set, pencil and ink on paper, Sheet # 1 of 6	
.09	DESIGN, Set, pencil and ink on paper, Sheet # 2 of 6, L 34" x W 22"	
.10	DESIGN, Set, pencil and ink on paper, Sheet # 3 of 6, L 33 15/16" x W 22"	
.11	DESIGN, Set, pencil and ink on paper, Sheet # 4 of 6, L 34" x W 22"	
.12	DESIGN, Set, pencil and ink on paper, Sheet # 5 of 6, L 34" x W 22"	

Remarks: (include special conditions and restrictions, etc.) _____

.13   DESIGN, Set, pencil and ink on paper, Sheet # 6 of 6, L 22" x W 17"

Other Units: (implies distribution sheets have been forwarded)

Reference: ENTERTAINMENT, Television (All in the Family)

SEE ALSO NMAH/2003.0330 FOR A HAT WORN BY CARROLL O'CONNER ON "ALL IN THE FAMILY".

Carl H. Schule REA CK
(verification and authorization by Curator)

Genevieve Gremillion
(Registrar or Designate)

1
No. Cont. sheets attached _____

(All papers which relate to this accession are to be attached to this memorandum and forwarded to the Office of the Registrar.)

SI-2670
9-21-76

RYAN LINTELMAN: Apparently the chairs were not the first choice for *All in the Family*'s living room furniture. In our "accession files," which detail the history of our acquisition of the show's furniture, there is a 2003 notation by one of the Smithsonian researchers stating that he had learned in an interview that the show started with a rocking chair, but found that Carroll O'Connor had had trouble getting out of it on cue.

DWIGHT BOWERS: Our accepting the *All in the Family* chairs was somewhat controversial. The public was not sure that they wanted entertainment artifacts at the Smithsonian, which up until then showcased the American flag and aspects of politics and American history. Entertainment history was considered a little suspect. I'm happy to say we've risen above that thinking.

The chairs remain popular, not only with the people who saw them when the show was new. I have been on the floor of the museum when teenagers have come in and asked for the Bunkers' chairs. Because that's the power of syndication.

RYAN LINTELMAN: In our "spotlight cases" we have some of our most well-known objects; there's a case for the *Wizard of Oz* ruby slippers, one for Jim Henson's Muppets, one for Prince's guitar, and then the *All in the Family* chairs. These are really the objects that we're pulling aside and making easy to find, because they are among the most popular things in the museum.

DWIGHT BOWERS: The chairs, and the little wood demi-lune table that sits between them, have the look of perhaps a used furniture store. They have no furniture pedigree. I'm sure the production designer picked things that would be in a typical home of that location and of that era, and that would have aged with the characters. When we look at the furniture itself, we see, oh, this doesn't look like the pristine living room of *Ozzie and Harriet* or *I Love Lucy*. This is a lived-in living room.

RYAN LINTELMAN: Carl Scheele worked with Mr. Lear, and as the show was supposedly drawing to a close in 1978, the donation was offered and approved. Carl traveled from Washington to Los Angeles to attend what was to be the final taping of the show. But right before he was to leave for his trip, the news was received that the show was being renewed for another season. And so the show asked if they could hold on to the furniture for another year before sending it to us; we had to say no, and that we would have to decline the donation. In the end, the show decided to reproduce the furniture. They sent the first set off to the Smithsonian and created a second set of chairs for the show's use; this second set now resides in the James Comisar Collection.

JAMES COMISAR, *founder and president of the Comisar Collection*: If there are any objects on earth that represent Norman Lear's tour of duty through television, it is these chairs. The original two chairs had come from a Goodwill shop in or near Santa Monica, California. Rumor has it that both of the chairs cost $20 in 1970. But when the producers had to re-create them, they couldn't find textiles to match the original fabrics. They ended up having to use material that was hand-loomed in England for $400 per yard and then distressed using tire brushes. And so those chairs cost $10,000 to remake.

BRENT MILLER, *Executive Producer of* Live in Front of a Studio Audience: For the *Live in Front of a Studio Audience* shows in 2019, we empowered our production designer, Bernie Vygza, to have the chairs re-created yet again. His set decorator, Ron Olsen, took on the challenge and of course had no reason to regret it. They and our art director, Rich Rohrer, ended up earning a Primetime Emmy nomination for Outstanding Production Design for a Variety Special. I can only imagine the look on Edith and Archie's faces if they only knew how much it cost to have their favorite chairs replicated fifty years later.

RYAN LINTELMAN: In 2022, the *All in the Family* furniture will join our new permanent exhibition called "Entertaining America." This will be the showcase for the entertainment collection that we've now been building for decades, illustrating how important entertainment is to the development of the nation, shaping people's minds and giving them space to talk about political and social developments. And the chairs will be an important part of the exhibit, because *All in the Family* brought the changes that were happening in American society into people's living rooms.

"HENRY'S FAREWELL"

WRITTEN BY: **Don Nicholl** • DIRECTED BY: **James Burrows**

STARS: **Woody Harrelson** as **Archie Bunker** • **Marisa Tomei** as **Edith Bunker**
Ellie Kemper as **Gloria Stivic** • **Ike Barinholtz** as **Mike Stivic**

GUEST STARS: **Sean Hayes** as **Frank Lorenzo** • **Jovan Adepo** as **Lionel Jefferson**
Wanda Sykes as **Louise Jefferson** • **Anthony Anderson** as **Henry Jefferson** • **Jamie Foxx** as **George Jefferson**

LIVE IN FRONT OF A STUDIO AUDIENCE: **'All in the Family' and 'The Jeffersons'**

★ EMMYS 2019: Outstanding Variety Special (Live) ★

AIR DATE: **May 22, 2019**

"THE DRAFT DODGER"

WRITTEN BY: **Jay Moriarty** and **Mike Milligan** • DIRECTED BY: **Pamela Fryman**

STARS: **Woody Harrelson** as **Archie Bunker** • **Marisa Tomei** as **Edith Bunker**
Ellie Kemper as **Gloria Stivic** • **Ike Barinholtz** as **Mike Stivic**

GUEST STARS: **Justina Machado** as **Teresa Betancourt** • **Kevin Bacon** as **Pinky Peterson**
Jesse Eisenberg as **David Brewster**

LIVE IN FRONT OF A STUDIO AUDIENCE: **'All in the Family' and 'Good Times'**

★ EMMYS 2020: Outstanding Variety Special (Live) ★

AIR DATE: **December 18, 2019**

NORMAN LEAR: The idea to do what became *Live in Front of a Studio Audience* started with Jimmy Kimmel. At first he wanted to do something on his show with the characters, and then that thinking evolved. Jimmy spoke with my producing partner Brent Miller, and Brent found that there were people at the network and the studio who would want to do the show on TV.

Seeing those episodes performed again, you realize that nothing has changed. Human nature is human nature. All these years later, you still recognize these characters and these situations. It was a very emotional experience, to see that set again. I talked to the audience each time, and I know they, too, were involved emotionally in seeing the show again.

BRENT MILLER, *Executive Producer of* Live in Front of a Studio Audience: One of the reasons we agreed to bring back these shows—aside from wishing to work with Jimmy Kimmel—is that it felt like the perfect way to pay homage to the writers and actors who created them. We didn't change a single word in those scripts. Ultimately, our special ended as a love letter to those shows, to Norman, and the team of people who worked so hard to make these shows relevant fifty years later.

JAMES BURROWS: *All in the Family* stunned you: where they went, what they said. And Norman's shows make you laugh. It was monumental what that show accomplished, and I'm not sure any other comedy ever successfully went into the same areas, although some did try. I worked with Norman only once years ago, on a pilot that never sold. That's why I was so grateful to work with him again on *Live in Front of a Studio Audience*, just to pray at his feet and say how instrumental he is. And also to tell him that it's nice to be working with somebody who's older than me.

WOODY HARRELSON: Norman has a progressive mind so he really pushed forward on important issues like racial equality, anti-war sentiment, and feminism. His shows gave voice to people and communities that weren't always given a seat at the table back then. He definitely had a big influence on America's national conversations because his shows were so mainstream—nearly everyone was watching them. I remember never missing *All in the Family*, *Maude*, *Sanford & Son*, and *Good Times*. I would watch them religiously every week, and I think that was true for a lot of Americans at the time. He definitely had a big influence on me, for sure.

Norman has an incredible level of vitality, energy, and enthusiasm for life. At ninety-eight years old he is a paragon of good living, which in large part is due to his positivity. He says yes to life and has deep compassion for everyone. He has an incredibly open mind and never became cynical. The main thing I've learned from Norman is that saying yes to life is the only way to go.

MARISA TOMEI: When I was younger and watching *All in the Family*, I certainly related to Gloria, with her clothes and her youthfulness. Mike, with some of his perspectives, reminded me of my uncle. And even Archie felt like a grandpa kind of guy. But Edith was always a little distant for me, and kind of a conundrum. I just didn't understand why, from my young perspective, she was always taking a lot of crap. And that was what was so wonderful about this opportunity to work with Norman on *Live In Front of a Studio Audience*. I was trying to figure a way in to Edith. I realized that in television, the writers tailor a character a lot to the actor, so I started researching more about Jean: her early singing roles, and how she was known to be an incredibly, almost saint-level person of kindness and humility. I started to understand the amount of love she carried, and why she could then understand Archie. I had been seeing her personality as a weakness. But when I was asked to walk in her shoes, I had the privilege of bathing in that field of kindness. That opened up the character and also gave me a beautiful place to be in for a few weeks.

JOVAN ADEPO: As a child, I had watched *The Jeffersons*, and to a somewhat lesser extent, *All in the Family*. It wasn't until I was a little bit older when I grew more acquainted with both shows, watching them on networks like TV Land. The themes in those shows were timeless, the subject matter transcending the years for which they were originally created. So I was really excited to get to bring these stories back to life for a new audience.

It was eerie being on the Bunker living room set, but in a good way. One by one, I would notice the cast members like Anthony Anderson and Kerry Washington, who was doing *The Jeffersons*, that night, and even Jimmy Kimmel, coming in to walk by and then sit in Archie's chair, when they had their own private time to do so. And just looking around the set, trying not to make noise, but being in awe. And of course the production designers had done a fantastic job re-creating the set. Every one of us had a moment where we were walking around the kitchen, touching the props, and looking at the books on the shelves and the photos on the piano. It was such a special privilege,

and I think everyone knew that. So everyone was very tender, and made sure to take a moment to take it all in and appreciate what was going on and where they were.

PAMELA FRYMAN: I was 100 percent a TV kid, so to be able to direct was thrilling. When Jimmy Burrows, who directed the first one, called me, he told me that I'd be really scared, because it was scary, but that it was worth it. It was unlike anything that I've ever done before, and I wasn't allowed to say no.

It can't be overstated how beautiful "The Draft Dodger" is as an episode of TV. It touched on so many important things, was so beautifully written, and so incredibly acted. And when that door closes at the end, and you're looking at that wreath that says "Peace," if you didn't feel something, I don't know what you're made of. Because in my chair, I had chills. It was perfect.

I learned early on that Norman Lear's shows equaled quality. They were always smart and about something. You laughed and you learned. As a director, I think I learned not to get in the way of that, and to do anything possible to enhance the lessons. You want to serve the comedy and not add unnecessary distractions. Norman's shows absolutely reflect his personality. He is always hungry to be educated and to talk about what's important. But there is a delightfulness to his personality, and nobody loves to laugh more than Norman. And he is grateful for it. I've never known anyone who appreciates every second of his life more than he does. And he loves to share in that joy.

ACKNOWLEDGMENTS

This book was made possible with the support of a number of great talents. Special thanks to the estate of Johnny Speight, the creator in Great Britain of the celebrated *Till Death Us Do Part*.

To my partner, Bud Yorkin, who found *TDUDP* and introduced me to Beryl Vertue, who represented the property.

A special and heartfelt thank-you to Jimmy Kimmel for his enthusiastic foreword; to the estates and the genius of Carroll O'Connor and Jean Stapleton; and to the immeasurable talents of Rob Reiner and Sally Struthers.

Many thanks also to everyone who contributed their memories, insights, and images; among them the casts, crews, studio executives, and especially the many brilliant writers across the years with whom I spent the most delicious time and without whose talent the show *All in the Family* could not have existed.

At Sony, thanks to Sony Pictures Consumer Products and Sony Pictures Television. A special thank-you to Ed Zimmerman for his contributions to the book, and for the treasure of his archival knowledge.

Additional and special thanks to our dedicated Act III support team (both past and present): Jean Anderson, Michal Beaumont, Sam Fagan, Ana Maria Geraldino, Jonathan Goldberg, Laura Reich, Eric Rodriguez, and Cindy C. Villa; with deepest appreciation and gratitude to Julie Dyer, Jackie Jensen, Brent Miller, Mark E Pollack, Liana Schwarz, and Paul Slansky, whose talent and dedication helped make this book a reality.

Finally, and blessedly, thank you to Robb Pearlman, who has been part of this book since he first tapped the project for Universe; the Universe Publishing team, especially Charles Miers, Colin Hough Trapp, Lync, and Elizabeth Smith; and, most notably, to the remarkable writer of this book, Jim Colucci.

CREDITS

Front and back endpapers, p. 4: ©CBS / Photofest; p. 2: Michael Rougier / The LIFE Picture Collection / Getty Images; pp. 6, 7, 217, 218, 219 (bottom): © American Broadcasting Companies, Inc. All Rights reserved.; pp. 8, 126 (bottom left): Courtesy of Putch Family Archives; pp. 9, 10, 11, 12, 13, 20, 25, 27, 28, 31, 32, 34, 37, 46, 74–75, 81, 85, 91 (top left), 99, 107, 113, 116–17, 126 (letter), 159, 160, 167–71, 177, 178, 197, 210–11, 212, 221: Personal collection of Norman Lear; pp. 14, 48, 94, 148, 194, 205 (left): CBS Photo Archive/Getty Images; p. 19: Edward S. Stephenson, courtesy of Tara Stephenson-Fong; p. 21: Those Were the Days. By Charles Strouse and Lee Adams © 1971, renewed 1999 EMI Worldtrax Music Inc. All rights on behalf of EMI Worldtrax Music Inc. administered by Sony Music Publishing LLC, 424 Church Street, Suite 1200, Nashville, TN 37219. All rights reserved. Used by permission.; pp. 37, 46, 74–75, 85, 99, 116–17, 126, 177, 178, 210–11: (background) iStock.com / olgakr; pp. 40–41, 91, 220–21: (background) ArthurStock / Shutterstock .com; pp. 91 (top right, bottom), 136 (bottom right), 143 (bottom right): Courtesy of Liza Stewart; pp. 122, 131, 136 (top, left and right; bottom left), 137 (left and right), p. 138 (left and right), p. 139 (all), 140 (sketch), 141, 142 (top), 143 (sketch), 144 (all), 145 (top left; bottom, left and right), 146 (bottom), 147, 167 (top), 207: Courtesy of Ritahouse & Rita Riggs; pp. 126, 140, 143, 210–11: (photo frame) Krasovski Dmitri / Shutterstock.com; pp. 136, 139, 143, 144, 207: (background) Chekmareva Irina / Shutterstock.com; pp. 190–93: (background) Courtesy of Michael Brittain; pp. 191 (top), 192 (bottom), 193 (top): Courtesy of Sondra Garcia; pp. 192 (top), 193 (bottom): ©2021 Viacom International Inc. / TV Land's "All in the Family" / Personal collection of Norman Lear; p. 205 (right): PictureLake / Getty Images; p. 213: Photographer Ron Olsen / Show Set: "Live In Front of a Studio Audience – All in The Family", (American Broadcasting Companies, Inc) / Courtesy of Ron Olsen; p. 214: Division of Cultural and Community Life, National Museum of American History, Smithsonian Institution; p. 219 (top): Photographer Craig Atkinson / Show Set: "Live In Front of a Studio Audience – All in The Family", (American Broadcasting Companies, Inc). / Courtesy of Pamela Fryman.

A thank-you to The Interviews, especially its executives Adrienne Faillace and Jenni Matz. Visit TelevisionAcademy.com/Interviews for more information.

p. 16: CARROLL O'CONNOR Interview, by Charles Davis on August 13, 1999, for The Interviews: An Oral History of Television; pp. 18, 29, 71, 93, 104: JEAN STAPLETON Interview, by Karen Herman on November 28, 2000, for The Interviews: An Oral History of Television; p. 19: FRED SILVERMAN Interview, by Dan Pasternack on May 29, 2001, for The Interviews: An Oral History of Television; pp. 28, 90, 101: JOHN RICH Interview, by Henry Colman on August 3, 1999, for The Interviews: An Oral History of Television; p.45: ISABEL SANFORD Interview, by Brad Lemack on April 3, 2002, for The Interviews: An Oral History of Television; p. 72: RUE MCCLANAHAN Interview, by Jim Colucci on May 4, 2006, for The Interviews: An Oral History of Television; p. 90: GEORGE SUNGA Interview, by Jeff Abraham on February 1, 2008, for The Interviews: An Oral History of Television; p. 93: PAUL BOGART Interview, by Michael Rosen on May 19, 2001, for The Interviews: An Oral History of Television; pp. 97, 114: BETTY GARRETT Interview, by Karen Herman on May 21, 2003, for The Interviews: An Oral History of Television; p.101: SHERMAN HEMSLEY Interview, by Karen Herman on August 17, 2003, for The Interviews: An Oral History of Television; p. 137: RITA RIGGS Interview, by Gary Rutkowski on August 19, 2003, for The Interviews: An Oral History of Television.

ABOUT THE AUTHORS

Producer, philanthropist, and activist **NORMAN LEAR** has the distinction of being among the first seven television pioneers inducted into the Television Academy Hall of Fame. He won his first two Emmy Awards in 1971 (for *All in the Family*'s premiere season) and his most recent one in 2020, for *Live in Front of a Studio Audience: "All In the Family" and "Good Times."* His memoir, *Even* This *I Get to Experience*, was published in 2014.

JIM COLUCCI is a television historian and freelance writer whose work has appeared in *TV Guide*, *Inside TV*, *Quick & Simple*, *InTouch*, *The Advocate*, *Next*, and CBS' *Watch* magazine, where he served as a deputy editor. He covers television and other entertainment media on his blog *Must Hear TV*, which had been an on-air report for *The Frank DeCaro Show* on Sirius XM radio for over ten years. He is the author of the authorized companion book *Will & Grace: Fabulously Uncensored* (2004), *The Q Guide to the Golden Girls* (2006), and the *New York Times* best-seller *Golden Girls Forever* (2016).

JIMMY KIMMEL is the host and executive producer of the Emmy Award–nominated *Jimmy Kimmel Live*, ABC's longest-running late-night talk show. Also a comedian and writer, he has hosted some of the biggest events in pop culture, including the Academy Awards, the Emmys, the American Music Awards, and the ESPY Awards, as well as executive-produced and hosted the Emmy Award–winning *Live in Front of a Studio Audience: "All In The Family" and "The Jeffersons"* and *Live in Front of a Studio Audience: "All In The Family" and "Good Times."*

First published in the United States of America in 2021
Universe Publishing, A Division of
Rizzoli International Publications, Inc.
300 Park Avenue South
New York, NY 10010
www.rizzoliusa.com

Publisher: Charles Miers
Editor: Elizabeth Smith
Design: Lync
Production Manager: Colin Hough Trapp
Managing Editor: Lynn Scrabis

2021 2022 2023 2024 / 10 9 8 7 6 5 4 3 2 1

Distributed in the U.S. trade by Random House, New York

Printed in China

ISBN: 978-0-7893-3973-7
Library of Congress Control Number: 2021937531

Visit us online:
Facebook.com/RizzoliNewYork
Twitter: @Rizzoli_Books
Instagram.com/RizzoliBooks
Pinterest.com/RizzoliBooks
Youtube.com/user/RizzoliNY
Issuu.com/Rizzoli